CHASING CHE

Patrick Symmes writes about Latin American politics, globalization, and Third World travel for a number of magazines, including *Harper's* (where he is a contributing editor), *Outside*, *Wired*, and *Condé Nast Traveler*. This is his first book. He lives in New York City.

CHASING CHE

CHASING CHE

A MOTORCYCLE JOURNEY IN SEARCH
OF THE GUEVARA LEGEND

Patrick Symmes

ROBINSON
London

Constable Publishers
3 The Lanchesters
162 Fulham Palace Road
London W6 9ER
www.constablerobinson.com

First published by Vintage Books 2000

First UK edition published by Robinson, an imprint
of Constable & Robinson Ltd. 2001

Copyright © 2000 by Patrick Symmes

Portions of this work were originally published
in *Talk* and *Harper's* magazines.

Grateful acknowledgment is made to the following for
permission to reprint previously published material:

- *Bronx Flash Music, Inc.:* Excerpt from "Big in Japan" by Marian Gold,
Bernhard Lloyd, and Frank Mertens. Reprinted by permission of Rolf
Budde Musikverlag GmbH. All rights in the United States and Canada
exclusively controlled by Bronx Flash Music, Inc.
- *New Directions Publishing Corporation and Souvenir Press Ltd.:* Poem
"A New Love Song to Stalingrad" from *Residence on Earth* by Pablo
Neruda, copyright © 1973 by Pablo Neruda and Donald D. Walsh.
Rights in the United Kingdom administered by Souvenir Press Ltd.,
London. Reprinted by permission of New Directions Publishing Cor-
poration and Souvenir Press Ltd.
- *Verso:* Excerpt from *The Motorcycle Diaries: A Journey Around South Amer-
ica* by Ernesto Che Guevara, translated by Ann Wright (London/New
York: Verso, 1995). Reprinted by permission of Verso.

A copy of the British Library Cataloguing in
Publication Data is available from the British Library

ISBN 1-84119-291-0

Map by David Lindroth, Inc.
Author photograph © Stephen Lewis
Designed by Suvi Asch

Printed and bound in the EU

10 9 8 7 6 5 4 3 2

for gusanos *everywhere*

ACKNOWLEDGMENTS

Special thanks to my mother, who actually said, "You're going to do it on a motorcycle, aren't you?" Also to Clara Jeffery, Ben Metcalf, and Lewis Lapham, to Dawn Davis and Marty Asher, to Richard Parks, and to Annie Dillard.

Regular thanks to Mr. Rojo and the pineapple people, to Isabel, Pascal, and Julie of Moquegua, Tito, and whoever it was that pulled me out of that ditch.

Much of this manuscript was written while on a Harper's–McLaughlin teaching fellowship at the UC Berkeley Graduate School of Journalism; I am also indebted to the Eight Oaks Foundation for the support which made this project possible.

CONTENTS

Because of the circumstances in which I traveled, first as a student and later as a doctor, I came into close contact with poverty, hunger, and disease; with the inability to treat a child because of lack of money; with the stupefaction provoked by continual hunger and punishment. . . . And I began to realize that there were things that were almost as important to me as becoming a famous scientist or making a significant contribution to medical science: I wanted to help those people.

—Ernesto "Che" Guevara, 1960

INTRODUCTION

You can still see the bullet holes from that day, scattered across the façade of the hotel they now call the Free Santa Clara. It was December 28, 1958, when a column of scruffy, bearded guerrillas with mismatched uniforms and outdated weapons entered this city in the flatlands of central Cuba. There was a sharp firefight with some military snipers hiding in the upper stories of the hotel; the guerrillas had more enthusiasm than skill and shot up the place pretty badly.

In the midst of the battle, the guerrilla commander, to confront a fearsome armored troop train bristling with weapons and loaded with government reinforcements, grabbed eighteen of his men and rushed to the outskirts of the city. The guerrillas commandeered a D-6 Caterpillar bulldozer, ripped up the train tracks, and hid on rooftops, behind trees, and on a small hill overlooking the site. It was a classic enfilade ambush: the train ground to a halt and the guerrillas opened fire from all directions. Pinned and disoriented, the government troops cowered where they could, unwilling to die for a regime they themselves despised. It was over in a few hours. With only one platoon of men, the commander—an enigmatic Argentine doctor known as Che—had captured 408 government soldiers and shattered the last resistance. Within days, Cuba's military dictator, Fulgencio Batista, had fled to Florida with a million dollars in his suitcase. The government collapsed, and Fidel Castro rode into Havana and the history books with a rosary around his neck and his handsome young Argentine commander at his side.

When I first came to Santa Clara in 1991 as a freelance magazine journalist, I was searching for Cuba's curiously powerful grip on the axis of history. And it was here, at the place that marked the apogee of Che Guevara's life, that I first glimpsed the true dimensions of his myth and the power and meaning it holds for millions of Latin Americans. I had already been exposed to the official version of Che's life: according to the museums in Havana and the books on sale everywhere, he was born Ernesto Guevara in Argentina; became a doctor and then a revolutionary; came to Cuba and won the battle of Santa Clara; then died fighting to emancipate the poor in Bolivia in 1967. The details were like shadows that did not bear scrutiny in the tropical brightness of Cuban orthodoxy.

I took a seat in the central plaza on a bench facing the battle-scarred hotel. At the other end of the bench was a young Cuban man drinking beer. He was short, thickly muscled, and his eyes were red. While we talked about Cuba he nipped at a large plastic jug of home brew—in Cuba you drink home brew or you don't drink—and complained. His father had gone to East Germany years before, the fellow explained, but now East Germany no longer existed. When his father had refused to come home, preferring the new, unified Germany to the old, isolated Cuba, he had been labeled a *gusano,* or worm, Castro's term for anyone who betrays his version of the revolution. The government had now cut off the son's mail and phone service, he claimed. He waited, hoping that his father would somehow extract him from history. He studied German at night and dreamed of Munich beer halls. The new world taking shape outside the island was one that this man, like many Cubans, could neither see himself nor imagine. TV carried only speeches by Castro and old cartoons. Russian magazines advocating democracy had been banned. Cuba now soldiered on alone, without a Soviet Union issuing fraternal subsidies. The official rhetoric of sacrifice rang defiantly in the quiet plazas of an economically destitute nation.

My friend looked right and left, and then reached for his wallet. He opened it and picked through the crowded interior until he found a small square of cardboard, faded and wrinkled. He handed it to me. It was a picture of Che, laughing, his beautiful face turned up toward some hopeful thought.

"If he were still alive," the man on the bench said, "none of this would be happening."

That line has stuck with me now for many years, a statement of sentimentality and faith that I have been unable to bury or forget. I have encountered one version or another of the young man's belief in every country I have visited in Latin America. Nor is the devotion he felt toward a cardboard picture of a dead man limited to our hemisphere—Che is an official hero in lands as diverse as Vietnam and Hungary, and an unofficial one in many other places.

Despite the best efforts of biographers to set down a factual account of Che's life—and the efforts of the Cuban government to curate an alternative, more palatable history—the myth of Che is essentially a living, oral tradition, an amalgam of a thousand fables, some of them true, others invented to suit the needs so clearly expressed on the bench in Santa Clara that day. I have been collecting shards of these stories ever since, writing down the tales passed through the dark of Havana nights—"I met him once," someone would begin. I have bought up the icons of his face, pure imagery reworked for other ends. Dead for more than thirty years now, Che has become ever more useful. His image has been appropriated for political, economic, and even spiritual purposes. He is the symbol of communist destiny, and yet also beloved of anticommunist rebels; his face is used to sell beer and skis, yet an English church group recently issued posters of Jesus Christ himself recast as Che. The affluent youth of Europe and North America have resurrected Che as an easy emblem of meaningless and unthreatening rebellion, a queer blending of educated violence and disheveled nobility, like Gandhi with a gun or John Lennon singing "Give War a Chance."

Against a tide of so many competing interpretations, I have

found it necessary here to retreat toward something approaching bedrock. Although this story has begun and will end in contemporary Cuba, it is mostly concerned with retracing the journey across South America that Che Guevara made in 1952, before he was famous, before he was known as Che, before he was anyone's myth except his own. I have followed where his own search for stories took him, and have sought an origin point of the man as he himself understood it.

You can never know where your journey begins, nor where it will take you in the end. That day in Santa Clara I tried to return the picture of Che my new friend had handed to me. He insisted that I keep it, and then we talked for a while more, and finally he asked me to promise him something. "Promise me," he said before we parted, "that you will tell people how it really is."

CHASING CHE

CHAPTER ONE

THE SILVER RIVER

Two hundred and twenty-nine miles due south of Buenos Aires the twin cylinders hesitated once, caught again, hesitated again, and then finally spun down into silence. The motorcycle coasted, ever slower, and came to rest by the side of the long ribbon of shimmery gray asphalt that stretched from one horizon to the next without interruption. The steel in the engine seethed and popped in the quiet of noon on the empty pampas.

I looked around, but there was little to see. The main tank had expired at two hundred and one miles, midway between two dots on the map. I'd reversed the petcock by my left knee while still moving, and steadily consumed another twenty-eight miles on reserve until the tank became, like the world, empty.

The Argentine pampa is a plain of near-mathematical flatness. I had departed Buenos Aires early and left behind its minor suburbs and depressing outreaches within the hour. I rode south on a two-lane tarmac that shrank away from my wheels even as the motorcycle pressed forward. Distant houses floated on lakes of light that evaporated with my rattling, wind-whipped approach. By mid-morning the houses were gone and the land approached two dimensions, a table of grass stretching out beneath a ceiling of depthless blue. This was an absurd landscape, an abstraction of emptiness that welcomed utopian projections and offered a hallucination of perfectibility. No clouds, no buildings, no animals, no traffic, no sound. And now no gasoline.

But in an imperfect world, I have come to believe, there is always some nagging flaw in the absolute. Off in the distance, through quivering air, the road curved gently to the left, and there, at the curve, was a singularity: a thin stand of poplars. Trees here are the work of man, so I stumbled up the road in my new cowboy boots and eventually came to a barbed-wire fence, inside which were the trees, a bay horse, and a listing shack of weathered gray wood. I climbed the wire and clapped twice.

Nothing happened, so I clapped again. The arid space of the pampas has bred a culture of distance, a fetishistic appreciation of personal space. You do not simply walk up and knock on a door here. Sound travels far on this featureless terrain, and you clap twice from a distance to give warning of your approach. It was traditional in older times for a visitor to clap when first entering earshot and then wait long enough for a kettle of water to boil.

A minute went by, and I clapped twice more, and then waited a while. Eventually I shuffled around in the yard and took a sideways peek out back. Just as I had hoped, a rusted Ford Falcon sagged there beneath one of the biggest poplars. I spent another full minute weighing the sin of siphoning some gas, and just as I stepped toward the Falcon the door of the shack opened, tentatively at first and then fully. A wiry gaucho appeared, sleepy in the midday heat, shirtless, and scratching himself. He was wearing the traditional outfit of baggy *bombacha* pants, a black felt hat turned up at the front, and soft riding boots (horseback is the gaucho's defining condition). We stood at pistol range. *"Buenos días,"* I said.

"Encantado," he replied—"Enchanted." I smiled and didn't say anything, eager to follow his lead. Jorge Luis Borges had written a famous story about a city slicker who blunders into a fatal knife fight with a gaucho. All I could remember about the story was that it was called "The South," and I was in no mood to become a metaphor.

"It's very hot today," the gaucho said, scratching his chin.

"Yes," I answered, "very hot."

"How are you today?"

"Fine, thank you."

"This is my son," he said, pointing to a face peering out from behind the door.

"Hello," I said.

"Enchanted," the boy said.

I was about to broach the topic of gasoline when the father spoke again: "You are from Buenos Aires."

This comment had ceased surprising me. I'd heard one version or another several times in the last few years, while hitchhiking in Bolivia or wandering Peru in search of personal revelations and lucrative magazine stories. Although I'd found few of either, my Spanish had become smoothly generic in the process, and the locals were never quite sure what to make of me. Often enough they assumed I was from Buenos Aires. The gaucho's assessment was less a measure of my voice than of my tangibles—my height, my blue eyes, my pink skin, my unscuffed boots, and my still-clean clothes. These were indelible marks that I came from the Other World, a place where rich, fair-skinned people lived, people with odd habits and the luxury of strangeness. Among the poor of Latin America, class trumps nationality every time. To a gaucho in a wood shack, the Other World could be that vague foreign land to the north where the gringos lived, and that seemed as close as a television set, or it could be cosmopolitan Buenos Aires, which seemed so much more distant than its two hundred and twenty-nine miles. The difference between the two is unimportant when viewed from below.

"I'm a foreigner," I told him. "I'm going to—" I paused there, because I really didn't know how far I was going. Chile? Peru? Bolivia? Somewhere north, or south, of there?

"I'm going to Patagonia," I told him, since this was not only true but likely. "My motorcycle has run out of *nafta.*"

The gaucho sympathized and then spent five minutes explaining in archaic tones that while he "would be enchanted" to give me some *nafta,* the Ford Falcon had not run for three years and the tank was empty. We thanked each other profusely, exchanged opposite hopes for the weather, and separated. I cut through his yard, gave the horse a wide berth, and then entered the stand of poplars, looking for the barbed wire fence. With my eyes raised, I missed what was in front of me and nearly put a boot down in the middle of a dusty dent in the ground. It was a small burrow filled with squirming puppies.

They were newborns, still blind, and at the last second I stutter-stepped and managed to miss crushing them but, nonetheless, their mother burst from the shade beneath the house and arrowed across the yard toward me, a yapping brown blur intent on murder. I went for the fence, and man and beast now engaged in an ancient contest, speed against speed, instinct against instinct. This race ended, improbably, in a tie: I got my left boot over the fence, and she got the right one in her mouth.

The dog held on for life, snarling and ripping at my heel. The boot was made of tough pigskin, and it held, at least for a moment. But the barbed wire fence now imprisoned me. Straddling it, one leg in safety, the other in combat, I was . . . exposed. With each yank and twist by the dog, one of the barbs was working its way through my denim jeans, tickling my testicles with ever greater urgency. I could feel teeth pressing on the vulnerable tendon of my right foot, while each rip and snarl drove me deeper onto the pointed steel. At some point, jiggling back and forth, the wire singing beneath me, the barb inching upward, I began to wonder just what I was doing there. It wasn't possible to laugh at a moment like that, although I later did.

I remember having only one thought at the time, while quivering back and forth on the wire, watching the dog try to kill me. And that was: It's only my first tank of gas.

Please, dog: It's only my first tank of gas. It's only my first day. It's only my first country. Please, dog: I have so many miles to travel, so many mountains to cross, so many months to come, so many decades still to unwind.

Please, dog.

———

It is easy to grow fat in Buenos Aires. In a restaurant decorated with stuffed bulls I ate half of a bloody steak cut to the dimensions of an encyclopedia and drank a bottle of Mendoza red cultivated on the foothills of the Andes. On the gleaming pedestrian lane of Calle Florida I sipped *café cortado* and ate éclairs while being thrashed at chess in the Cafe Richmond by an old man in a tweed suit who did not like to talk. Wine, more meat, more wine, more pastries. They say an Argentine is an Italian who speaks Spanish and thinks he is German. The political implications of this formula are deadly, but it guarantees a rich diet.

At night I slept on the roof of an apartment building in a glass cubicle, and was awoken each morning by a parrot named Federico, as in Fellini. The parrot, like the doorman at the entrance eleven stories below, was a Paraguayan. If you waved at either of them, they said *"Hola,"* a trick the parrot had learned from the owner of my glass house. She was an elderly woman named Pibita, or "little girl" in Argentine slang. Little Girl would totter out to the balcony in the mornings, light a cigarette, and remove the cover from Federico's cage. His greetings (*"Cómo te va?"* he asked relentlessly, mockingly) sent me off to another day of looking for my wheels.

The ship carrying the bike from Baltimore had arrived just after my flight, during the gap between Christmas and New Year's. Nothing was going right. First my luggage had disappeared from the airplane somewhere between America and Argentina, and now no one could find my motorcycle. I wandered the city in a daze, exhausted by the incongruous glamour of this South American Paris, a city so steeped in the present that history could seep into the streets only with oblique gestures and concealed motives.

But it was there, this troubled memory. The first thing I saw when I stepped off the plane into a muggy December heat wave was a teenager in a red T-shirt bearing the unmistakable likeness of the man I had come to South America to find, the man known to Argentines as *"El Puro,"* the Pure One. To the rest of the world he was known simply as Che.

Argentines love nicknames, archaisms, and Italian slang, which render their dialect of Spanish indecipherable or untranslatable on many occasions. The "Che" of a million T-shirts and dorm room posters was born here in Argentina as Ernesto Guevara Lynch de la Serna. This name meant many things. In reverse order, "de la Serna" was his mother's maiden name, the "de la" revealing aristocratic roots; "Lynch" was his father's patronymic, indicating the family's descent from a noted Irish-Chilean admiral and providing just the European patina that Argentines crave; "Guevara" indicated traditional Spanish stock, the blood of the conquerors; "Ernesto" was the Christian name of his own father, indicating roots, generations, and tradition (abbreviated usually to "Ernestito," or "Little Ernesto," it was doubly a reminder of his place in the particular world that the young man in question came from, the petty aristocracy of Córdoba, the country's second city, a refined town of churches, universities, and culture in the dry high plains of the northern interior).

One by one, Ernesto Guevara Lynch de la Serna would discard these various meanings until he was reduced to a single three-letter nickname that was an embarrassment to his roots: "Che." The word is really just a verbal tic, a lower-class habit more common in rural Argentina than in the big cities. It means, alternately, "you," or "hey, man," or "uhm," and can be used any number of ways. "Hey, che, come here." "Pass me the salt, che." "I think Avenida Roosevelt is . . . che . . . che . . . che . . . three blocks north." It is a disreputable term.

Che became himself through a deliberate process of shedding his names, his past, his class, his family, and his country. Born on June 14, 1928, in Rosario, a major city on the swampy lowlands of the Parana delta, he developed asthma as a small child. Following medical advice, his family removed itself to the higher, drier ground of Córdoba. His mother, Celia, was an extraordinary figure with wealth, beauty, and brains. A political radical, she was the first woman in Argentina to open her own bank account. She filled her house with books and an endless supply of intellectuals, Spanish Civil War veterans, poor artists, rich relatives, and street children, an environment guaranteed to stimulate a child and likely to teach him contrariness. The senior Ernesto Guevara was a genteel and lovable bum, a civil engineer who never got a business off the ground and wasted his wife's inheritance on bad investments and keeping up appearances. As their prospects dimmed, the Guevaras moved through a series of humbler and humbler houses, eventually ending up on the edge of Alta Gracia, an airy town outside Córdoba filled with German sailors who had stayed in South America after the battleship *Graf Spee* was destroyed outside Montevideo during World War II. In this confusing crossroads of cosmopolitan provincialism, the young Ernestito learned to battle everything: his asthma, his parents, his neighbors, the ideas of his class. He grew up an impoverished aristocrat, moving from dining room debates over fascism to gang warfare among bands of poor children who lived directly across the street. He was fond of shooting at birds with a tiny rifle his father gave him, and he attacked his relentless, suffocating asthma by denying it existed: he took up rugby and taught himself to play through the pain and regular collapses.

He was restless and believed in doing everything himself. When his mother contracted cancer, the thirteen-year-old Ernesto decided to invent a cure, and he set up a basement laboratory where he subjected rodents to unspeakable "treatments" like injections of petroleum-based solutions. Unlike the guinea pigs, his mother survived, but Ernesto retained his interest in medicine and enrolled in the University of Buenos Aires medical school at the age of eighteen. His initial vocation was asthma research, a case of "physician heal thyself."

During the summer of 1951, Guevara bought a tiny motor to attach to his bicycle and set off across northern Argentina. This month-long expedition by moped had been something of a lark, an adventure conducted entirely within the orbit of his own world, but it laid a template that I recognized. I'd begun my own wanderings with a few short journeys around New England on my father's tiny Honda Supersport, rides that at the time were meant only as vacations but that began a process I could no longer control. I had learned to travel, to trust in the road and those along it; this was the dangerous lesson that Guevara took away from his moped journey. From now on he would be a traveler, his relentless curiosity given a vehicle (two-wheeled or otherwise) and a course—outward but, on a spherical planet, always toward home.

By late 1951 this urge had become irresistible. In December of that year Guevara laid plans for a motorcycle trip across the hemisphere; it was a trip from which he would never come home, even when he returned. One journey leads necessarily to another, and the moped of 1951 gave way inevitably to the motorcycle of 1952. On this trip he would go deep into Patagonia and as far north as Miami, from the swamps of the Amazon to the peaks of the Andes. Guevara would return to Argentina after eight months, a changed man—a man, as he himself put it, "in transition to some other conception of life." He was a traveler now; the act of discovery is not merely the basis of travel but is also the quintessential revolutionary act. Every long journey overturns the established order of one's own life, and all revolutionaries must begin by transforming themselves.

Movement became the continuum of his much-examined experience: "Yes, you'll always be a foreigner," his mother would write him years later; "that seems to be your permanent fate." After finishing medical school in 1954 he set off again, first for Bolivia, where he wanted to see a "peasant revolution" that he had heard about. Learning of a similar upheaval in Guatemala, he crossed Peru and transited Ecuador to reach it. He was now a sympathizer of leftist movements but still a visitor, and when that Guatemalan government fell in a 1954 coup as Guevara watched, he acquired a fixed target for his enmity: it was the CIA that had sponsored the coup, and it was the United States that he blamed for the repression he saw. Chased out of Guatemala by events, he worked in Mexico as an itinerant street photographer until he made the acquaintance of a shabby band of Cuban troublemakers and joined—as the expedition's doctor—their foolhardy attempt to invade Cuba. Within three years he was a legendary battlefield commander and the head of Fidel Castro's Second Column. After their triumph in 1959 he took on the role of the official internationalist of the Cuban revolution, dashing about the globe on diplomatic missions. Even so, he grew restless with Cuba, renounced his duties, and left again in 1965 for a failed military expedition to the Congo. Committed by his own public declarations to wandering the earth until death, he made his final trip, to Bolivia, in 1966. On the eve of his departure he wrote his parents that he once again felt "the ribs of Rocinante" between his heels. Rocinante was, as everyone in Latin America knew, the horse that bore Don Quixote on his endless travels, and the line could as well have described the motorcycle between his heels in 1952 as his fatal misadventures in Bolivia fifteen years later.

On October 9, 1967, Guevara died in a schoolroom where the Andes peter out into the Argentine plains of his birth, close enough to his home to smell familiar flowers on the last breeze of his life.

The motorcycle journey of 1952 was but one episode, yet it was here, on this route, that young Ernesto had stripped away the life he had been given to expose the life he sought. His later travels would shape his character and have a more direct bearing on his ideology, but it was this first journey that interested me, simply because it was the first. This was the trip where Ernesto became Che, both figuratively and literally. He would inherit the nickname Che for the first time; he would conceive of himself as a revolutionary for the first time; he would leave behind one life and begin another.

Almost forty-four years later, New Year's Day came and a blizzard of paper fell from the sky. The streets were empty of people, and I shuffled through long strips of computer printouts and reams of records that clutched at my ankles, as though I were a solitary ticker-tape parade. It is an Argentine custom on January 1 to toss paperwork from the previous year out the window, thus discarding the past with the evidence.

The first days of January crept by in a sweaty haze of this confused paperwork and futile wandering. The motorcycle was in one warehouse or another. It hadn't been unloaded yet, or it was waiting dockside, or it was locked up in a container. I stood in a crowd of couriers at the customs broker's office in a chrome skyscraper high over the port. While someone typed up paperwork that would prove useless, I peered over the vast estuary of the Río de la Plata, the misnamed Silver River that ran, brown and broad, over the horizon to Uruguay. The customs broker finally gave me a note insulting the customs inspector, who replied an hour later with a note blaming the customs broker. The heat wave was relentless, my repetitive thrashings at chess were depressing, and I began to bloat from eating éclairs. The *porteños*, as natives of B.A. are known, were arrogant and amused by my poor dress. I still hadn't recovered my luggage and was stumbling around town in the same T-shirt every day.

In the early blackness of each morning, long before first light, I would lie awake in the glass house high above the avenues, listening to the stirring of the city as it came awake. Every dawn it was the same: in darkness, the small squealing of unoiled garage doors opening eleven stories below, and then the early express buses filling the shadowy gray light with the hissing of their air brakes, and then, with the blue dawn, the rattletrap Fiat taxis shooting through the intersection tooting their horns. In time a cool half-light would fill the glass shed from all directions, and the traffic would build, the air now an orchestra of tinny, high-pitched dirt bikes and knocking diesel trucks and the unsteady idle of old cars caught in stop-and-go traffic.

Eventually, as I lay immobilized with dread, Little Girl would come onto the balcony, light a cigarette, and pluck the cover from Federico's cage.

"Cómo te va?" he always asked. Roughly: "How's it going?"

"It isn't going at all, Fed," I'd tell him.

I always said it in English, so he wouldn't understand.

I once took a bus in Buenos Aires that zigged and zagged out of the city. We turned constantly, stopped incessantly, and drove slowly. It was a local run heading out of the core at breakfast time, and since we were going the wrong way the bus wasn't half full. It took a long time.

My companion was a young Argentine grad student named Mercedes Doretti, an attractive but grim woman who seemed to be fighting a perpetual battle to control her frustration. Given her job—poking at dead people all day—this was understandable, and we didn't talk much on the way. We debarked at an anonymous intersection in a suburban neighborhood of low cement apartment buildings that had seen better days. I followed Doretti a block and then we came to a long, high wall and crossed through a raised, ornate gate just wide enough to admit the only kind of car that ever entered. Inside the wall was the Avellaneda Municipal Cemetery, and we walked through. It was huge, but without the glamour of Recoletta, the famous Buenos Aires cemetery where the upper classes buried their dead in elaborate, fantastical crypts that imitated Egyptian pyramids and Roman temples and Greek oracles, as if the dead were now simply confined to smaller versions of the lives they had just left. Here in the prosaic suburbs the dead were mostly underground, but a few sepulchers and crypts with hints of ornate Latin style dotted the more desirable pieces of real estate, like the side groves or the corners where two footpaths met. Location location, even here.

We came at last to the far side of the cemetery, a back corner ruled off by its own wall. It was a rectangle a few hundred feet per side, a small space in which three hundred and forty-three people had been murdered.

A grave diggers' shed and a storage building had been confiscated and used, first by the killers, now by their pursuers. The killers had been Argentine police and military men, usually in civilian clothes. They saw themselves as clinicians purifying the country of contaminating elements. The protagonists called their crusade *el proceso*, a neatly blank euphemism for the killing that became known to the rest of the world as "the Dirty War." The slaughter began in 1976 when a military junta overthrew the government. The prisoners were brought here in Ford Falcons and Renaults. A few of them were Marxist guerrillas, but most were just left-wing students, union activists, members of fragmented Trotskyite/Catholic political organizations, or naive kids who had played at the romantic game of clandestine life, running food to a safe house or passing messages for someone the military didn't like. A few of the prisoners brought here were academics or journalists or human rights advocates, but the disappearance of those types was too noticeable. The poor and forgotten bore the brunt of Argentina's psychotic urge to purge itself, to burn out the weakness and cowardice it saw when it looked in the mirror.

There is still no telling how many died in the Dirty War. For one thing, the notion of a particular, distinct period of killing is inaccurate—even before the coup, the police and military were locked in a war with "subversives," and police torture had been present for decades in Argentine life. But the killing began in earnest in 1976 and petered out with that decade. In that time, it was usually said, some ten thousand Argentines had "been disappeared."

"This figure is, of course, too low," Doretti noted caustically. To be counted in that tally, there had to be either an identified body or a credible record that someone had been seized by the military or federal police. Many prisoners had passed through the bureaucracy of the Naval Mechanics School, a torture center operated by the Argentine navy in Buenos Aires. Between four thousand and forty-five hundred suspects were brought into the school, and the great majority were tortured in one way or another, often for months, before being killed. Thousands of bodies had been tossed from airplanes into the Río de la Plata, the great sheet of water that gave Argentines their identity—they called themselves *Ríoplatense,* or "of the silver river"—and that now absorbed their dead forever. Other bodies were taken far out into the pampas for disposal. There were poor families who had no paperwork even to prove that their sons had ever existed—driver's licenses and school records being less common in the poorest parts of the major cities, exactly where the death squads were most active.

"Twenty thousand," Doretti said when I asked. "Maybe even thirty."

Then came the pursuers. It began with the mothers, as it usually does. The ordinary women of Argentina began to protest the disappearance of their sons and daughters. The Dirty War was still in full swing when they began meeting on Thursday afternoons in front of the Casa Rosada, the presidential palace. They held up signs with pictures of their missing children and marched in a circle. They tended to wear black, and since they were old women the military rulers did not dare do much about them. The greater the death toll, the stronger the opposition. By 1982, the junta in charge of the country was under domestic and international pressure to answer the charge, leveled by a group of old women in black, that the professed defenders of the nation were, in fact, its murderers.

As cowed men with guns are wont to do, the generals overreached. Desperate for some credibility with their countrymen, they fixed on an obscure nineteenth-century territorial dispute—the Falkland Islands—and launched a surprise attack. This is an oversimplified account of modern Argentine history, certainly, but in many ways the forensic work here in the cemetery was made possible by Britain's Royal Navy. Argentina's speedy and humiliating defeat in the Falklands destroyed the credibility of the military regime; the leaders were arrested, and their replacements agreed to elections and a restoration of democracy.

In a frenzy of exposure, some mass graves were ripped open with bulldozers, destroying any chance at identifying the dead. To avoid more such mistakes, Doretti and a few others had founded the Argentine Forensic Anthropology Team, receiving training from the American scientist Clyde Snow in the technique of uncovering and identifying bodies. One room in the shed was now filled with boxes full of bones, each box labeled with the date of its discovery. A skull, a femur, a tibia, and a few shards were laid out on a long, high table as though an autopsy were in progress. Instead of taking a body apart, however, a couple of other grad students were putting this one together. There was no doubt about the cause of death here: they rolled the skull over and showed me a bullet hole in the back.

Outside, there were two large pits in the ground. One by one, the three hundred and forty-three victims had been led into this small rectangle of dirt, forced to kneel at the edge of the pit, and then snuffed with a pistol shot. Sometimes the bullet made a tiny hole on the way in but blew out large chunks of the face as it exited, but the killers refined their methods with steady practice. Done properly, a shot down through the neck was cleanest.

I climbed into the pit, which came up to my shoulders. The soil was black. The remains had all been skeletonized by now. Doretti and her colleagues worked in silence all morning while I watched. They excavated inch by inch, took photographs, isolated individual bones in the dirt and noted their location, type, and surrounding material on clipboards. The dead had been dumped one atop the next in chaotic fashion, and it was vital to preserve the integrity of each skeleton, to observe the way bones had fallen together like cards in a disordered deck. The edges of a few bones were visible, and I brushed at the black soil with my fingers until it occurred to me what this crumbling black earth clinging to my hands was: human flesh. It had been composted by worms and bacteria and time into something unrecognizable, but its origin was clear. I climbed out and stood alone in a corner of the yard.

I waited there, uneasy, hoping to see something in the pits that was worth seeing. There are those who claim that the dead are some-how abstractly beautiful, and others who find some cold and material lessons in mass killing. I have seen enough mass graves, and find them uniform in their sordid plainness. The slaughter is always done in some out-of-the-way place, behind a factory or a fence. The space is always small and claustrophobic. The soil always seems in ferment, warm and busy with the steady work of converting one form of carbon into another. Often there are fragments of bone—teeth in a neat row, or shards of something bleached white by the sun. The graves collect rainwater and are usually soggy and bubbling with gasses. My reaction to these sights is much the same, regardless of where on earth I stand: I have found that the sorrow is cumulative and that hardness eludes me. I have not learned any lessons from the dead.

For some reason, I felt sorry for the men who had done this killing night after night. It was too easy to demonize them, to attribute this burst of evil to a few particular actors, or to simply blame the political ideology of the killers for what had happened. The fact is that Latin America in the 1960s, '70s, and '80s was one long bloodbath, a southern version of the "ancient boneheap" that Orwell saw in Europe, "where every grain of soil has passed through innumerable human bodies." It was hard to assign some particular meaning to these acts when the hemisphere was covered with graves fresher than this one.

In Argentina, however, it was a particularly intimate form of cruelty that had filled these holes. The Argentines had avoided the race-tinged wars of Peru or Guatemala, where a brown underclass fought against a social order controlled by whites. The Mexicans and Brazilians had suffered, but across divides of class. The rich in Nicaragua lost their money, the poor their lives. But here the killers and the killed were somehow one. The most racially homogeneous, middle-class society in Latin America had murdered itself.

Was any group more responsible than others? Certainly the individuals who ordered this and the ones who carried it out had to be punished (a few leading military officers had been imprisoned, but the ranks of the police and armed forces were still filled with men who had participated in one way or another). But to describe these acts as political—as the results of policies set by groups with calculated agendas—seemed inadequate. Responsibility for the killing was amorphous and shared, a product of individual actors, of Argentine history, of ambition, of human nature itself. The military had not launched *el proceso* in a vacuum. During the 1960s and '70s, Argentina was besieged by a series of guerrilla movements directly inspired and often supported by Che. The scale of these guerrilla movements defied precedent: by 1976, Argentina was home to the largest guerrilla army ever assembled in Latin America, larger even than the Sandinistas in Nicaragua. The guerrillas earned more than $60 million from kidnapping Argentine businesses, and they controlled an enormous Wall Street investment portfolio that disbursed funds to other guerrilla groups across Latin America. Convinced that they had decoded history, the guerrillas embraced their own version of *el proceso,* eagerly filling up their measure of horror and shameful deeds. In the memorable phrase of Jacobo Timerman, a journalist who was himself disappeared by the military for a while, all these guerrillas achieved with their bombs and assassinations was "to grease the wheels of the killing machine." The guerrillas acted and the police and military reacted, each action resulting in retribution and a cycle of violence that lost all meaning as it gained its own, self-perpetuating rhythm. Even though the great majority of the killing had been done by the right-wing military, blame could not be apportioned out like some mathematical formula.

All the hunters of utopia believed equally in the cult of action and the need for heroes. The left had sown seeds that the right propagated, and this black soil was the result.

Despite the occasional war, Argentines adore the English, and, back in the center of Buenos Aires, the man in tweed proved himself no exception. When he learned I was American his scorn was ill concealed. We sat in the basement of the Richmond, riven by the increasingly empty board, until he announced the final verdict, *"Heke-mahtay,"* the local pronunication of "Checkmate."

I went upstairs, ordered an éclair and foamy, milk-fed *cortado,* and then sat by the window watching the pedestrains watch each other. The Calle Florida was a place of display and ornament: tiny shops with glazed fronts, marching citizens in their finest, the air washed by the smell of bougainvillea. B.A. was a city of talk, a hyper-analytical labyrinth of words. It was a nocturnal society that assumed its full animation only under cloak of darkness. Like New York it was defined by how it spoke, and it birthed bilingual writers from the amniotic fluid of endless chatter. The conversations began famously late, usually after midnight. I got lost once near the port around 11 P.M. and slaked my thirst in an empty bar. I finished my glass of Mendoza wine at 11:30 and rose to pay my bill; another customer came in. I decided to have one more. By 12:30 the place was packed and a trio of Brazilian jazz musicians banged away on rumpled instruments. Four hours later I was locked in a debate about Che Guevara with a truck driver who smuggled goods over remote Patagonian passes. When I wandered home toward the glass house, I stumbled in the darkness with Julio Cortázar:

> *You see the Southern Cross*
> *you breathe the summer with its smell of peaches,*
> *and you walk at night*
> *my little silent ghost*
> *through that Buenos Aires*
>
> *always through that same Buenos Aires.*

There were dinner parties with high-ranking police intelligence officers and diplomats and twenty-three-year-old doctors in miniskirts. Society offered a collective thrill in the act of language, in the cultivated B.A. accent and the Italianate flourishes of their own argot, called *lunfardo*. The chatter was partly defensive; whether it is true or not, Argentines loved to claim that there were more therapists per capita in B.A. than anywhere in the world, a class of professionals paid to listen much like the stylish young men in the parks were paid to walk dogs. Night concealed unmet aspirations, squandered talents, and stymied hopes. The unsuitable reality was overpainted where possible: plastic surgery was covered by the national health plan and therefore ubiquitous, while anorexia was epidemic and bulimics vomited up their tensions in private, the inevitable self-loathing of a society that celebrated the tummy tuck and Sigmund Freud.

Aside from cheap beef, Argentina provided meager sustenance

to its people. Only speech was free, so anyone could afford as much as he wanted, and like the Italian clothing people wore it was put on to conceal the poverty of sidelined idealism. They were relieved merely to be alive, to have escaped a nightmare, and denial was sometimes more necessary than we outsiders cared to admit. The local comedian Enrique Pinti pedaled an exercise bicycle on the stage of the Liceo Theater eight times a week, spewing out a venomous history of the nation at such an incredible clip that even the *porteños* could not understand him. They roared with laughter, but his bitter words washed over them, as if the enactment of self-examination was all that mattered. Like his nation, Pinti pedaled faster and faster and yet never went anywhere or, as he liked to point out, lost any weight.

Now in broad daylight the *Calle Florida* was full of kiosks selling newspapers, and I bought three. They were filled with Che. *Clarin*, the *New York Times* of Argentina, ran an entire Che page with a photo of the man they called the "First Commander" in battle fatigues, quotes from the war diary he wrote during the Bolivian campaign of 1967, and a history of the various *Guevarista* guerrillas who fought in the north of Argentina in the 1960s. After the 1959 victory of the Cuban revolution, Guevara had quickly looked toward his native Argentina, eager to spread his doctrine of Marxist revolution. "We mustn't be afraid of violence," he said then. "Violence is the midwife of the new societies. But it must be loosed at exactly the right moment, when the leaders of the people have found the most favorable conditions."

Coincidentally, he was the leader and the moment was now. By 1960 the first cell of Argentine guerrillas was in action in Tucumán Province, in the north. The group, called Uturunco, was wiped out within months. In 1963, an Argentine journalist who had covered the Cuban revolution launched, with Guevara's support, the People's Guerrilla Army in Salta Province. The journalist called himself "Second Commander" and planned to turn the budding revolution over to the First Commander, *El Che*, but the People's Guerrilla Army was wiped out long before this could happen. The few guerrillas who escaped that failure are believed to have starved to death in the Andes, but this gruesome fate did not deter many more pretenders. A third guerrilla group, the Peronist Armed Forces, established a base in Tucumán in 1968 and was captured within weeks. Another group rose from the ashes of that defeat, taking the name Montoneros—Mounted—to reflect Che's doctrine that a mobile guerrilla force could outfight any conventional army.

Che was no hypocrite. He was willing to face the consequences of his ideology, and in the Cuban war he had led from the front lines and been wounded repeatedly. He was shot in the left ear once; another bullet entered his neck and exited at his shoulder; another struck him in the chest but bounced off, spent; and he was wounded in the foot in the Sierra Maestra Mountains in December 1957. (He also shot himself in the cheek when he dropped his pistol during the Bay of Pigs invasion, but nobody is perfect.) His love of combat was paired with a seductive eloquence. He spoke about creating a "New Man," an idealized, revolutionary citizen who would be motivated by morality and justice rather than paychecks. Yet always, war came first. He called for "two, three, many Vietnams," and lit the fuse of revolt in country after country. When his surrogates all failed, Che led his own campaign in Bolivia. He died there in 1967 with his hands tied, executed by a sergeant reeking of beer.

The repeated failures of the rural strategy pushed guerrilla warfare into the cities by the late '60s. The specific doctrines Che taught were modified or set aside after his death, and a hundred doctrinal schisms appeared within the guerrilla movements across the continent, yet Che's most important contribution was intact: the myth of the heroic guerrilla shooting his way into power. The Montoneros began attacking in the urban centers of Argentina, using assassinations and bombings to destabilize the military-civilian regime. The war moved from the pleasant abstraction of mountain ambushes to the bitter reality of neighbor executing neighbor.

Marxists call this doctrine "deepening the contradictions." You deliberately seek a vicious response from security forces; the worse the repression, the better the prospects for revolution. The connection between guerrilla assaults and counterrepression was direct and explicit in Che's thinking: "The objective conditions for the struggle are beginning to appear in Argentina," Guevara told a fellow Argentine in the early '60s. "There's unemployment and therefore hunger, and the working class is starting to react to this. Such reaction sets off repressive measures, and repression stirs up hatred. That's the exact point at which objective conditions need reinforcement with subjective ones, that is, with an awareness of the possibility of victory by violent means. . . ."

But even Che, who knew the taste of his own blood, could not foresee the ferocity of the reaction he would induce, and therefore the cost of these doctrines. "See you at the final victory," he used to salute his comrades, because he believed not just in the possibility of victory, but in the inevitability of it. Yet in the end the theoretician and guru of guerrilla warfare had miscalculated how deep the contradictions could get. In the end, the contradictions got about shoulder deep.

SEARCH RENEWED FOR REMAINS OF "CHE" GUEVARA, *El Chubut* trumpeted. Improbably, just weeks before I had set out for South America to retrace his youthful motorcycle journey, Che's body had been located after thirty years of mystery. An American biographer, Jon Lee Anderson, had learned the secret while interviewing the Bolivian military men present when Guevara had been buried secretly in the little town of Vallegrande, in southeast Bolivia. Now these same military men, retired and fat, led an encampment of about sixty journalists and several members of Dorretti's Argentine Forensic Anthropology Team back to the field. On December 1, as I was loading my motorcycle onto a container ship in the Baltimore harbor, the digging began. The exhumation was going slowly—so far they'd turned up three *other* guerrillas, but no Guevara—but the Bolivian minister of the interior assured the world that the body would be found momentarily now that work had resumed after Christmas.

SEARCH FOR CHE COMPLICATES, another paper declared. But it was just a matter of time before he would be among us again.

The imminent resurrection of such a potent figure in Latin history had sparked a necrophilial argument among three nations. In Buenos Aires, the Socialist Party introduced legislation requesting that the body be brought home to Argentina to provide "a necessary period of analysis, criticism and reflection." Cuba declared that Guevara's remains should be shipped "home" to Cuba. Bolivia announced that the body already was home, since Guevara himself had said that "wherever a man falls, that's where he stays." All parties had mixed motives: the Argentine left wanted a symbol of its own victimization; the Cubans wanted a relic to breathe life into their comatose revolution; the Bolivians hoped to generate tourist revenues.

And, according to another report in *Clarin*, Che himself was about to invade Argentina. This Che was no dead body but the Spanish heartthrob Antonio Banderas, who was due in Buenos Aires momentarily to play Che in the film version of *Evita*, Andrew Lloyd Webber's trashy musical. In the original stage version, Mandy Patinkin had played the role of "Che Guevara," a young idealist in a beret who occasionally burst into song while wandering the set trying to interest Evita in an insecticide he had invented (as a teenager, Guevara really had peddled his own bug killer, but not to Evita). There was a vague implication that the failure of his insecticide plan shattered the young Guevara's idealism, pushing him toward guerrilla war.

The apt casting of Madonna as Evita had infuriated Argentines, and now the appropriation of Guevara's image added salt to the national wound. In a calculated concession to Argentine fury, the British director announced that Banderas would not play a character called "Che Guevara" but merely a character called "Che." In a city of semioticans this was a dodge with real implications: by removing the specific reference to Guevara, the character became universal. All Argentines are known as "Che" to people in neighboring countries, just as all Frenchmen are called "Pierre." By playing "a Che" rather than "the Che," Banderas was suddenly a stand-in for the entire nation, a common man. The insecticide subplot was discarded, and Banderas instead became something of a Greek chorus, following Madonna through the movie with a swaggering commentary on her empty promises to the Argentine people. Though this might have insulted Evita's remaining defenders, it was a closer fit with the actual character of Ernesto Guevara.

Despite being dead—actually, because of it—Che was more popular than ever. A brewery in London made Che Beer. Swatch produced a line of watches bearing his picture and the word *REVOLUCIÓN*. You could buy Austrian skis painted with his likeness, or Canadian refrigerator magnets. It wasn't just the fluent capitalism of the First World that appropriated Che's image. The Cubans minted money on Che T-shirts, Ecuadoreans manufactured Che mud flaps for South American trucks, and Che was again one of the most popular figures in Argentina, where the government had once hunted his simulacrums through the slums. A weekly magazine reported that, thanks to the exhumation in Bolivia, his name had been cited in more Argentine media reports than anyone but the country's finance minister, who was still alive.

I was staring at that list, wondering why history bothered coming back around, when I noticed who was third in the rankings. Right below the little iconic photo of El Che in his beret was a picture of a handsome, fair-haired man named Alfredo Astiz. Known to the press as "the Blonde Angel," Astiz had been a young naval lieutenant during the peak of the Dirty War. He had specialized in penetrating "subversive" groups like Mothers of the Plaza de Mayo. He was directly responsible for the kidnapping and death of scores of people, including two French nuns abducted from a Mothers meeting. He shot one prisoner in the head and stood by watching while many others were tortured. Although not as cruel as some of his colleagues, Astiz had been cruel enough. Yet he had paid no price for his actions. He survived an unsuccessful prosecution for murdering a seventeen-year-old girl, and his navy career prospered. Despite surrendering his command in the Falklands war without firing a shot, Astiz became a lieutenant commander. He bragged in a television interview that he was untouchable. He was seen now lounging at the beach or dancing in discos.

Astiz was back in the news because the French government was attempting to prosecute him for the murder of the two French nuns. Argentina refused the French request, and the gesture would later come to nothing. It was merely a coincidence of timing that Astiz was in the papers during the same weeks that Che's burial site had been identified, yet there was something oddly symbolic about their mutual return to prominence. There they were next to each other in the news columns, two such different men—Marxist guerrilla and navy officer—yet both Argentine, both sons of the cultured leadership class, both combatants in a secret war. They were opposites in theory but startlingly close in origin, men who had lived clandestine lives in the service of political warfare, men obsessed with honor who nonetheless made the many compromises that a commitment to violence requires. They shared in a heroic subculture, in the rituals of extreme danger, intrigue, and secrecy. Like warriors everywhere, Astiz gained stature through the existence of his enemy; the radical left and the radical right existed in a kind of symbiosis, flip sides of the same coin, the one necessary to the other. This point was not lost on Astiz, of all people. In the text accompanying the photo, he was quoted as saying that he "admired" Che Guevara for his idealism and unwillingness to compromise. He might have been a communist subversive, but he was still *El Puro*, the pure one.

I had come to South America to find some youthful, original Guevara, perhaps a young man who predated the various encrustations of legend, the Ernesto who came before the Che. But with even a right-wing military murderer declaring himself a fan of the man, it was beginning to seem I had set myself an impossible task. You could ride across South America, you could see what he had seen, you could even reach all the way to his grave site in Bolivia. But if everyone agreed that Che was a hero—right-wing killers, Hollywood executives, guerrillas in the field, marketing experts, Fidel Castro, and church fathers—then no one really agreed on anything. Who, really, was Ernesto Guevara Lynch de la Serna? And who is Che?

"**O**h, it's a very bad moment for Che," the T-shirt salesman told me. "Nothing but smalls." He was a rotund, mustachioed fellow who cared more for rock bands than politics. It was lunchtime now, and en route to the Richmond for my daily defeat I'd spotted his shop in a commercial gallery and paused long enough to see how the Che shirts were moving.

"I sell three or four of these an afternoon," he went on, "five on Saturdays. There's a Che mania right now. It started a couple of years ago when a few bands that are fashionable with very young people—Los Fabulosos Cadillacs, Rage Against the Machine—started having Che banners at their concerts and so on. Then it really picked up with the search for his remains in Vallegrande. Now, with Antonio Banderas coming to town, forget it."

I asked him what the movie would be like. "They say he isn't going to be Che Guevara, just a typical Argentine Che. But I don't believe it. It's going to be just like when I saw the musical in London, Che and Evita dancing together. I have some Che backpacks if you want."

I didn't want. My own clothes and luggage had reappeared mysteriously at the airport, and I no longer needed shirts or gear, however iconic. I walked to the Richmond, but the man in tweed was absent from his usual seat. I let a coffee burn into my stomach and read the papers. Above the fold was an article detailing the triumphant march of stock prices on the Argentine *bolsa*. Below the fold an intrepid reporter had settled the mystery of Argentina's disappearing cats. As a rather gory photo showed, the children of the new shantytowns were roasting them over trash fires. With a kind of routine reluctance I called the customs broker from the house phone. "It's here," he said. I glanced at my watch: their office closed at three, and with luck I might just have time to do the paperwork and ride away. I jumped into a yellow-and-black Fiat cab and headed for the port, a route that passed behind the Casa Rosada. The taxi was running fast—this is a nation of frustrated Formula One fans—and up at the Plaza de Mayo I caught a sudden glimpse of a tiny crowd, some banners, and a cloud of smoke drifting through the air.

"Tear gas," the driver announced. "Roll up your window."

We barreled along toward the port, passing a dark green beast lumbering the other way up the avenue. It was an armored truck topped with a comically tiny spout for shooting water at the *delincuentes*. I asked the driver what cause had brought peaceful Argentina back to the brink of civil unrest.

"Well," he said, meditating for a moment while cutting off a bus. He looked in the mirror, not to check the bus but to see my face. "What day of the week is it?" he asked. Thursday, I said. "I think on Thursday it's the teachers."

Across Latin America, for the first time in a generation, the left had gone silent, reduced to these clockwork motions of the If-it's-Thursday-they-must-be-teachers variety. Once upon a time the ratio of missing cats to rising stocks would have provoked a guerrilla movement or at least the magical-realist flights of rhetoric upon which the hemisphere's left depended for life. But even the Spanish language had been captured by the values of capitalism now. Regional debate bristled with financial acronyms like NAFTA, GATT, and MERCOSUR. Latin America had become a net importer of capital for the first time in decades, hyperinflation was almost forgotten, and the World Bank and the International Monetary Fund dictated endless cuts in social spending to governments throughout the region. Even Fidel Castro was talking about efficiency and profit repatriation, and you could earn a master's of business administration at the University of Havana. It was a moment of transition in Latin America, when generations of history were being undone, when old arguments fell silent. This did not mean that the suffering and deprivation across Latin America were lessened, as the missing cats demonstrated. Global capitalism generated great wealth and then distributed it with blind indifference to need. Worldwide there were one and a half billion people living on less than a dollar a day; that number *increased* by about two hundred million in 1993. "People who find themselves at the juncture of worlds passing and worlds coming." Henry Adams noted long ago, "tend to be crushed like insects."

Latin America got the good along with the bad, and the world coming was in heavy evidence at the port, where the docks were so crowded with European luxury cars—Range Rovers for the *estancia* set and Alfa Romeos for the soccer players—that it took half an hour of wiggling between mirrors to find the dock foreman. He grunted when he heard what I wanted and led me into a long brick warehouse, up a ramp, and into a garage filled with new cars. In the corner was a motorcycle covered with plastic. He whipped off the cover with a great flourish to reveal a gleaming Honda chopper.

It was a lovely motorcycle, but not mine. The foreman implied that I should just shut up about my BMW dirt bike and take the Honda, but I persuaded him to keep looking, and we rode a passing forklift down the waterfront a block, each of us clinging to a side of the machine until it reached a prefabricated steel hangar. Inside were pallets of shrink-wrapped VCRs and, behind them, a twelve-year-old, blue-and-orange BMW R80 G/S that looked familiar. The saddlebags were still attached, which astonished the foreman (like most Argentines I've met, he felt that his countrymen were a race of thieves). I rifled quickly through the contents—a tent, sleeping bag, fishing rod, and a six-month-old copy of *Notas de Viaje,* or "Notes of a Trip," written by none other than Ernesto "Che" Guevara. The book was his own road diary from the 1952 trip, a guide to where he had been, what he had seen, how he had felt. It was to be my road map to the past and present of South America.

"Get it out of here," the foreman barked, but when I inserted and turned the key nothing happened. The green diode on the tiny dash should have glowed brightly, indicating that the clutch was in neutral and that the bike was ready to run. Instead, the diode was dark. I heaved at the kick starter for several minutes as he watched without patience, and just when I had given up hope, the bike caught, faintly, and ran with a low, hesitant gurgle, as if still nauseous from a month at sea.

I repacked the saddlebags and rolled out of the port. I had not brought a helmet to my chess game, and so I set out into traffic bare-headed, like a true *porteño*. The great avenues were filled with sprinting taxis and messengers on dirt bikes, and I raced along until my eyes began to water and the battery regained some strength. When an ambitious Renault shot across four lanes of traffic, nearly flattening me into a grease smudge—I remember only the rear window, with its NO FEAR sticker—I turned onto smaller streets. I began carving a series of turns at random, testing brakes and acceleration, adjusting the mirrors, throwing the bike from side to side on the straightaways to relearn its balance and gain confidence in its purchase on the ground. After a period of aimless dodging I looked up and saw that I had entered La Boca, the Brooklyn of Buenos Aires. Boca is a tough, working-class Italian neighborhood paved with cobblestones. The locals are guarded against outsiders and believe only in the invincibil-ity of the Boca soccer team and the divinity of Eva Duarte Perón. Like Guevara, she had been subjected to several exhumations since her death long ago, both literal excavations of her body and cultural renovations of her image.

I sprinted out of one intersection and a hundred feet later hit the brakes, hard, sliding deliberately over the slick cobblestones. You had to know the bike instinctively, even in its flaws. As I sat playing with the controls—the red kill switch, the headlight, the horn, the turn signals—I noticed that I had come to rest in front of a construction site. Someone had daubed the corrugated fencing with a spray-painted message for foreigners who came to tamper with old myths: MADONNA IS A WHORE.

The next morning Little Girl stood on the sidewalk, waving and crying out *"Ciao, ciao"* in her smoker's rasp. The Paraguayan door-man waved too; perhaps somewhere up above, Federico cried out his final *"Cómo te va?"* I made it five minutes down the road before being pulled over by the first cop I saw. He was a motorcycle policeman with shiny jackboots and an Italian Ducati. He took my papers in one hand but only pretended to read them while actually running his eyes over my bike.

"How fast does it go?" he said. This stumped me. What can you say to a policeman who asks how fast you have driven? "I don't know," I replied. We had a lengthy discussion by the roadside about German engineering, the reliability of driveshafts versus chains, and the torque problems generated by a monoshock. Neither of us could explain the monoshock.

On the day his trip began, Guevara had pulled away from the house with family and friends watching. As he turned to wave farewell, he lost control and nearly collided with a trolley car. He was almost finished with his hemispheric journey before leaving the block. I expected better luck, and got it when the trooper let me go.

I still don't know if this was a reasonable expectation.

Five hours and two hundred and twenty-nine miles later, I forced my right heel down into the dust, the brown bitch still firmly attached. I pushed down on the barbed wire with both palms and then pirouetted, bringing my left leg backward over the wire in a high arc and swinging it down in a trajectory that the dog understood only when it was too late. My boot heel connected with her neck just as she let go, and with a long, aggrieved yelp the mother of puppies went flying tail over tooth into a thorn bush. We mustn't be afraid of a little violence.

Limping back to the bike, I assumed the worst, but when I yanked off the boot there was only a slight scrape that had not drawn blood. My brother had thrust the boots on me, just hours before my departure, to replace the sneakers I had foolishly planned to wear.

My preparations for this trip had been shoddy by any standard. I'd spent only a few months conceiving a plan, and I didn't have a Swiss Army knife, enough money, a motorcycle license or insurance, a repair manual, shirts with epaulets, a photojournalist vest with twenty-two pockets, any arranged interviews, a good map, a sleeping bag suitable for ascending Mount Everest, a stove that burned four kinds of fuel, or, it would turn out months from now, a tire pump that actually worked. The things I did carry included a spare clutch cable and spark plugs, one inner tube (for some reason I thought only the rear tire would go flat), a six-year-old Macintosh PowerBook 100, a pair of $18 rain pants, a stove whose fuel cannot be purchased in South America, and a rotten Korean War surplus sleeping sack that dribbled feathers. My girlfriend had handed me a compass at the last minute. I was ill prepared and underfunded, but I had decided to go anyway.

The last-minute boots were like a forecast of good weather. If people kept taking care of me, I would come through. I pulled the right boot on and looked around, and although there was still nothing to see out here, nothingness has inviting qualities. I'd been reading one of the first travelogs ever set in Argentina, an 1826 tract by an English captain of engineers known as Francis "Galloping" Head. He earned his nickname by riding vast distances over the pampas, and he came to love their spareness:

> [*I*]*t is beautiful to see the effect which the wind has in passing over this wild expanse of waving grass; the shades between the brown and yellow are beautiful—the scene is placid beyond description—no habitation nor human being is to be seen, unless occasionally the wild and picturesque outline of the gaucho on the horizon. . . . The country has no striking features, but it possesses, like all the works of nature, ten thousand beauties. It has also the grandeur and magnificence of space, and I found that the oftener I crossed it, the more charms I discovered in it.*

Sometimes a few drops of gasoline trickle down the walls of an empty tank to fill the carburetors again. I reached for the tiny dashboard, the size of a paperback book, and twisted the key. The little green neutral light glowed like an emerald. The procedure was always the same, an ingrained routine for every motorcyclist: choke on; hit the starter button and wait for the roar; choke off; left foot up on the peg; left hand pulling in on the clutch; left toe knocking the shift peg down one click into first gear; check the neutral light is out; ease the clutch out with the left hand while twisting the right wrist for throttle; right foot up on the peg as you pull away and gain speed.

Seven tenths of a mile later the bike died again and coasted to a stop, and I set off to look for the next gaucho. I found a white fence and followed it to a driveway, which led to a boxlike one-story house with a bright red roof. Halfway to the house I stopped and clapped twice. Nothing happened, so after a few moments I covered half the remaining distance, clapped twice, and waited. I felt ridiculous standing in the sun at noon in the middle of a field covered with horse shit while clapping, but I waited. Again nothing, and I advanced a third time—close enough now to hear a radio blaring inside the house. I went up and banged hard on the door.

In time the gaucho appeared, wearing the usual baggy *bombacha* trousers and black hat turned up in front. We went around back to a shed where, hidden behind enough bridles and saddles to outfit a squad of dragoons, there was yet another dusty Ford Falcon. The gaucho cut a yard of garden hose, retrieved a sun-bleached two-liter Coke bottle from the trash ditch beyond the tomato plants, lay down on the ground, and methodically began sucking gas out of the Falcon's tank. For some reason the gas would not keep flowing after each pull on the tube, as if gravity were weak.

I insisted on taking a few mouthfuls myself, but the gas hit me like a drug. I spat a few ounces of fuel into the Coke bottle and then fell about the floor, hacking and wheezing and spitting. "It is not easy," the gaucho said, and took another mouthful. Eventually he filled the bottle halfway with a mixture of gas and spit. The next gas station was four miles down the road, he told me. The math looked good: half of a two-liter bottle would last about ten miles. He refused payment of any kind, and I stumbled back to the bike, fed it, and set off again.

The miles rolled by. After five there was no sign of the town, just the same unrelieved flatness and the sky overhead. Six miles passed, and seven. At eight miles I saw something on the horizon and grew hopeful; at nine I saw it was just a tollbooth; at ten I drove through it without slowing. The bike shuddered once, then again, but kept running on gaucho spit.

The road bent around another windbreak of poplars and there was the town, a half mile away. Then the engine died. I was going about seventy miles an hour when it quit, and now the math didn't look so good. I lay down on the tank to cut wind resistance and drifted silently sixty, fifty, forty, thirty, twenty miles an hour. The gas station was at the far end of town. It was going to be close.

I drifted down the main street, wobbled the last few yards, and curled up at the pump like an old dog on his bed. I bought nineteen liters of gas and one of Quilmes beer. I rode all the way back and left the beer on the gaucho's front step—because I had to, and because in the end the dog did let me go.

CHAPTER TWO

FELLOW TRAVELERS

Like Guevara, my first stop on an itinerary filled with larger things was a forgettable beach town called Villa Gesell, where I arrived with a sore ankle around three in the afternoon. The South Atlantic was an unappetizing brown here, discolored by the coast-hugging outflow of the great Río de la Plata estuary, which drains an enormous swath of the flatlands of Argentina, Brazil, Paraguay, and Uruguay. The streets of Villa Gesell were filled with sand, and I steered my way tentatively around the drifts and past the vacationing surfer boys from Buenos Aires dressed in the same NO FEAR T-shirts as their California cousins. I picked an empty restaurant for a late lunch and, wary of thieves, carried my saddlebags inside. I read while I ate.

> *The day of departure arrived. A nervous emotion invaded all of us. Surrounded by a noisy multitude of little boys attracted by the spectacle of the motorbike and our unusual dress, the departure began.*

That was a diary entry describing Guevara's departure forty-four years before, but not the one written by Guevara himself. This was from the road diary of a man named Alberto Granado, the other half of that "us." Guevara did not make his trip alone; his *Notas de Viaje* was filled with references to Granado, who had shared the motorcycle seat and all his adventures with him. But I had learned only a few months before that Granado too had kept a diary of the trip, describing the same events, the same places, and even the same conversations. Like Guevara's diary, which had languished in obscurity with the Guevara family for decades, Granado's diary had been forgotten for decades, and then finally published in Cuba in 1986, thirty-five years after their trip. I had a friend visiting Havana purchase a copy, which I now laid before me on the table beside my lunch. The edition was printed on flimsy paper with smudgy ink, under the grand title *Testimony: With El Che Across South America*. It had arrived just two days before my own departure, and this was literally the first chance I had had to crack the pages. This parallel account of the young Ernesto Guevara's travel experiences would allow me to corroborate basic facts about the trip and flesh out the picture of how travel had changed Ernesto.

Aside from a few qualities these two fellow-travelers shared—both men were from Córdoba and both were pursuing medicine—there was one overwhelming reason why Guevara wanted Alberto Granado along for the trip: Granado owned the motorcycle they were traveling on. The dilapidated 1939 Norton was mockingly named La Poderosa, or "the powerful one." (Actually, the Norton was named La Poderosa II; the original La Poderosa had been Granado's bicycle.)

This fourteen-year-old English bike was to carry both men into what they understood would be the greatest undertaking of their young lives. The twenty-nine-year-old Granado's friendship with the twenty-three-year-old Guevara was intense and would become the bookmark of the former's life. Not only did Granado journey across South America with Guevara, but Granado was already in 1952 a devoted Marxist who would play a crucial role in crystallizing the revolutionary instinct of his younger companion. Years later, when Guevara was the famous Che and living in Havana, Granado would move there to be near his friend and lend his help in the building of socialism. Forged in the experience of travel, their friendship would endure until Guevara's death in 1967.

Granado's account of the trip ran parallel to Guevara's own

notes, but I was only halfway through my *milanesa* sandwich and just one page into Granado's account when I realized that the two volumes were different in some important ways. The divergence began with the fundamental question of why the two Argentines were undertaking the trip in the first place.

Unlike Guevara, whose motorcycle "diaries" were, in fact, a polished memoir he had written after returning home, Granado's account was raw, a live diary written each night, filled with immediacy, sometimes eloquent, often dogmatic, usually hasty, and always larded with the obscure practical details that seem of enormous importance at the time. If Guevara had never become famous as the *Guerrillero Heroico* of the 1960s, no one would have plucked these scribbled entries from a desk drawer and given them their grand title.

In Cuba, the myth of the man they called the *Guerrillero Heroico* is an elaborate and official cult. Granado, a devoted supporter of the Cuban regime, was careful to do his part by heightening the noble motives behind Che's motorcycle journey. In his introduction, Granado wrote that he and Guevara traveled with political goals:

> *One had to know the world, but first Latin America, my*
> *suffering continent. And do so not with the eyes of a tourist,*
> *who looks only for landscapes, comfort, and ephemeral pleasures,*
> *but with the eyes and the spirit of a son of the people, who needs*
> *to know the beauty of the continent, the riches it contains, the*
> *men and women that inhabit it, as well as the internal and*
> *external enemies that exploit and impoverish it.*

Guevara's account put the emphasis on something slightly less noble: he wanted to have some fun. "I was restless," he wrote, calling himself "a dreamer and free spirit" interested in "faraway places, sailing tropical seas, traveling through Asia."

Asia proved beyond reach, but Guevara and Granado were tinkering on the motorcycle one October morning in 1951 when they realized that their means of travel was right in front of them. Instead of Asia, the two could make a journey across their own hemisphere as far as the roads would take them. Guevara claimed credit for the idea and said they planned to go as far as North America on La Poderosa. Granado also took credit for the plan, which he said was to go only to Venezuela. Perhaps it was inappropriate to admit that the *Guerrillero Heroico* had dreamed of making it big in the USA.

Side by side on the table in front of me, the cheap, smudged pages of Granado's Cuban account contrasted sharply with the glossy look of the British edition of Guevara's diary. The differences in tone were just as wide. Granado's language was enough to kill the soul— "bourgeois-democratic freedoms" and "the suffering proletariat" leaped off the page while "capitalist exploitation" lurked behind every tree in South America. Yet Guevara, who disclaimed all higher motives, wrote like a true searcher. Where Granado offered moral certitude, Guevara embraced his own limitations and biases:

> *So, the coin was tossed, turned somersaults; sometimes coming up heads, sometimes tails. Man, the measure of all things, speaks through my mouth and recounts in my own words what my eyes saw. Out of ten possible heads I may have only seen one tail, or vice versa: there are no excuses; my mouth says what my eyes told it. Was our view too narrow, too biased, too hasty, were our conclusions too rigid? Maybe so . . .*

Whatever the twenty-three-year-old Ernesto was searching for—literary inspiration, adventure, or a solution to the world's problems—he mounted the motorcycle with his eyes and mind open to the world he was about to enter. His at times brutal self-doubt was a sign of fundamental honesty, of an integrity uncontaminated by ideology or the habits of rigid thinking that political commitment required.

Guevara's spare *Notas de Viaje* had been dressed up considerably for its debut in English as *The Motorcycle Diaries*. The rather short narrative of the trip had been padded with letters that Guevara wrote home and long excerpts from his father's memoirs. ("Years later, thinking back over his continuous traveling," Ernesto Guevara Sr. wrote, "I realized that it had convinced him of his true destiny.") The thrust of this English edition could be judged by its cover: The letters *C, H,* and *E* dwarfed everything else on the book jacket. That oversized type was something of a lie, for in fact the diaries had not been written by a famous revolutionary and Marxist superhero named Che. They were written by a young and unknown skeptic named simply Ernesto. One was a famous figure; the other was an unknown. Che was a political leader; Ernesto, I was beginning to believe, was a much more complex figure, a young man in search not of the world but of his own small place in it.

But before they could discover the world, Granado and Guevara had to get moving. They stayed a few nights with Guevara's relatives in Villa Gesell, stocked up on food, and then rolled onward. I decided to not even spend a night, but ride hard for the south and a more important conversation awaiting me there. I tucked both oddly mismatched diaries into my saddlebags again, paid, and passed out of town by the brown ocean.

In his entry on Villa Gesell, Alberto Granado noted his astonishment at even this rather silty bit of water. The cause of his excitement was simple: raised in the mountains, this was the first time he had set eyes on the sea. Guevara also noted his friend's discovery:

> *For me, the sea has always been a confidant, a friend which absorbs all you tell it without betraying your secrets, and always gives the best advice—a sound you can interpret as you wish. For Alberto, it is a new, oddly perturbing spectacle, reflected in the intensity with which his gaze follows every wave swelling then dying on the beach. At almost thirty, Alberto is seeing the Atlantic for the first time and is overwhelmed by a discovery which opens infinite routes to all points of the globe.*

Granado was less poetic. Writing in Villa Gesell on January 6, he said the ocean and other sites "give me a material base to tell myself how marvelous and important for our future formation this until-now hypothetical voyage is going to be."

Riding away at almost four in the afternoon, with just a few hours of sunlight to guide me to Miramar, the difference between these two views of the same ocean sat with me, ill digested. To Guevara, the sea was something mysterious and yet personal, a confidant, a friend with whom you shared secrets. To Granado, the same ocean was a "material base" for his "future formation." The sea itself could be incorporated into this larger mission, a crusade whose outlines I was only beginning to see in the pages of his book, and one that would come to haunt me—and perhaps Guevara, too—as the three of us rode into the months ahead.

For a few hours the main road to Patagonia ran southwest, following the coastline as it turned from the tropical embrace of the Rio de la Plata and bit into the pampas. From now on South America would grow narrow, pinched by the corset of two oceans eager to meet at Cape Horn. The farther south you went, the more this narrowing seemed to squeeze the blood from the land, numbing it into a pale, cold wilderness. By the end of the day I was riding almost straight into the lowering sun, racing down the empty road at eighty miles an hour, hoping to reach shelter before darkness arrived, at around 9 P.M. in the Southern Hemisphere's January summer.

Miramar was the great resort town where Guevara and Granado arrived on the sixth of January, 1952. It had taken them three days of travel to cover the distance I had done in eight hours, dog bite and lunch included. Modernized roads played a part, certainly, but the most important difference seemed to be in our motorcycles. Guevara and Granado were devoted to their old companion, La Poderosa, while I had bought my bike used—on a credit card—just two weeks before shipping it to Buenos Aires. I barely knew how to put gas into it and certainly hadn't given it a name—the idea of naming my motorcycles had always seemed plain silly. They were machines, not horses or humans, and if the BMW was really an entity of fuel, electricity, and physics, then giving it anthropomorphic qualities would be a distraction from its true nature. Alberto Granado had no such overrational qualms: the Powerful One was the perfect name for a motorbike that wasn't. The Norton was not particularly large to start with and definitely inadequate for two riders. Thirteen years old by the time they hit the road, La Poderosa was overloaded with an assortment of luggage, including a heavy canvas tent, waterproof saddlebags filled with personal goods, a pair of camp cots, a teakettle, food, a medical kit including Guevara's asthma medicine, a pistol, and—they being Argentines—a barbecue grill. On this underpowered, overburdened, battle-scarred machine they planned to cross the hemisphere. Or at least hoped to. Guevara was so apprehensive about their chances of success that, "to save face, just in case," he told friends that he was only going to Chile on the bike.

My own odds looked better. The maps showed more roads, on straighter routes, in better condition, and everything about motorcycles and camping equipment had improved. Like La Poderosa, my BMW was more than a dozen years old, but I was traveling alone and therefore lightly. My engine was larger, and the technology of motors had improved immensely in the almost half-century interval since La Poderosa left its factory in England. My bike could handle the trip.

The driver was another question. I didn't plan to reach North America, but even if I followed their route on the motorbike only as far as Peru, and then turned toward Che's grave site in Bolivia, that was still months and thousands of miles away across various borders, the steepest mountains and driest deserts in the world, through unknown hazards ranging from dogs to thieves to guerrillas. Listening to my pepper-grinder engine all afternoon, I half wished that I had lied and told my friends that I was only out for the short jaunt to Chile. I had been singing as I rode, an occupational hazard for motorcyclists locked inside their own helmets hour after hour, with an audience of one. Having run out of gas once today, I had somehow become fixated on an annoying Mexican folk song with its nonsensical lyrics about a cockroach that runs out of fuel and comes to a halt:

> *La cucaracha, la cucaracha*
> *ya no puede caminar*

There were many versions of that song in English, all of them cleaner than the original. Back in Chihuahua, the original lyric had complained about a shortage of *marihuana* that stops the cockroach in its tracks. In my case it had been gasoline, so like many a gringo before me I cleaned up the lyric:

> *La cucaracha, la cucaracha*
> *ya no puede caminar*
> *porque no tiene, porque le falta*
> *gasolina pa' comprar*

Just at twilight I saw Miramar rise ahead of me. The blue ocean had shouldered aside the brown estuary by now and reclaimed the coast. Wild, foaming breakers cut into a line of cliffs that seemed held in place only by the roots of the tall white apartment blocks lining the sea. The two-lane road that ran along the coast into the city resembled a camel market. Vehicles of every sort tried to move in every direction at once, a Ford Falcon jammed with an extended sunburned family backing out of a beach-side parking spot into the path of a Mercedes that was in turn swerving around a boy carrying a surfboard toward a waiting dune buggy while clouds of impossibly young motorcyclists riding impossibly loud dirt bikes swept through every channel of pavement more than a foot wide, anyone at any moment liable to be skewered on the end of a twelve-foot-long fishing rod shouldered indiscriminately by a wandering grandfather who found walking the side of the road too painful on his bare feet and therefore used the middle. The entire high-season population of the town emptied onto the beach each day and spread up the coastline, then was inhaled back into Miramar's trashy bars and steak restaurants at the approach of night.

I crawled through the interwoven madness until I reached a traffic circle at the very edge of town, put down the kickstand, and dismounted. I needed to orient myself, find a place to stay, and rest my aching butt. Nose-deep in a guidebook, I didn't notice the sound at first. Then it became too loud to ignore. I looked up and saw that a half dozen dirt bikes were independently circling the roundabout. Some had two passengers; all were tiny, whiny machines without the slightest redeeming value. The drivers—not one of them wore a helmet, and several were barefoot—patrolled round and round, occasionally gunning their engines in solar flares of testosterone. They were all looking at me.

The first one stopped within seconds of my looking up. He was about sixteen and still had sand on his flip-flops. "What kind of *moto* is that?" He'd never seen a BMW motorcycle before. I told him it was German.

"How fast does it go?"

That was the same question the policeman had asked me this morning in Buenos Aires. This time, having driven eighty miles an hour at one point during the day, I had an answer to give him. He grunted and drove on.

The second bike stopped a minute later. The driver and his passenger both looked about fifteen. The kid in back was wearing another one of those NO FEAR T-shirts. I'd believed that line once too.

"How fast does it go?"

I added ten to the figure I'd just named. They grunted.

The third bike, the loudest yet, had a genuine grown-up for a driver. He gunned the engine every few seconds.

"What kind of bike is that?" German, I told him. "How fast does it go?" I added ten to the figure I'd just named. No grunt this time, just a grave nod. We were a couple of motorcycle guys talking motorcycle stuff. He was polite enough to ask if I needed any help, and pointed me toward a campground before roaring off in a cloud of oil-laden blue smoke.

Two more of my colleagues of the road caught me before I could leave the roundabout. Each time I added ten to the previous figure, until I was going a hundred and twenty miles an hour standing still. The last boy finally whistled appreciatively.

La Poderosa must have been a sight when it pulled into Miramar with its two passengers and tied-down exotica. In 1952, the city by the sea was an aristocratic reserve, a swank summering destination for the traditional elite of Argentina. Guevara was here to visit his girl-friend, María del Carmen Ferreyra, known as Chichina. She was a seventeen-year-old Córdoba girl from one of that city's best families whom Ernesto had been courting for some time. According to *My Son El Che* (written by Ernesto Guevara Sr. after Che's death), Chichina was "a charming young girl. . . . My family and I were all convinced he would marry her."

The Guevaras did not have much money, although they still had some of the trappings of aristocrats, like a home in Buenos Aires. Ernesto Sr. had lost much of the family fortune by poorly timed investments in the cultivation of *yerba mate*, the bitter green tea con-sumed ritualistically by Argentines. But the Guevaras still had one thing that mattered more than money—a good name. On the father's side, they were distantly related to various muckety-mucks, includ-ing that noted Chilean Admiral Lynch. On the maternal side, the de la Sernas were notably upper class, the source of what little money the family still had. In the hierarchical social structure of those times, the family was therefore "impoverished aristocrats," the noun being more important than the adjective. Ernesto Guevara was still of a suitable class to court Chichina.

Alberto Granado was not. Granado was a short, husky fellow with few social graces, a long history of political radicalism, and enough talent to become a biochemist, a position similar to pharma-cist that in Argentina comes with the medical title "Doctor." Granado carried this humble background on his shoulder. A self-declared

Marxist, he put his training in class analyses to work as soon as he met Chichina and her friends in Miramar.

"The stay here has been very beneficial," he wrote with characteristic gravity in his diary. "I have gotten to know many people of a social level that I have never encountered before, and frankly it makes me feel proud of my own class origin. Never in my life have I met, much less rubbed elbows with, this type of people. It is incredible how they think, how they reason. They are types who believe that by divine right or something similar that they deserve to live unconcerned with everything but their social position. . . ."

Granado spared Chichina from his disdain, noting that she was unusually intelligent and open-minded for a member of the oppressor class. Then he raged on for a full page about the spoiled rich kids surrounding her. Granado's didactic tone broke for a moment when he fell into a rare description of the sea at night, its dimensions and infinite movements still new to him. Yet even this was part of the struggle to Granado.

"What alienates me," he wrote, summarizing the night scene, "is the way all these people who accompany us, and claim to feel profoundly the beauty of the night and of the sea, don't feel like I an enormous desire that all the world would be able to admire and enjoy so much beauty."

After a make-out session with Chichina, Guevara also indulged in a little class analysis. The couple fled the cold (and in those days, deserted) beach and apparently took shelter and pleasure in a car. "[I]n the great belly of the Buick," Guevara wrote with relish, "the bourgeois side of my universe was still under construction."

My own night in Miramar was thoroughly proletarian. The campground was jammed, and in the belly of my tent I tried to sleep despite the blaring competition among three cassette players and the gas lanterns hissing around me. The dusty campground was filled with the improvised rigs of Argentine families on vacation. A group of Boy Scouts approached and tried to buy my tent out from under me, but fled when I named what I'd actually paid for it.

Times were always hard in Argentina, but now they were hard in some new ways. The reigning economic doctrine was the same here and across the Third World: neoliberalism, which simply means loosening capital and tightening belts. The IMF had forced Argentina to cut a billion dollars from its government budget—an austerity visited largely on the poor through education cuts and higher prices for food. The minimum wage was $325 per month—or about one third the basic cost of living over the same period. Social spending, traditionally the highest in Latin America, had been cut sharply. Almost half the children in Argentina under fourteen lived in extreme poverty. Unemployment was officially less than 20 percent, but unofficially somewhere north of there. Nonetheless, Argentina had certain things other countries in Latin America could only imagine—an enforced minimum wage, for example, and social programs of any kind, however reduced. One result was that Miramar was now a bastion of pudgy parents in ill-fitting swimsuits, young couples sleeping in tube tents, and sullen kids affecting the look of the American underclass while bobbing to rap.

This middle class had risen over the last decades, partly rooted in the policies of the Peróns—the bombastic Juan and the diamond-encrusted Evita. They had won their popularity in the late 1940s by tossing economic promises to the people in my campground—the ordinary working poor, the "shirtless ones." Even though the welfare state they promised was incomplete and partly responsible for bankrupting Argentina, it created pensions for the old and jobs for the young. An Argentine auto industry thrived behind protectionist walls, producing obsolete Ford Falcons into the 1980s: this was inefficiency by free-market standards, but not to the factory workers who took home First World industrial wages year after year. Argentina was still not a First World country, but ownership of even a battered old Fiat was a stunning achievement measured against the economic conditions in Peru or Brazil. Meat was cheap, university was almost free, and people could now afford, once in a while, a trip to the beach.

The throngs in my discotheque/campground were proof that Granado's "enormous desire" had come true, that ordinary people were now able to enjoy the one-time reserves of the elite. Egalitarian reforms are not nearly so chic as the high societies they displace. If you were part of the elite, you could regret the crowded conditions at formerly quiet beach resorts. You could be horrified by the noise, the trash in the streets, and the poor taste in music. But even an aristocrat would have to concede that this was a small price to pay for a more just society. Argentina had changed, and for the better.

This thought comforted me until 3 A.M., when the last radio went dead and I quickly followed its example.

One of the women who grew up around Chichina remembered Alberto Granado as "an unpleasant young man, someone you didn't want to be seen with." That was the worst thing you could say about someone in Córdoba society.

According to Granado, that kind of class snub was beneath Chichina, and I had to agree after meeting her. I had traveled to Córdoba without knowing quite what I would find, but Chichina agreed to meet me for a half-hour discussion on the steps of the city cathedral at 10 A.M. She was slim, dressed in a pants suit, with neat brown hair and a grace undiminished by six decades. Chichina was a biologist by training but now worked in Córdoba's municipal archives as a historian.

We strolled through the leafy center of the city past churches, libraries, and convents. The half hour easily became an hour as we chatted comfortably on topics from religious art to sculpted fountains, then viewed local architecture designed by various relatives. We discussed the latest newspaper article by Jorge Castañeda, a Mexican biographer of Che, and reviewed her life during the Dirty War. We agreed on the cult of Evita Perón, disagreed on economic globalization, and pondered, at least briefly, the fate of Africa, the Internet, Cuba's health care system, Greenwich Village, the publishing industry, and race relations in Peru. In short, she talked about everything except Ernesto Guevara. She had warned me about this in advance. During a phone conversation while I was still in New York she said that I was wasting my time coming to see her. ("No," was how she put it, "I won't talk about it.") Now, repeatedly and with growing steeliness, she brushed aside my questions about Ernestito Guevara.

Yet *Che* Guevara she would talk about. The difference was important to her: Ernestito was an item from her own past that she wanted to forget or at least control. Che, however, was an abstraction, a political generality that her historian's mind could not resist. We stopped for a *café cortado*, and she spoke with ease about this famous man called Che. She was fascinated by the ongoing search for his body in Vallegrande, Bolivia, and quizzed me on the latest theories about where the corpse had gotten to. "We have a tradition with corpses, you know," she said, ticking off a frighteningly long list of Argentines who had been posthumously dug up, moved, mutilated, or otherwise denied their long rest (Juan Perón, for example, had posthumously traveled the globe). She liked the theory, already being advanced by some Bolivians, that the CIA had secretly stolen the body, and she was horrified by the cultish behavior that had sprung up around El Che. "Che Guevara is now a consumer product; it's incredibly ironic," she said with a long, passionate laugh. And she was confident that he went to Bolivia to kill himself, aware that his was an impossible mission. "Don't you think it was suicide?" she asked me. But all this seemed totally unrelated to Ernesto Guevara, the young man with whom she had been in love. She had deliberately set aside that part of her life, that romance of youth that happened to make her a tangent of history. She wanted her own history, and had it. She had married, raised children, become a biologist and historian, done things that were worthy in their own right, become a figure in her own right, not simply someone's girlfriend from long ago.

But her relaxed tone was really not so relaxed. It was a device, as if to say that this talk of Che Guevara was just another topic of conversation, an abstract set of data for the historian in her to consider. Her own stake in it was hidden away, sunk beneath the depths of a carefully constructed life. Only two accidents parted those waters.

The first came when I asked for her address, to send her a copy of any articles I wrote about Guevara. Searching for a blank piece of paper, she began flipping through my notebook, and there stumbled on a list of questions I had written the night before, when I still hoped she would break her promise and speak freely. There were three questions in the notebook. Chichina spoke English, but she handed the notebook back and asked me to translate them.

I read them out as I had written them. "Number one: What did Guevara say about purpose of 1952 trip?"

"He just wanted to travel, that's all. Young people always want adventure. Nothing more. He wanted to go. So he went."

"Number two: How did he seem different after the trip?"

"I don't know," she said immediately. "I only saw him twice afterwards." She was agitated now, feeling ambushed.

"Number three: What specific memories do you have of his departure?"

"No," she said, cutting the air with her hand as if slapping away the question. She got up from the table and left the coffee shop. She was too polite to run away, however, and I caught up to her quickly and apologized. This did not fool her for a second, but it did restore some form and manner to a day that had stretched from an assigned thirty minutes to four hours. We began walking back into the center of town. She wanted to show me one more local site that she was particularly proud of, the University of Córdoba law school building, which had recently been redesigned by a relative who was a noted architect. Entering a long, dark passageway, we pushed against a current of outgoing students to reach a traditional Spanish interior courtyard, which had now been joined to a large modern building with an asymmetric staircase that pierced a series of floating walls. We stood side by side, admiring the bold work. Then we turned around to leave.

That's when she saw the sign. It was handmade, filled with urgent exhortations to the student body. The topic was obscure, but the message was not. Across the top, in foot-high letters, it read VENCEREMOS, or "We will win." This had been his slogan. And below that, taking up most of the poster, there was the picture of him.

The same picture as always, the relentlessly pure gaze into history crowned by the militant beret. He looked very youthful, a hand-some young man. It was the face she had once kissed in the belly of the Buick. We both stopped cold.

"It is an icon," she said acidly. "It has nothing to do with him." The students milled past us. "It's just a way of saying which side you are on, that's all." And then, as she slipped out into the darkness of the passageway, so faintly that I could barely hear her, she spoke one last time. "They don't even know who he was," she muttered.

As is customary in Latin America, I had left the motorbike parked on a sidewalk in Córdoba during the interview. I was fiddling with the lock a few minutes later when a handsome man in a beautiful long wool overcoat and a beret stopped, eyed my American license plates, dirty clothes, and strapped-on luggage, and asked some friendly questions about where I was from and where I was going. I told him I was retracing a motorcycle journey that Che Guevara had once made.

"I knew him," the man said plainly. "The last time I saw him was when he got back from that motorcycle trip."

Like most people, the fellow mixed up old dates—he placed the trip in the late '40s, not the early '50s—but I believed him because he emphasized that he had barely known Guevara. They were just casual acquaintances, he said. Years after schooling together, he'd seen Guevara on the street "a few blocks from here."

"I said to him, 'What have you been up to?' and he said he'd been all over South America on a motorcycle, crossing the Andes to Chile, all the way to Peru." The man recalled two things about this conversation. The first was that when he congratulated Guevara on the trip, saying how proud he was that an Argentine had crossed South America, Guevara had immediately replied, *"No soy argentino; soy americano."*

To be *americano* doesn't mean to be from the U.S. of A. It means to be Pan-American, "of the Americas," and sounds just as awkward and politically correct in Spanish as it does in English. The implication was clear: the trip had made him an internationalist. "Before, he never—never—spoke of politics to me," the man said with a shrug.

The second surprise came when, midway through their conversation, the man referred to Guevara as he had always called him: Ernestito, or Little Ernesto. Guevara rejected his own name for a new one. "He said, 'You know what they called me on the trip? Che.' He was proud of it!"

Five minutes later, after a lecture on the sin of letting Madonna play Evita on film, the man in the beret was gone. "She wasn't a whore!" were the last words he called out to me.

In Miramar, Guevara wrote, "The two days I'd planned stretched like elastic into eight." His tone was at once self-mocking ("the bittersweet taste of the goodbye mingling with my inveterate halitosis") and self-conscious. Every voyager conceives his own departure, a place and moment that often differs greatly from the physical point of departure because it is the demarcation of another frontier entirely. Up to this point, the motorcyclists were still within their home orbit. They had stayed with Granado's relatives in Rosario, at the Guevara house in Buenos Aires, with Guevara's relatives in Villa Gesell, and then in Miramar they were introduced into Chichina's comfortable society. Now, on the outskirts of Miramar and their familiar world, the true voyage began, the enormity of the Southern Hemisphere at once summoning and cautioning them. There would be no more Buick bellies, no relatives handing them stocks of canned food. In leaving Chichina finally, painfully alone, Guevara had also severed himself from his own desires. It was time to submit himself to the discipline of chance, to confront expectation with reality, to conform years of hope to some version of the actual earth.

Our destinations had to be, necessarily, the same, yet I could not follow every mile of their route. Not only were the details vague— even with two diaries for corroboration, I had little more than a list of towns they passed through—but it also seemed pointless to reenact their every move when it was their experience of discovery that I was after. They were heading into a wild, undeveloped Patagonia, toward a place called San Martín, and I would have to find my own way there.

During that 3:30 A.M. argument in a tango bar in Buenos Aires, the truck driver and smuggler had dismissed my planned route to San Martín, explaining that the unpaved roads and wild terrain of '52 were gone, replaced by a paved superhighway lined with convenience stores. Working with my pen and a cocktail napkin, he drew a route that went due south, deeper into Patagonia. It was a divergence from the path of Guevara and Granado—the two G's, as I was beginning to think of them—but the trucker was sure it was wilder, more the old Patagonia. "You want to see what it was like back then," he said, "then this is the way. You'll really be on your own."

Before I fled my dusty Miramar campground the next morning, headed west and south, I studied the map of Patagonia. The lines that portrayed roads first grew thin, then dotted, and finally petered out in blank spaces, like capillaries disappearing under skin. Of his own departure from Miramar, Guevara wrote, "I finally felt myself wafted away on the winds of adventure, towards worlds which I fancied stranger than they were, in situations I imagined much more normal than they turned out to be."

That morning, before pulling out of the campground, I took a black marker and wrote the words YES FEAR in thick letters across the back of my helmet.

CHAPTER THREE

BIG IN JAPAN

There are moments on a motorcycle when all the glory of motion is distilled into one purposeful package. Chasing curves over a swelling landscape, a motorcycle enters the pure expression of physics and is bound to the road in a way no car will ever know. The rider and machine are literally balanced on the infinitely thin line where centripetal force meets gravity. Despite this state of suspended disaster, the sensation of risk is largely a sensation; the motorcycle is in harmony with the road, and risk comes overwhelmingly from other drivers. Any moment of travel on a motorcycle is a light and essential moment, an agile rebuke to a life conducted in one place. The raw force of the engine is not hidden beneath a hood, but alternately purrs and growls a few inches from the knees, demanding the consciousness of power. Sealed behind glass, insulated by climate control systems and music, the driver of a car knows nothing about the directions of the wind, the lay of sunlight, the small changes in temperature between a peak and a valley, the textured noise of differing asphalts, or the sweet and sour aromas of manured fields or passing pine forests. Engaged in all the senses and elements, balanced in the present tense, a rider on two wheels can taste moments of oneness with the road.

Alas, this wasn't one of those moments. After three hard days and two bad nights I came finally to a sliding, squirming halt in a thick pebbly gravel at the end of Valdés Peninsula. The truck driver had been right. I was on my own.

National Route 3, as the road south was called, had been pock-marked, scarred, and prone to sudden fits of gravel, all in all a merci-less experiment in moving fast down a dangerous yet utterly boring route that lasted hour after hour, morning and afternoon, day after day, interrupted only by brief interludes in hideous gas stations manned by surly men dishing overpriced fuel. This shakedown cruise was pure pain: the new Plexiglas windscreen on the bike proved too short by a few inches, so that a sixty-five-mile-an-hour wind slipped over the top and tugged at my helmet all day, pressing the chin strap into my neck; the tip of my nose burned red and then peeled; my shoulders and behind complained incessantly; I became very dirty. Later I would miss the Ruta Nacional 3, of course, but I didn't know that at the time.

Patagonia is immense and more impressive than lovely in its austere vastness. With every mile south the land turned a lighter brown. Green grasses faded to tan clumps on a canvas of powdery soil. Where the road cut near the sea I saw a churlish and black Atlantic dressed with constant whitecaps. It was an ever-diminishing landscape: flatter, emptier, windier, a desert without sand, hot by day and cold by night. The last hundred miles out the peninsula were on a loose gravel track that caught the wheels and threw me down twice. I'd topped up my tank in the pathetic town where the gravel began, and each time the bike fell over gasoline trickled out of the carbure-tors, wetting the stones. The dark stains evaporated quickly in a wind that ripped off the Atlantic at twenty-five miles an hour, an offshore blast that smelled only of fathomless distance, of the great expanse of ocean east toward Africa and south toward the ice.

Valdés Peninsula is a geologic oddity, thrust far into the cold cur-rents of the South Atlantic yet home to the lowest point in South America, a broad, white salt pan some thirty-five meters below sea level that I had passed quickly on my way in. This featureless plain was the dullest tourist site I'd ever seen, but every day a bus pulled to a halt beside it, disgorging groups of visitors who were expecting the Patagonia of wall calendars. The buses progressed around the peninsula, pausing at ocean vistas and heading always to the north point, where, if you arrived at high tide, you might see one of the local orcas charge the beach, scattering—and only occasionally catching—the seal pups that played tauntingly in the surf. The rest of the peninsula was satisfyingly empty, a landscape without utility poles or houses or pavement.

I'd finally come to a halt at Caleta Gonzalo, a zipper of a bay at the ocean end of the hundred-mile peninsula. Twice a day, Caleta Gonzalo opened along its length and closed again, breathing water in and out in an enormous tidal swing that exposed almost ten miles of mud, then reflooded it. Steep cliffs dropped down to a beach where a dozen obese sea elephants brayed and dozed. Despite the briny stink of the tidal flats, the beach looked attractive. I'd driven back and forth for miles, scaring up a rare Patagonian fox and several loping guanacoes but failing to spot even a single dip or hollow to shield my tent from the wind, nor any man-made structure to provide lee shelter. From on high you could spy the magellanic penguins as they waded into the water and fell over with a cute belly flop. In an instant these waddling land creatures were reborn as subsurface birds, their useless wings now fins that helped them school in speedy flocks through the undersea.

Everywhere, the elements sounded their warnings. A blood-orange light fled the setting of the sun behind me, and the wind already carried a premonition of how cold it would be in half an hour. I needed shelter quickly. Night was minutes away, and in this unpopulated zone I was ready to ignore the No Camping signs sprinkled thoughtfully along the cliff, but I knew why they were really there. At high tide the beach would disappear, and the water came in like a flash flood. If you were asleep on the beach you would never make it. A month before my arrival a careless camper had been killed that way.

I drove south on the bay road, rounding bluff after bluff in search of any sheltered spot, but the ground was flat everywhere and scoured by the violence of the air. If I'd had a car I could have slept in it, but instead I needed protection from elements that cared nothing for "oneness."

Hurrying along, I almost passed the little farm nestled in a dell where the cliffs briefly faded away and a cluster of buildings touched the high-water line. There were four sheep ranches on the Valdés Peninsula, and these buildings were an outstation on the biggest, which ran more than 40,000 head.

This is where my filth came in handy. If there was one thing I was learning to admire about the young Ernesto Guevara, it was his unmitigated gall. As story after story in his diary showed, the man was absolutely shameless, a master at the traveler's art of scamming, borrowing, begging, or otherwise landing accommodation, favors, food, clothes, money, introductions, jobs, dance partners, and liquor. When it came to freeloading, Guevara was a prince. "We aren't that broke," he once wrote to his mother after cadging a bed in a hospital, "but explorers of our stature would rather die than pay for the bourgeois comfort of a hostel."

Menaced on both sides by barking black dogs, I rode down the driveway of the ranch, dismounted, and clapped twice. Then I waited the customary two minutes, the black dogs barking all the while, circling slowly as I stood stock still. I spent the time preparing a little speech. I had to sound needy, yet not desperate. I had to plead for a roof, neither so demanding that I would offend nor so tentative that I would be rejected. I had to balance a humble tone with the subtle implication that I was a person of enormous importance, deserving of aid. For proof of the latter, I carried in my breast pocket a letter of introduction from a New York magazine, ready to spring forth like a passport from the Other World.

When he came out—a fat, greasy fellow in a sun-bleached PARIS ELLE T-shirt, his hair wild in the wind—he didn't wait for my speech. He looked at the setting sun, the distant horizon, and above all the dirt on my clothes.

"Come in, come in," he said, "you had better spend the night." His name was Florio, and he had the buttery handshake of a man who handled sheep. He waved at the dogs, who fell silent, and led me inside.

My bed was the floor of the cookhouse. After three twelve-hour days of riding my ugly cockroach of a motorcycle, I slept soundly and long. The broken cement felt like a down mattress.

The hens woke me when they strutted into the shed and bobbed nervously, emitting feed-me clucks. The tin roof played a twangy tune, like an instrument in the wind that had risen during the night. Outside it was blowing hard enough to send an unhappy hen rolling beak-over-talon past the shed from time to time.

Florio listened to the radio, measured the wind, and sent his son David out to tell me that I was grounded. It was gusting to forty-five miles an hour now, and I could not drive. The boy told me this and kept talking. The dam of solitude first leaked and then gushed. Nine years old, living in isolation with his father and 40,000 sheep, the boy needed nothing so much as to speak. As I stood silently with him in the sunshine, both of us leaning against the wind, he unleashed everything at once, a gale of words about the neighbors, who lived an hour away, and the level of water in the well, which was low, and the whales and sharks that came into the bay. He named the starving cats that wandered the yard eyeing the chickens, and explained the work histories of both black dogs, along with the good qualities of various birds, the murderous nature of foxes, and which of every animal that walked or swam was good or bad, which cherished or hated. He talked of the orcas that came into the bay to hunt seals and tasty sea lion pups, and of the tourists who came on great lumbering buses to watch the orcas hunt, and of the water truck, which was three days late, and of the strange English boy he met once at a boarding school, a boy who spoke very oddly, almost as though he had different words for things.

"*Myaw myaw myaw;* we couldn't understand anything he said," David explained. The fever or speech ran on, burning at the boy so

badly that he twitched and jumped and jumbled words, hunching
down to tell me about the coloration of chicken eggs, then jumping
up to describe the stars we would see at night, and the paths of airplanes, and the cost of soccer balls, and his fervent desire to drink
Coca-Cola. "I go through mountains of shoes my father says I'm
crazy he can't believe it but I don't do anything except when it's raining and the mud gets everywhere and the rain kills the chickens that
one lays white eggs it's the only one the *patrón* comes to visit sometimes and I showed him but if it's an east wind it's cold and wet
and that kills the chickens or the fox comes and gets them which
is why they sit in their bush all night where the dogs don't chase them
I like the cats better my kitten is better will you take a picture of
him?"

By my watch he talked for twenty-five minutes without interruption. What finally stopped him was that I belched, and at this he
fell over in the dirt and chicken shit and began laughing his head off,
the fever of an entire solitary winter broken by a fit of endless giggles.
He'd never heard a foreigner belch before. Before he could start talking again, I asked him if he'd ever heard of Che Guevara.

David looked broken by the question. My tone told him it was an
adult matter, something serious and from the outside world, but I
was mouthing words as meaningless as those of the strange little English boy at boarding school. This was something from beyond the
realm of foxes and sea elephant pups and good and bad winds. "Does
he play football?" he asked tentatively.

Later I risked the short trip to the north shore, but the orcas
never came and the seals sunned themselves unmolested. When I got
back Florio was still sitting inside at the same table, his ear tuned to
the transistor voice of the world. There was no news from the atmosphere.

In the morning I lay on the floor listening to the roof, which struck a
lower tone than the day before. The shed was decorated with old

shears and handmade knives hanging from the wall, their rusty points dangling down in the general direction of my sleeping bag. The tools were waiting for October, for the 40,000 sheep to finish converting grass into wool and then to line up in the chutes and paddocks and march in steady panic under these sharpened edges.

Little David came to the door carrying the same message from his father that I had heard in the tin roof: the wind was down in the twenties. David stood just inside the doorway of the cook shed, silent but clearly crestfallen by my decision to abandon him to the sheep and cats and chickens and orcas. He watched with wide eyes as I handled each of my possessions in turn, brushing stray down from my sleeping bag and stuffing it away, nestling my tiny cook stove in a saddlebag, dropping my flashlight into the zippered tank bag that would fit on the bike between my knees, one piece of kit after another. You could carry a lot if you packed carefully.

"This is the airplane that brought you here," he said. I turned and saw he was pointing at one of the last things I packed, the book of outdated hotel listings and dubious restaurant recommendations that was supposed to be guiding me across South America. It lay open to the very first page, an advertisement for SAETA, the Ecuadorean airline. Like all airline ads it showed a clean jet rising up in a blue sky. I told David that I had come on a different airplane.

"From where?" he said. I turned to the map of Argentina in the guidebook and showed him the Valdés Peninsula and how it lay far to the south of Buenos Aires.

"Is Buenos Aires in your country?"

This was serious. I unpacked my big map of South America and explained that Buenos Aires was in his country, while mine lay still farther to the north. He pointed to the north of Argentina: "Here?" Farther north, I replied. He looked slightly defeated by the news that there was more than one airplane, but I gave him a set of batteries for his transistor radio, which had died months ago. Now, like his father, he could have a one-way conversation with the world. I said good-bye to Florio, who looked relieved to see me go and asked that I send David a book, which I did.

Driving out the peninsula, the wind knocked me over twice more, sending me into knee-scraping mounds of pebbles. When the bike blew over the second time the windshield cracked. Gasoline leaked from the carburetors again; I watched the liquid evaporate from the stones in horror, quickly righting the bike each time but losing several pints that I could not afford to lose. Yesterday's trip to the north shore suddenly seemed a foolish waste of fuel. I hit the reserve tank with an hour still to go. Somehow I made it to the steep ridge of hills at the neck of the peninsula, but the motor began to cough and hesitate on the way up the last hill. I threw the petcock from *Res.* back to *Auf* and got one last burst of power that pushed me up to the crest at a wobbly five miles an hour. It was two paved miles from there to the gas station, but all downhill, and I eventually coasted into the little settlement of Puerto Pirámides like some pathetic bicyclist. I mailed a postcard to my girlfriend and bought a vanilla milk shake and a full tank of gas, and then sat on a chair on the beach drinking the milk shake, watching the tide surge right past the No Parking signs, up and over the legs of the chair, and while I sipped my milk shake the water ran forth and back beneath me, chilling the aluminum. I said over and over to no one in particular that this was a very fine town indeed. Six days, and already I was talking to myself.

Several weeks evaporated in a selfish blaze. I rode west, up the Chubut Valley, heading toward the Andes and circling slowly north toward San Martín. The valley was a green ribbon in a red world. The wind blew so strongly that I began to read the landscape of low mesas for its aerodynamic qualities. Wherever a break appeared to the south—a wide arroyo or an expanse of unvegetated sandy stone between hills—the wind would be waiting in ambush. I learned to hike out like a sailor in a small boat, shifting my weight almost off the left side of the bike and stretching that knee wide to give me some balance and control. I managed to stay upright through several days of travel up the valley, but once, when I dismounted to take a photograph, a gust carried the bike right off its kickstand, snapping the right mirror and cracking the windscreen again. I put some duct tape on the Plexiglas fault lines and had the mirror welded back on in a truck stop.

The towns here were settled in the last century by wandering Welshmen, a breed celebrated in Bruce Chatwin's legendary *In Patagonia*. The Welsh had come to this land to escape the English imperium then obliterating their homeland, and Chatwin's 1979 book had painted a melancholic portrait of a lost colony, a dying experiment in national survival. South America had been home to many such experiments: defeated Confederate soldiers built a slavers' colony in the Brazilian interior; and the flatlands of Paraguay had been settled by blue-eyed Mennonites fleeing modernity. Chatwin's book had the odd effect of fetishizing exactly what the Welsh had been fleeing: their Englishness. The valley now attracted tourists who studied the red-brick houses, walked through the small-gauge railroad tunnel the colonists had dug, and visited an excellent little museum full of agricultural implements from the Industrial Revolution. These were all emblems of European culture, and it was their situation in this distant land that created such an appealing contrast.

I wasn't sure what there was to mourn. The Welsh had come, and built, and never disappeared. Their language had mostly died out, but the original colonists had always been eager to find their place in this new world. They had studied Spanish and posed for photographs clutching the blue-and-white banner of their new homeland, proudly Argentine. They themselves had not died out but merely changed, and this was a triumph, not a failure. Chatwin's book had infuriated some of the remaining Patagonian Welsh, and even two decades later the *Buenos Aires Herald*, the English-language paper in the capital, carried occasional acrimonious letters accusing the author of condescension. In Gaiman, I ate cake in a red-brick tea-house run by a white-haired matron who inquired hopefully if I was myself Welsh. We spoke in Spanish, naturally.

At the head of the Chubut Valley the Andes appeared, looming sharply in the distance. The green suddenly spread out, filling fields to the horizon. I followed the smell of rain up into those mountains and began to dissolve myself in their waters for days at a time, fishing pole in hand. I slept on the ground, alone in valleys and forests or sometimes in small campgrounds where kids from Buenos Aires tugged guitars at night and hiked by day. The waters absorbed whatever was put into them, an alchemy that transformed a thousand wants and a million particulars into one constant. For days and then weeks, I passed ten or twelve hours a day immersed to my waist in water that was cold and clear like iced gin. It flew through fuming channels, it swirled over deep bubbled pools, it gathered in slow wide draws running green with weeds, it curved left and right, and if you climbed up a stream, slowly shuffling over the rocks to keep your footing in a pair of cheap sneakers, you would move up from pool to pool during the course of a day, stopping sometimes to drink straight from the waters or to pull one lonely sandwich from the sling over your shoulder, and eventually when you looked up from reading the stream you would see that your eyes had climbed level with some vast sheet of a lake, as though you were now a fish yourself, rudely waking to the dry world.

Rivers cut through the dust, and I simply disappeared. I remember nothing of three days spent on one river except that once, as I stood immersed in a deep bend, hidden by the bank, a pair of silent gauchos cantered by herding a dozen unbridled chestnuts and leaving a fine golden dust suspended in the sunset long after they passed without noticing me. When I slept by a ford, with my head against a tree, I was awoken twice in the night by wet horses tromping blithely on each side of my prone form, their hooves scattering dust in my face as water rained from their bellies. There was that afternoon when I taught a dozen lonely Korean teenagers—youth missionaries carrying the word of Christ through Patagonia—how to fish. But mostly there were hours and days of silence, punctuated by a passing gaucho tipping his hat or a nun filling a water truck or a violent explosion of small life. A cloud of ducks settling into a run around me; a hooked rainbow trout yanking and leaping angrily; twenty thousand nymphs clambering up through the water column one noon and floating past or lodging on my legs, struggling to shake off their own skins. I cupped one of these struggling shape-shifters from the passing river while the trout slapped at the surface around me, feasting without mercy on the helpless. The black nymphal shuck split open, and a tan caddis fly emerged, fluttering unsuccessfully at first as its wings dried, but eventually achieving its first flight and ascending from the pool in my palms toward a brief residence in the sky.

I often returned long distances through the woods at ten or eleven at night, trying to follow the Southern Cross toward my camp and wade fast rivers in darkness. These were the moments of hard alertness within my calm joy; to mistake one crossing in the moonlight for another, to pick the wrong footing in the boiling, chest-deep currents, to be swept alone from a deep rapid in the dark, all these were possible a dozen times each night. But the waters did not betray me.

Inevitably, I closed on San Martín. In a place without calendars or clocks, I sensed that February had arrived, and with it came a cold rain that finally washed me out of the hills and down a steep road that traced its way between a mountainside and the shore of a tremendous lake, Lago Lacar. I paused in the rain long enough to survey the view from a high overlook. Deep blue and cold, five hundred yards wide and twenty miles long, the lake had the same effect on Guevara that the mountains were having on me. Camping on its edge, he and Granado were captured by the dreamy beauty of the place:

> There, in the shade of the huge trees, where the wilderness had held back the advance of civilization, we made plans to set up a laboratory when we got back from our trip. We imagined enormous windows looking out over the lake, while winter painted the ground white; an autogiro to get from one side to the other; fishing from a boat; endless excursions into the almost virgin forest. Often on our travels, we longed to stay in some of the wonderful places we saw, but only the Amazon jungle had the same strong pull on the sedentary part of ourselves as this did. I now know, by a fatalistic coincidence with fact, that I am destined to travel, or rather, we are destined, because Alberto is just

*like me. All the same, there are moments when I think with
profound longing of those wonderful areas in the South of
Argentina. Maybe one day when I'm tired of wandering, I'll
come back to Argentina and settle in the Andean lakes, if not
indefinitely at least in transit to another conception of the
world.*

Looking down on the lake, I could almost see him half a century
later, bent with age, a respectable citizen retired from his medical
practice at the lakeside, a car parked in the driveway instead of the
dreamed-of autogiro, but otherwise a model of contentment.

Maybe he'd be out there now, sitting in a rowboat, waiting
patiently in the rain in the middle of the lake. If you were a dreamer,
it was easy to believe that eventually something would bite.

Even in 1952 San Martín de Los Andes had been a tourist destination, and when I finally rolled out of the hills with my fingers frozen
to the handlebars I found a town without a trace of indigenous color
or life, only windsurfing shops and clouds of soaked backpackers lin-
gering under the eaves of the main street. San Martín breathed in the
mobile pesos of those Argentines who could afford to sit by a lake and
stare at the mountains. Like every resort town, it was a transient
place, with a summer population that swelled with busboys and
chambermaids and from which the life ebbed each fall in slow disappointment.

In a coffee shop I thawed my fingers around a *cortado* and borrowed a phone book to search for a name that did not exist. In their
diaries, both Guevara and Granado had mentioned a notable night
spent at the *estancia,* or ranch, of a local family. I hoped to find the
family, but neither diarist had noted where they lived except to say it
was a short distance outside the town. The chance of finding them
was reduced by the fact that the two G's had each spelled the family

name differently. Granado's diary mentioned them as the "Von Put Camers" while Guevara, in a letter to his mother, had spelled it "Von Putnamer."

Neither name was listed in San Martín, and I patiently worked my way through the subdirectories for the surrounding rural communities without luck. I even checked combinations of the name (Putnamer, Put Camer, Von Put Namer, Camer, Vonputnamer, Von Camer Put) but it was a dry hole. San Martín was a land of transients. Time, no doubt, would have wiped away much of the trail left by the motorcyclists. I handed the phone book back to my waiter with a sour look.

"You didn't find what you were looking for?" he said with evident sympathy.

To be polite, I explained that I was searching for an old German family from the region, the Putnamers or Putcamers or Von something-or-others. It had all been long ago.

He closed his eyes tightly, like he was on a game show. "25260, I think. Yes, 25260."

I went over to the house phone, picked it up, and dialed. Mr. Oscar Von Puttkamer answered on the first ring. Caught unprepared, I had no reasonable explanation for my call. I didn't know how to spring on him the odd bit of news that a young man his family had briefly entertained in their home forty-four years before had turned out to be of some great importance to Latin American history. Rather than mention Che Guevara's name, I simply mumbled a not-untrue explanation that I was a North American journalist, researching the history of the region.

"Be here in five minutes," the voice said. "I will tell you everything you want to know about it."

His house was four blocks away. I took down the directions.

I was still replaying the conversation in my head—what did he mean that he would tell me about "it"?—when I reached the motorcycle, plugged in the key, and twisted it clockwise. The green neutral light gave off a faint glow—very faint.

As soon as I had unloaded the bike in Buenos Aires, I had

noticed that the battery was weak. I put this down to carelessness by the longshoremen, who had probably left the ignition on during the day or two that the bike had waited in a warehouse. On my journey down the Argentine coast it had run well enough, but once I turned inland the green light had begun to fade. Each morning the bike was harder and harder to start. During three weeks of inland travel, I'd burned up battery juice by driving with the headlight late into the night. Sometimes, on the cold mornings when I had set off to fish some high mountain stream, even heaving on the kick starter was barely sufficient to start the bike.

Now the green diode looked wan and sickly, and when I hit the starter button the engine turned over only once and then choked on a *ga ga ga* sound from the solenoid. I pressed the button again, and this time the motor turned over and caught, and with the pepper grinder back in action I drove a block, made a right, drove a block, made a left, drove a block, and saw Oscar Von Puttkamer standing in the street, waving at me.

It turned out that both of the boys were wrong about the spelling. The Von Put Camers and Von Putnamers had never existed, but the Von Puttkamers were right here where they had always been. A barrel-chested man with a dense brown beard and a florid face, Oscar looked German enough to slip down to the beer hall in a pair of lederhosen.

Looks were deceiving. Oscar invited me inside his "city house"—he had an *estancia* outside town—and offered me a choice between coffee or *yerba mate*. Made from spare lawn clippings—or so it tasted—*yerba mate* was crammed by the fistful into a tankard, doused in boiling water, and the resulting green swamp was inhaled through an ornate filter-straw. There was no denying the ritualistic appeal of passing the *mate* gourd, but coffee seemed safer terrain for the novice. Oscar sent his wife off to make a round and let fly. He had been waiting a long time to tell someone "what happened."

I still hadn't mentioned Che Guevara's name, but Oscar never doubted for a second why I was calling. Just a few years before today, Che's *Notas de Viaje* had been published for the first time in Italy. A friend drew their attention to the entry about the Von Puttkamer family. He had never read the actual passage and asked to see my copy, which I produced. I read him the brief passages referring to the family:

> *Late in the afternoon we stopped at an* estancia *whose owners, very welcoming Germans, had in the past put up an uncle of mine, an inveterate old traveler whose example I was now emulating. They said we could fish in the river flowing through the* estancia. . . .

I broke out Granado's diary to see if there was anything worth quoting. Oscar asked what I was looking at, so I told him. He had never heard of Granado, of course, but I explained who he was and mentioned that he had also written about the *estancia* visit that day in 1952. "What does it say?" Oscar asked.

Guevara had been delighted by his stay with the Von Puttkamers and even praised one of the men in the family as being "the best" despite supporting the posturing Perón. Granado's diary was less flattering, but Oscar had a right to know what others said about his family. I read him Granado's entry for January 30, 1952:

> *A few kilometers along we encountered a road leading to an estate. We entered to try to buy some kind of meat to lunch on. Fate put us on the path to this establishment, which demonstrates the extent of the penetration by German Junkers, Nazis of course, in Patagonia.*

I looked up from the book briefly. Oscar's face had turned red at the phrase "Nazis of course," and the flush was rising visibly up his cheeks as I now read on. Granado went on to complain that the Argentine military junta had tacitly supported these "Nazis" in Patagonia:

> *They spoke of this in the first years of the Second World War, but later the news was silenced. The owner of this place is a*

*relatively young German, with the typical appearance of a
Prussian official. His last name says it all: Von Put Camer.*

*The construction of the central house of the estate imitates
the buildings of the German Black Forest. They have brought
deer here, which over the years have adapted and reproduced in
the surrounding zones.*

I stopped there, because each sentence seemed to push Oscar's
head closer to exploding. The lower half of his face had turned a
deep, sanguine purple, edging toward bright red in his upper cheeks.
The skin under his sideburns was purple, but only to a precise line
midway up the ear. Above that line he was pale, white, and almost
sweaty. It looked as though someone had drawn a line across his face
and then slowly filled him up with blood.

He couldn't hold it in. "You know why they say this?" he burst
out, and just as suddenly stopped. Neither of us could answer that
question. Oscar was tongue-tied; I fixated on the thermometer of his
temples. "Well," Oscar vented, and again: "Well." He grabbed big
mouthfuls of air and then, finally, sputtered out a family résumé.
"It's true," he began, "there were always Von Puttkamers in Germany's highest military circles. The Von Puttkamers were one of the
great military families of Prussia. But . . ." He fell silent for a
moment, looking for something to attach to that "but . . ."

"You know who Bismarck was married to?" he continued. "A
Von Puttkamer! Well . . ." Again, the pause that said he was not sure
quite where he was going with his point. "It's true there was a Von
Puttkamer on the German general staff! But . . . but the Von Puttkamers were always on the general staff!

"But . . . uh . . . it's true there were many Von Puttkamers in the
German army during World War Two. Something like twenty-six of
them! But . . . well." Pause. "Yes, it's true there was a Von Puttkamer in
the room when they blew up Hitler!" Pause. "But . . . but the Von Puttkamers were professional soldiers!" Pause. "They were not Nazis!"
Pause.

Oscar's clipped gestures and red face were fulfilling Granado's caricature of a Prussian functionary. The cycle was self-reinforcing: the more he tried to defend his family history, the more he was digging himself into a hole. That just made him more desperate, which in turn made him defend things which needed no defending—he denied that the family had introduced European deer into the zone, and even became defensive over the architecture of the old "Black Forest" house that Granado had found somehow sinister.

Oscar had a point, even if he couldn't make it. The Von Puttkamers were a great military family long before Hitler arrived on the scene, but *these* Von Puttkamers weren't even small villains. Oscar hadn't even been born when Hitler died, while his father and uncles and female relations had spent the war in Argentina.

Guilt flows with the steady creep of osmosis, however, and the strange association of Patagonia with Nazis was by now both popular image and old news. That the German influence here long predated Hitler did nothing to lift the cloud that shadowed the psychology of people like Oscar. German settlers had been coming to South America for generations before the war, filling up the emptiness of Patagonia with farms and sheep ranches, building towns like San Martín and Bariloche to the south into enclaves of proud Germano-Argentines.

As Adolf Eichmann learned at the cost of his life, it was wrong to assume that these Germano-Argentines were fellow fascists ready to provide fugitive Nazis with camouflage. Eichmann, the functionary who planned and directed the logistics of the Final Solution, had survived the collapse of the Nazi regime and emigrated to Argentina, where he spent several years in odd jobs—laborer, vacuum cleaner salesman, factory manager—in different parts of the country, including Patagonia. Eventually he was spotted by one of the very "Germans" he had assumed would protect him, a man who had fled the Nazis and now informed on the modest bureaucratic killer. Commandos from the new state of Israel kidnapped the fugitive and shipped him to Israel for a historic trial. Testifying from inside a bulletproof glass box, Eichmann said that he was "only following orders" when he personally oversaw the extinguishing of millions of European Jews.

Eichmann was the most famous Nazi refugee in Argentina, but hardly the only one. Klaus Barbie, the former Gestapo officer and "butcher of Lyon," had been a frequent visitor to Bariloche. During the 1950s and '60s, Barbie lived in Bolivia, where he taught his Gestapo skills to the local secret police. To escape the rigors of this employment he would head south on vacations to the comforting Alpine vistas of Bariloche. When I'd been in Bariloche years before, my hotel keepers had been a pair of elderly Slovenians with Austrian educations and pretensions. They were honorary members of Patagonia's German community and recalled meeting Barbie on the local ski slopes in the 1960s, although he was using a false name. ("A very ordinary man," the husband said. "We had no idea who he was.") Barbie was finally deported from Bolivia to France in 1983 to stand trial. A few months before my arrival yet another Nazi—now in his seventies— had been plucked from the streets of Bariloche. As a young SS captain, Erich Priebke had overseen the massacre of 335 Italians in a cave beneath Rome; he had spent the subsequent decades living openly in Bariloche, and had even been president of the local German-Argentine Friendship Society. He was deported to Italy, tried for the massacre, cleared, retried, and eventually sentenced to house arrest.

Oscar hadn't even been alive during the war. Born and raised in Patagonia, an engineer by training, he drank *mate,* spoke Spanish with an Argentine accent, and knew more English words than German. In fact, he could not conjugate one verb in that tongue. He was Argentine through and through. Yet here he was sputtering in defensive fury against charges that his family were "Nazis of course."

I apologized and explained that I was merely repeating what someone else—this Alberto Granado character—had said about the Von Puttkamers. The temperature of Oscar's face seemed to drop a few degrees, and we returned to the present of coffee cups and hospitality.

I still resented Guevara's ability to cadge bed and board from strangers. Determined, as the Cubans say, to "Be Like Che," I screwed up my shamelessness and mentioned that I was looking for a place to stay the night. The historic parallel—Che stayed with you, and I'm following his route—apparently didn't occur to Oscar, who merely agreed that it was very tough to find a bed in town during high season. I malingered around the house for a few minutes, but it was unlikely that he or his wife would offer me a bed after I had labeled him a Nazi.

"Why don't you come out to the country house tomorrow at ten o'clock," he finally said, "and I will show you where Guevara was."

This was the best I would get. We went outside and stood around the motorcycle. Oscar was pleased that I drove a German machine, but proved he was really an Argentine by asking how fast it went. I boasted about the speed and how reliable the bike was ("Like a cockroach," I told him, "it's ugly but impossible to kill"), but when I turned the key the green light glimmered only dimly. Nothing happened when I pressed the starter button. I kicked over the engine, and kicked again, growing sweaty and embarrassed. For more than five minutes I tinkered with the choke, switched the key on and off, and swung the engine over without the slightest response. The green light faded and then died. Perhaps I would have to spend the night here after all.

At the last second the bike unexpectedly roared to life. Oscar looked relieved. Just as I pulled out, it started to rain again. I drove around and around the town getting soaked, but all the cheap hotels were full. Like the two G's, I tried to camp on the lakeshore but was instantly routed by a glowering park ranger. It grew dark.

A priest charged me seven dollars to sleep on the floor of his church.

At 9:30 the next morning the bike died again in a gas station at the end of San Martín's main street. Nothing I did would restart it.

The attendant gave me directions to a repair shop, and I slowly pushed the bike down the street and into a garage filled with grease-blackened pieces of engine. A young man of about twenty came over and explained that the mechanic was in Chile at a soccer tournament.

"But I might be able to help you," he said. Not without some preparation, however. First, Manolo introduced himself; second, he asked how fast the bike went; third, he turned on and adjusted the radio; fourth, he made *yerba mate.*

While we waited for the electric kettle to boil, Manolo stuffed a *mate* gourd rim full of the grassy green herb. He offered me the first sip, a traditional sign of hospitality. I would have preferred to add some sugar—in fact, I would have preferred to toss the stuff on the ground—but I dared not antagonize a mechanic. I choked down a boiling mouthful without complaint.

Manolo sipped at the second pour and stared at the motorbike. He stared and stared at it. "What's it called?" he finally asked. I told him the motorcycle wasn't called anything. "It has to have a name," he said. "You have to give it a name, like a girl."

Gusts of moist wind blew in the open door of the garage, and I waited. Manolo sipped, stared, and sipped some more, drawing in his cheeks. He leaned against a wall beneath a cartoon of Argentina's president sitting on a toilet. The caption read FUCK THAT SHITHEAD MENEM. The minutes stretched out and the tranquillity became unnerving. Manolo poured a third dose of water over the same leaves and went back to leaning against the wall with the metal straw poked into his mouth. Finally, after ten minutes of this contemplation, he took a single step toward the bike, reached out a hand, and then froze.

"What song is this?"

My head snapped up and my ears located the sound of the radio.

> *I had no illusion*
> *That I'd ever find a glimpse*
> *Of summer's heatwaves in your eyes*

The tune . . . the lyric . . . it was all a bit familiar, but not enough. An alarm tolled in my subconscious, but the jangling keyboard drowned it out. The name eluded me.

> *You did what you did to me*
> *Now it's history I see*

God . . . it was . . . that awful song . . . what was it called? "Beehon sha pawn," Manolo said tentatively.

> *Things will happen while they can*
> *I will wait here for my man tonight . . .*

"BEE HON SHAPON," he announced more urgently. "OOH YOO BABY!"

> *It's easy when you're big in Japan*
> *Aah, when you're big in Japan tonight . . .*
> *Big in Japan-be-tight . . .*

"*Grande en Japón,*" I announced.

"Quick, tell me what the words say," he ordered, and began waving his hands to encourage me. "SING!"

I had no choice—I was immobile without his help—so I sang along as fast as I could, trying to follow the tune while conducting instantaneous translation, neither of which I did very well.

> *yes baby it's big in Japan*
> *very big in Japan*
> *tonight it's . . . uh . . .*
> *the sea to the east is very blue*
> *life is very easy*
> *if you are a big man in Japan*
>
> *you did, uh, something to me*
> *history*

something something road again
something
if you are a big man in Japan

The song faded out, and Manolo's animation died with it. His disappointment was palpable: why did such great songs have to end!

"I've been to Japan," he said after a moment. He'd never been out of Rio Negro Province before or since, he explained, but one time he had traveled with the provincial Kung Fu team all the way to Tokyo. "At the tournament, they played this song all the time. I love this song." He crooned out again, "BEEHON SHAPON, OH IS TEN SEE SO BOO."

He went over to the bike and crossed his arms. "Take out the spark plugs," he ordered. I did. The thin elements at the ends of both plugs were blackened, covered with thick carbuncles of soot. The plugs were only a month old, but they looked like they had been in the bike for years.

"This is your problem," he said. I carried a spare set, so I screwed them in under his supervision ("Careful! Like it's a girl!") and turned the key. The green light burst into life. The engine turned over cleanly on the first try and ran smoothly.

I pushed the bike backward out of the garage, letting the engine idle to recharge the battery. We stood around, looking at each other fondly. I asked what I owed him. He declined any pay.

"Thank you for translating that song," he said, and shook my hand.

It was almost one o'clock by the time I found the Von Puttkamers' *estancia*.

It wasn't much of an *estancia*. The original parcel that Guevara and Granado visited had been divided among the three sons. The old Black Forest mansion had gone to the oldest brother, who, just two years before, had sold out. The new owners, apparently agreeing with Granado that the house was suspicious, knocked it down and put up a new, very ordinary ranch house. The second brother kept his land but leased it out and lived in the city. Only Oscar kept his feet on the soil.

And what soil it was. The land lay along a valley floor, golden hills ranging up and down each side while a blue river bisected the view. There is an arid, spare beauty to Patagonia, a kind of spartan perfection that I have never seen better represented than in this land. The slim strand of barbed wire cutting through a field; the scarce, tough scrub brush and low bunches of tawny grass; the transparent, icy blue of a river sparkling through the branches of the drooping willows that feasted on its banks and nowhere else. I sang on my way up the road, first a verse of *"Bee hon sha pon"* and then the old reliable *"La cucaracha,"* as the landscape unfurled its perfection and filled me with anticipation. I stood on the pegs, rising to meet the wind, yelping with joy and delirious with my smooth-running, green-lighted speed through the winding valley, up its gentle hills and down again to the sweeping curves of its yellow, dusty floor.

The Von Puttkamers' house and outbuildings appeared out of a science fiction tale about the colonization of Mars. First I saw a few quick-growing poplars waving from the distance; inside their embrace was a very modest, one-story home and a few utilitarian outbuildings. As I pulled in the driveway I saw that the surrounding half dozen acres were planted with potatoes and young fruit trees and cut everywhere with irrigation canals. The whole place felt wrested from the grip of the earth.

Oscar came trundling out of the house, his plaid work shirt whipping in the inevitable wind. "We thought you were coming earlier," he said with a touch of resentment. I told him of my mechanical difficulties and he became understanding. Farmers knew the uncontrollable whims of machinery and therefore of time and travel.

The living room was filled with cheese sandwiches, Germanic bric-a-brac, and children, and there was a great deal of confusion at the start as the family tried to feed me and I was subjected to examples of the English language. This ritual had become familiar to me after much practice. Latin Americans suffer from an inferiority complex, a feeling (largely correct) that they come from one of the forgotten regions of the world. When a gringo like me said that Argentina was one of the forgotten regions of the world they were profoundly insulted; nonetheless, they could say it themselves and often did. They knew what "First World" meant more than First Worlders did. It meant that movie stars came from Hollywood, that music came from New York and London, that machinery came from Japan and Korea, that fashion and old buildings came from France and Italy. It was in Washington and Geneva and Peking and Moscow where the fate of nations was decided, where wars were started and stopped, where the stage was lit and the curtains raised and lowered. Argentina produced wheat.

This is not entirely fair, but Latin Americans are not entirely fair to themselves, either, and I had never met a people who belittled themselves more than Argentines. You were ill-advised to answer "I love it" when taxi drivers asked what you thought of Argentina. The correct answer was the one they gave: *"Argentina es mierda."* I was amazed at the number of shopkeepers who ventured the English phrase, "Arhentina ees booshit." Everyone was nationalist, everyone was patriotic, everyone loved Argentina—and yet they hated it with a passion. The level of self-loathing was only slightly lower in the rest of Latin America.

Thus the ritual of accented English, which could happen anywhere from the Café Richmond to the Von Puttkamers' little *casa* in Patagonia. Argentines asked for respect from others that they did not give themselves, and they asked for it in English. People in Buenos Aires loved to go to Disneyland on vacation, or at least Europe (Little Girl had been to France four times but had never set a foot in Patagonia). Oscar's son, about thirteen, was brought forth to mutter in memorized English, but the main show came from Mrs. Von Puttkamer, who taught English at a local school. She spoke correctly, with a slight Minnesota accent earned by spending a year in the land of snowbound Scandinavians.

I was into the cake when at last Oscar got to break in. He had been a toddler of only one or two when Guevara visited, he explained, too young to remember it himself. I showed him a line in Guevara's diary ("one of the owner's sons seemed to think these disgustedly dressed and apparently famished 'doctors' a bit odd . . .") that might have described him. "Just think," Oscar roared, "Che Guevara probably looked into my crib!" He laughed, but after only a moment the joy died on his face. "Of course," he added, "I hate everything that son of a bitch did to us.

"Hijo de puta," he said. Oscar began ticking off the guerrilla groups that had appeared in Argentina on the heels of the Cuban revolution. The Uturuncos; the Revolutionary Popular Army, the Montoneros; no matter how many times the army wiped out one cell another appeared, until bombs were roaring in the cities and policemen were gunned down on street corners. Like most of the Argentines I'd met, Oscar remembered this public madness better than the silent terror that followed the military coup of 1976. He knew in an abstract way that the death squads of the right had killed ten (or was it twenty?) thousand Argentines, not Che or his followers on the left. Some of these groups weren't even followers of Che's specific ideology, but despite the statistical burden of responsibility on the right, somehow Oscar could not help but blame Che. "He provoked the greatest conflict in Argentine history," he said. "Look at us now."

The remark was explained only by his sad tone. Oscar limned the problems of Patagonian life, from irrigation and the planting of windbreaks to the cost of tractor parts. He was soon complaining about how much he paid in taxes and how this prevented him from expanding production on the ranch or building a bigger house. Yet he was not Granado's evil landlord exploiter, either. He had the broad shoulders and massive forearms of a man who did manual labor all day. He had built this small but comfortable house with his own hands ("My son helped," he announced, making the boy beam), and he showed me the practical workmanship. Nothing fancy about it; it wasn't even German in styling. Alberto Granado would have liked it because it wasn't that much grander than the shack nearby where the two *peones,* or farmhands, lived.

In private later, these two elderly men would tell me that the boss was *muy simpático* and the Von Puttkamers were *buena gente,* accolades that would fill several pages if translated from the gaucho's spare idiom of loyalty to the American vernacular of empty praise. Forty-four years before, Granado had taken a dim view of the work arrangements on the Von Puttkamer *estancia,* calling it capitalist exploitation. As was proving usual, Guevara drew a more subtle lesson from the life of the *peones.* In an evocative sketch of the predawn rituals of the farm, he wrote of the gauchos who crowded around the kitchen stove. These hard men took their *yerba mate* straight and laughed at the visitors who added sugar, a custom of northern Argentina considered unmanly in the south. When Guevara described them as typical of the "subjugated Araucanian race," it lacked the hollow ring of Granado's lecturing, for Guevara saw in that dark kitchen that it was his own kind—the white outsiders—rather than some abstract economic doctrine that subjugated the men. The *peones* were:

> still wary of the white man who in the past brought them so
> much misfortune and still exploits them. When we asked about
> the land and their work, they answered by shrugging their
> shoulders and saying "don't know" or "maybe," which ended
> the conversation.

The motorcyclists had slept that night on the floor of the Von Puttkamers' kitchen, and, given a second chance in my moping presence, Oscar now lived up to the tradition of hospitality. The family had to rush away to a nearby city for a few days, but he offered to let me stay alone at the *estancia.* I accepted with two conditions. The first, that I would camp outside rather than use their house; the second, that I be allowed to fish in the Río Chimehuin, flowing across the valley floor.

Guevara and Granado had fished there, although how much luck they had was subject to opinion. Ernesto wrote that Alberto "cast his line, and before he knew what was happening, he had a fleeting form glinting in the sunlight jumping about on the end of his hook." The future guerrilla prince went on to detail the cooking of this one fish and noted with hungry precision that "Alberto cast his line again and again, but he didn't get a single bite despite hours of trying."

When I turned to Granado's diary, however, the fishing had suddenly improved: "we" had caught "various" trout, he stated vaguely.

I knew a harmless fisherman's lie when I heard it. Yet this made me recall a series of these discrepancies I'd seen in the two diaries, differences of both fact and tone. The fishing was bad or it was good. The Von Puttkamers were "wonderful" or "Nazis of course." Where Ernesto noted the beauty of the landscape, Alberto wrote of "the ferocious face of capitalism." The two diarists couldn't even agree on how they ended up at the Von Puttkamer *estancia* in the first place. Granado described it as an accidental encounter while searching for something to eat, but Guevara's diary mentioned his tramping uncle who had stayed with the Von Puttkamers before, and a few days later, in a letter to his mother, he mentioned staying "at the Von Putnamers' estancia, friends of Jorge's," as if the family was well known to the Guevaras (although not well enough known to spell their name right). These were small differences, but given how intimately the two men had experienced the same moments—they were as close as the two ends of a motorcycle seat—it was surprising.

Oscar showed me where to get water, gave me a key to the front gate, and hurried off, a curious man who radiated a mixture of gratitude, excitement, social awkwardness, patriotism, self-loathing, pride, and guilt all at once.

I threw my bags under a tree, changed into fishing clothes, and strolled across the valley and into the glinting waters of the Chimehuin. All evening the trout rolled out of their lies beneath the willow branches and slashed at a brown, feathery fly. I pulled in seven of the rainbows, but I can only see the last one in my mind's eye now, shining silver in my hand in the darkness. I built a fire, roasted the fish, and ate under the stars.

In Bariloche I put up with the same Slovenian couple from five years before; they didn't remember me but said they did. Guevara had come here after San Martín, moving once again and chipper after casting off the seductive spell of both Lago Lacar and all the wine and beef he and Granado were cadging from a series of visits with friends of friends in the area. When finally frustrated in a plan to steal five bottles of wine from a barbecue they were working at, the boys knew they were getting rusty from sitting around. They made the trip to Bariloche along winding roads past one enormous lake after another, fingers of water reaching up toward the mountains and the Chilean border. Their business in Bariloche was simple: check for letters at the post office—Guevara had asked his mother for mail—and then get over the border.

Disaster struck. Waiting at the post office was a letter from Chichina. She broke off their relationship, firmly and completely. Guevara was devastated, utterly shocked that, just because he had abandoned his medical studies to run off to points unknown with no fixed schedule or planned return, his girlfriend would desert him. He began to have hallucinations; at night he saw her green eyes glowing in the dark and could not sleep.

There was nothing to do but apply the geographical cure, and the boys threw themselves into the complicated crossing to Chile, which involved a series of seven lakes connected by short land hops. Brokenhearted, and therefore without pride, Guevara waved his medical credentials around and pleaded poverty; the ferry captain gave both men free passage in exchange for working the bilge pumps, and La Poderosa was lifted on board.

I knew that it was going to be hard, forty-four years later, to convince the ferry captains to even talk to me. In 1952 the ferry route was the only route, and the boats carried cargo, people, animals, anything that could fit. Now the trade was all in tourism. I'd been over the route years before, coming the other way. It was a staggering set of views, worth it despite having to constantly shuffle from bus to boat to bus to boat to bus to boat to bus, all the while being instructed by a tour guide with a microphone to "sing your national song" for the rest of

the passengers. A series of Bolivians, Germans, Chileans, Danes, and Frenchmen had belted away, even during lunch, and the thought of repeating that day now made my imminent rejection bearable.

"Use the road," the clerk at the ferry office said dismissively, just as I'd feared. They wouldn't even consider taking my bike. The schedules were too tight, and there was no loading or unloading facility for cargo on the high-speed catamaran ferry that ran out toward Chile each morning. Cargo went on the road, a well-maintained gravel track that shot over the border to the north of here and that hadn't existed in 1952. You could get to Puerto Montt in Chile in half a day on the northern route.

But I turned south. I was still laboring under the impression that bad roads were going to teach me something important about South America in 1952. The quick, modern route would never inspire the same idealism in me that Ernesto had found on his road. Perhaps my motives were not so purely spartan, either; the truth was that, like the two young men I was following, I simply wanted to see wild things. The south promised adventure, which is why Guevara had come this way in the first place. On my map I noted obscure gravel roads that crossed the border at several points, and I connected a set of these dotted lines over the fold of the map, into Chile, and eventually to Puerto Montt. It looked like it could be done in a few days and would be as wild as anything Guevara and Granado had found during the several days it took them to complete the Seven Lakes route. They'd gone bushwhacking, hiked a mountain, and just ridden around looking at stuff, so I figured I might as well do the same. This southern route followed rivers and lakes, and there would be some fishing along the way and then at the end a ferry up to Puerto Montt, almost like the boys had done on boats plying the more direct line.

In the end it took a few smoky days to reach the border. Several forest fires were burning out of control on the dry Argentine slopes of the Andes. I spent my last night in Argentina sleeping beneath a burning mountain, the sky a mass of low clouds underlit with orange. In the morning I left behind a tiny Argentine border post and passed through several miles of no-man's-land. The road went down and entered a dense, temperate rain forest of gargantuan ferns and thick-leafed lenga trees. It began to rain, an indication that I was probably in Chile. The border post soon appeared, and after completing reams of paperwork to obtain a permit for the bike, I was forced to drive it through a trench filled with yellow disinfectant solution, like a sheep at dipping time. A strutting Chilean *carabinero* impounded some bread and cheese I was carrying and then looked at the back of my helmet.

"What does it say?" he demanded.

I translated the words YES FEAR literally, and he stared at me. "You know," I said, "like the surfers." He kept staring. "The ones with the NO FEAR T-shirts," I added. "Only, I *am* afraid, so . . ." Eventually he gave up staring. Some things don't translate.

The rain kept up, but there was no place to stop, and I rode along happily, down and up, but mostly down. The rivers were narrow and fast, filled with white flume, and I saw two salmon leap a cataract, their wet bodies twisting through the air in tandem. A few miles farther downstream I crossed the Futaleufú River on a tiny bridge named after a military officer. Sealed up in my rain gear, I saw a quick view of a microbus parked at the side of the river and a pair of kayakers loitering in an eddy, waiting to descend. By afternoon I had reached the Carreterra Austral, the only north-south road in these parts. The road is somewhat famous in Chile: it was pushed through the deep forests of the south on the personal orders of General Augusto Pinochet and was always cited as an example of his good works for the nation. Having overthrown the country's elected president in 1973, killed more than 3,000 of his countrymen, and ruled Chile despotically for seventeen years, Pinochet should get credit for every single thing he deserves. Unfortunately, the road proved to be the same mixture of mud and gravel as the roads in Argentine Patagonia. The main difference was that on this road the bridges were all named after military officers martyred at the hands of the leftist guerrillas that Pinochet claimed he had saved the country from. Since the guerrillas were few and inept, there were actually more bridges than officers, and so even sergeants and a few privates ended up being honored in outsized plaques attached to unimpressive one-lane bridges.

I was singing to myself, as usual. I started with *"Bee hon sha pon"* but then, inevitably, *"La cucaracha"* began to wend its way back inside the helmet. The road was empty, and there were few vistas in the rain, so I tried to distract myself from singing by composing some notes about Chile in my head. There were always lots of these mental gymnastics on the road. Sometimes if I didn't want to sing I'd compose indignant letters to the editors of various newspapers, or deliver nonsensical commencement addresses and rambling Nobel acceptance remarks.

I'd just fixed on the metaphor of Chile as a land of holes in the ground, of anonymous graves and buried secrets, when I struck an actual hole in the general's road. I was thrown hard to the left, over-corrected to the right, and shot sideways into the bushes at thirty miles an hour, shattering the windscreen, snapping off various bits and pieces of the motorcycle, and cracking a rib.

Lying on the ground in the rain with the motorcycle on top of me, I smelled smoke and listened intently to sounds: the way each droplet of rain singed into steam when it struck the hot motor; the way the turn signal clicked aimlessly, as if we were going somewhere; the way the tires of a truck splashed through the mud as it passed above me on the road.

Two minutes later the truck came beeping backward down the road and stopped. A man I cannot remember and his beautiful daughter, who I can, came down the embankment, tied a rope between the bike and the truck's bumper, and then dragged the machine slowly up to the road. We propped the bike on its kickstand and banged on various bent pieces with hammers. I threw the shards of the windscreen into the bushes. After a few minutes the man apologized and said he had to make it to Argentina by nightfall.

I thanked him, and he stood there looking at me. "You know you are bleeding," he said.

After he left, I plucked one of the mirrors out of the under-growth and looked. It was true. A small trickle of blood ran down my forehead. I grazed my fingers across the outside of the helmet, which showed only a tiny scratch where I had smashed face-first into the gravelly root ball of a gargantuan rain forest bush. Somehow the force of the crash had passed cleanly through the hard outer shell, two inches of foam insulation, and the lining without damaging a thing, and then broken my skin instead. I pulled off my gloves and found another cut, a bloody scrape on the back of my left hand. There was only a faint scratch on the outside of the glove. My rain-coat was ripped through on the left side; the leather jacket under-neath had suffered a heavy scrape but held. The skin under there was unmarked, but beneath that something was clearly wrong. I couldn't think or move much, and I was having trouble breathing, but it wasn't bad for a motorcycle crash.

Alberto and Ernesto had gone down some thirteen times by this point. I stood in the middle of the road, in the rain. This was an empty quarter of South America. No one approached from either direction. For a while I wandered around, collecting the broken and muddy possessions scattered across the scene, trying to fit shattered pieces of plastic together, or tie things up, or tape them closed, or wipe them off.

But mostly I just stood there. Once in a while I would shuffle over, turn the key, and look to see if the little diode came on.

CHAPTER FOUR

MYTOPIA

Five days and a hundred miles later, the little green fishing smack backed away from the rocks and, turning east, began to plow up the fjord on rough seas. Like most working boats, this one had too many useful qualities to have any elegance at all. A modest sailing mast speared the deck, but diesel engines did the pushing, and the passengers crowded onto benches in the converted hold.

The surface of the fjord was black and blue like a bruise, and as we pitched heavily away from the ocean the prow slammed showers of spray up and over three Chilean police officers. I stood with these men in featureless green uniforms, their collars turned up against the cold. Eventually a few guitarists in dark glasses and wool sweaters joined us. The cops tried to shield their pistols and the musicians their guitars, but we all got a little wet. I managed to avoid vomiting yet again, at first because the pain in my ribs made it unthinkable and then because the sea grew easy as we moved deeper into the fjord and the walls closed in. Although the cliffs rose almost straight from the water, green vegetation covered them like a carpet. This was temperate rain forest, a confusing mix of conifers and deciduous trees grown to eerie proportions. The climate was soggy and, above the water, so densely green that neither brown earth nor gray stone interrupted any but the very steepest slopes.

We passed sea lions loitering on smelly boulders, and skin divers taking shellfish from the bottom, and long pens of farmed salmon.

After an hour the boat grounded on an unprepossessing mudflat at the head of the fjord, a gentle green cirque of mountains and trees. A blue tractor rolled out of the woods, came slowly across the flat, and began to load up with boxes of supplies that we passed down from the boat. A little path led up the mud. The score of musicians clambered down from the bow, distributed their instruments, and then marched in a ragged column toward the woods. I followed their laughing progress up and into the tree line, beneath a high gate made of hewn poles. A sign over our heads read REÑIHUÉ.

"Region X," the bureaucrats in Santiago had labeled this paradise. They did not mean to capture the mystery of the place in that blank name; they were simply extending the system of Roman numerals that the Pinochet dictatorship had superimposed on Chile's ancient provinces. The tenth region was where the great forests began, a narrow wilderness of old trees, forgotten islands, and saltwater fjords. The forests of Region X held most of the few remaining groves of alerce, the towering, talismanic trees of the deep south that were sometimes more than two thousand years old. The wood of the alerce—properly named *Fitzroya cupressoides* after Captain Fitzroy, commander of the *Beagle*, which carried Charles Darwin through these parts—is endangered in most parts of Region X.

But not here, in the curious little kingdom of Reñihué. I had come following the musicians, who had come following a man, who had himself come following the trees. It was the man, named Douglas Tompkins, who brought us all here with his love of the vast southern forest and his fortune that was even vaster. Founder of the North Face and Esprit de Corps clothing companies, Tompkins had grown disillusioned by the retail world. In 1990 he sold out his share of the business to his ex-wife and her partners for over $150 million. In 1991 he began buying land in Chile. The purchases were done quietly at first, and before anyone had quite realized what Tompkins was doing, he ended up with a thousand square miles of spectacular forested terrain that literally cut the country in two, running from the sea to the mountainous border.

If Chileans were surprised to find a foreigner controlling so much land in their midst, Tompkins's next move astonished them: he announced he was giving the land away. The "ranch" would become a 700,000-acre national park called Pumalín, or "mountain lion," a legacy of the public, preserved forever. He was paying for an environmentally sensitive infrastructure of trails and campgrounds for visitors, and the park land itself would be turned over to a nonprofit foundation run by a board dominated by Chileans. The reaction to this generous, farsighted offer was pretty much what you would expect: Tompkins was accused of being a "secret Jew" (he isn't Jewish) founding a new Israel, or of being some kind of pseudo-Nazi, or of planning to build a nuclear storage dump on the land, or of being a closet communist. A former defense minister called Tompkins "irritating and out of place."

The majority of Chileans were not openly hostile to Tompkins, but there was widespread befuddlement at the idea that a wealthy man would give away huge tracts of land. Philanthropy is a weak tradition in Chile, and landholdings have always been the measure of wealth in Latin America, the determinant of status, even of identity. You were a landowner or you were nothing. You did not simply give away land. There *had* to be some other motivation for the curious gringo's actions, it seemed. And, in fact, there was. Tompkins wasn't simply giving a national park to the people of Chile. Just as his enemies feared, his plans were much more radical than that.

I plunked my sleeping bag onto the floor of the schoolhouse and watched a few army-issue down feathers escape and begin to drift around the room. Like all the buildings in the compound—the various residences, a plant nursery, and a barn, a dozen buildings in all—the schoolhouse was not simply a schoolhouse but an act of charity and economic largess with a purpose. Tompkins and his wife, Kristine McDivitt Tompkins, a former CEO of Patagonia (the clothing company, not the region), had paid local workmen to build the schoolhouse with local wood, using traditional construction techniques from the region. Reñihué was not just a ranch but a fantasy of an esthetically pleasing, environmentally minimalist lifestyle. There was no electricity anywhere in the compound. There were also no phones and certainly no fax machines. The only communication with the outside world came through a single radio and a grass airstrip where Tompkins landed his Husky. Heat in the buildings came from burning wood. The enormous vegetable garden supplied lettuce and herbs and root foods to complement the locally harvested seafood. The raised garden beds and virtually the entire compound were linked and divided by wooden boardwalks. Even the soil itself was safe from human trampling here.

Three dozen folk musicians were already living in the schoolhouse when I arrived. They were members of various traditional groups from the surrounding areas of southern Chile, mostly young people although each group tended to be led by an older man with some invisible moral authority. Each *conjunto* claimed a section of floor in the schoolhouse, and the two-story building vibrated with music. With a dozen hungry musicians I watched the *peones* dig a hole in the ground near the barn. The hole was lined with rocks heated in a fire and then filled with fat clams taken from the fjord and lumps of potato-dough bread. The hole was covered over and the contents steamed for a couple of hours. Then we dug everything out and nibbled like gluttons. Dogs and cats mingled with the several dozen people who came in and out. I found a few Americans in the crowd, friends of Tompkins's wife who were on a kayaking vacation. They were pilots and former stewardesses, all trained in first aid. The women quizzed me: "Have you coughed up any blood? Is the pain sharp and electric or wide and dull?" The men took turns squeezing me in bear hugs.

"If you go to a doctor, all he'll do is tape you up and tell you not to ride your motorbike for six weeks," one of the men said, and I believed him because he spoke with the trained voice of the airline captain. The truth was that I'd fractured a rib without breaking it, and it would heal. In the meantime I found it impossible to laugh, breathe deeply, or sit up in bed. In the mornings I had to crawl out the side of the bed, roll over onto the floor, and rise to my hands and knees before I could stand.

I wandered stiffly around Reñihué looking for Tompkins and finally caught him at the airplane hangar, in the company of a local Chilean politician he was wooing. He proved to be a tall, utterly lean man with the slightly remote look of Bruce Dern. He was warming up his Husky to fly the politico home, and I asked him for an interview, to which he replied "Maybe later." Those two words were the first and last ones he ever spoke to me.

The plane taxied for a moment, turned, and pounced into the air with a sacrilegious roar. The sound of the motor circled off the surrounding peaks and the little plane grew smaller and smaller, struggling for height as it headed down the fjord. Aside from his wife, about thirty people—musicians, forest workers, and a few of the local villagers from across the fjord—watched it disappear. Wherever he went, he carried their future with him. That was $150 million flying into the clouds, and the good people of Reñihué had many reasons for wanting to see him come back safely.

It rained the final and third afternoon, but I set out with my fishing pole into the gloomy forest, following a narrow, barely passable trail through overhanging ferns and across flooded creeks spanned by wet logs skinned of bark. After forty-five minutes I reached the Reñihué River, which rampaged through the landscape in enormous open bends and side channels choked with downed trees. Dimly visible beneath the rain clouds were the slopes of a high range in front of me. I waded far out into the crushing current, slipping and twisting for purchase on the stony bottom, and eventually made it to a long gravel bar with its own side channels and pools. The water was silty with glacial dust, and the rain sheeted down, but over the next two hours I managed to pluck a pair of fat rainbow trout from holds behind a log and a bush. I pocketed the fish and waded back through the dusk, unable to recognize where I had crossed the deepest currents, tripping on sunken logs and crashing into the water face-first twice. Soaked, I battled back up the trail in almost total darkness, slithered over the wet log bridges, and arrived in the kitchen of the schoolhouse four hours after I left, sneezing and bruised and covered with thorns and convinced that Tompkins was a genius who had to preserve the land exactly as it was. Anyone with the slightest sense could see that this was a magic place.

I put the trout in tinfoil inside the wood stove. The flesh was bright pink, turned the color of salmon by the pectin in the shells of the *pacora*, miniature green crabs. The musicians and some of the American kayakers stopped around and looked at the fish. "It's a salmon," they announced one after another, and I couldn't win the argument no matter how many times I explained that all trout in Patagonia were pink on the inside. I was just finishing up when the musicians left the building in groups, one after the other.

The concert was easy to find, since Tompkins, back safely from his air excursion, had fired up the generator to make that rarest of things: electricity. The hangar, emptied of aircraft, was filled with light. Little boys gathered in from the darkness like moths toward the flame and stood in the light-throw of the front door, wrestling and jumping about.

There were over a hundred adults inside, and I found a seat by sharing a hay bale with an older man from the village across the fjord. I quickly picked out four or five Americans by the fact that they were wearing at least $500 worth of brightly colored outdoor gear each. Tompkins and his wife both appeared in dark wool sweaters made locally, which nonetheless did not particularly make them blend in with the hundred or so small, dark-skinned Chileans.

The *encuentro folklórico*, as it was called, featured one band after another, all of them playing more or less the same style of southern Chilean music. The bands typically featured four or six acoustic guitarists, a few percussionists, and a troupe of dancers. The style was fast and energetic, a quick-stepping, guitar-driven dance music. Since most of the bands were from the island of Chiloé, which you hit if you went straight out the fjord and kept going, most of the music was about lonely fishermen and unrequited love. While the Chiloéan musicians tended to wear wool caps, the smaller number of mainlanders wore cowboy hats and sang about lonely cowboys and unrequited love. One after another, the groups got up, thanked Tompkins, and then played four or six songs and sat back down. The most rocking number featured a lot of quick-stepping cowboys slapping their boots on the ground. The slowest number was a traditional *cueca*, or "handkerchief dance," in which a man and woman spun in a slow circle while clutching opposite corners of a white kerchief. It was a pretty dance, and eventually Tompkins and his wife were prevailed upon by the crowd to take hold of the cloth and dance. They did well.

Gradually I realized that almost everyone in the barn—perhaps a hundred out of a hundred and fifteen—was a musician. There was no audience. Near the end Tompkins got up and gave a speech. He said that the purpose of the *encuentro* was to let Chilean musicians play for Chilean musicians. He hoped their beautiful music would continue to flourish and that they would all return next year. He said that the global economy was a threat to their traditional culture. He spoke a correct but accented Spanish and stumbled a bit pronouncing *monoculturización*. A band leader stood and praised *"el patrón"* for having the concert. He led a cheer for Tompkins that seemed to pain the recipient deeply.

Patrón is a common term in Latin America, but in English "the patron" had a medieval ring that I could never get out of my ear.

When Tompkins ran Esprit in San Francisco, he banned the chewing of gum by his employees. Smoking was banned; also coffee, which he must have felt endangered his workers in some way. He once closed a factory in San Francisco rather than allow the employees to unionize, explaining that a union was incompatible with his vision of a new workplace paradigm. This utopian streak flourished in the free space of southern Chile, fueled by an unlimited budget and welcomed by economically hungry locals. Tompkins was popular, as the sincere and formal messages of thanks from each band in the barn showed. Everyone called him "Don Tompkins," an honorific slightly less freighted with feudal baggage than *patrón* but still indicative of his authority.

Tompkins was a good *patrón*. He built the schoolhouse in which I was sleeping for the use of the village children. He hired their fathers at above-market wages to build his walkways and maintain trails and roofs; he sold their locally woven sweaters at a little gift shop and paid handsomely for the food they harvested from their waters; and he treated the locals with respect touched only lightly with condescension. In a profile of Tompkins, *Outside* magazine compared Reñihué favorably to Tolstoy's utopian farm estate in Russia—never mind what this said about social progress in a century.

Tompkins was not simply out to save the locals, however. He was planning on saving the surrounding forests, then all of Chile, and eventually the world. The master plan for this was called Deep Ecology, a stew of radical environmentalism and technophobia that aimed at nothing less than overturning the profit motive in Western civilization. Deep Ecology argued that recycling and trail cleanups and other popular forms of environmentalism were "shallow" ecology. Tompkins had launched the Foundation for Deep Ecology to advocate for these views. Brochures lying around the schoolhouse explained the foundation's agenda: a serious decrease in the earth's human population and a rejection of economic growth, profit, and "technology worship" as the guiding principles of life. "Basic economic, technological, and ideological structures" would have to be changed and "the resulting state of affairs will be deeply different from the present."

Culture, ecology, and economics had been fused at Reñihué into a seamless vision of the correct way to live. There was no separating these elements: the forest could only survive if the locals were paid well to do something other than cut it down; the locals could only survive if their traditional lives, from folk music to wood craft to weaving, were preserved; the foreigners could wash their money of its original sin by planting lettuce and banning telephones.

It was no wonder Tompkins was hated by some segments of Chilean society. He denounced free trade agreements exactly at the moment Chile's government, major press, and business elite were pushing hard for a NAFTA-like free trade agreement with the United States. Tompkins blasted "market-based economic systems" in a country obsessed with *el libre mercado*. He bought and took off the market 700,000 acres of forest in an economy where forest products were a crucial source of foreign exchange and a region where timber jobs were a staple of life. He advocated a population decrease in a Catholic country where mentioning birth control was still controversial. His schemes were self-consciously radical, and no matter what you thought of them—I found them a mix of technophobic nonsense and visionary thinking—it was obvious why Chileans reacted with confusion, shock, and sometimes hostility. Deep Ecology promised to "quell the present drives of our society," but a lot of poor people in Chile felt their best shot at a future was in those capitalist drives. Virtually all of the rich people felt that way.

Tompkins was doing good, but of what kind? The Grand Tetons of Wyoming were saved by the Rockefellers, who knew that some things belong to the world and were willing to finance the transaction of preservation. The problem with Tompkins wasn't his plan to save the land, it was his plan to freeze the people in place. The conflation of a natural ecosystem with a "natural" culture was dangerous; it condemned the Chileans to not becoming what they might become. The *encuentro folklórico* was designed to preserve the old ways, but what was so pure about their music anyway? The guitar was invented in Arabia, not Region X. Much of the best music in the world— including their folk songs—was the result of cultures blending, subverting one another, and twining into new forms. In every practical way, Tompkins had created a better space for himself and those around him—but he had also created an illusion. Inside his magic circle of money, he had stopped the tide of life like some antipodean King Canute. But outside the fjord the regular world went on without him, still polluting, still consuming, still spending, still assimilating cultures and creating anew. He seemed to have withdrawn from all hope of collective action; of grasping, dirty, public life; of patient, blundering adaptation. I left Reñihué grateful for its beauty and, perhaps, the example. But this wasn't activism; it was defeatism.

I had little doubt what Che Guevara would have said. Tompkins was exactly the well-meaning bourgeois reformer that violent revolutionaries always find so threatening. But I could also hope that Ernesto Guevara would have been grudgingly impressed by Tompkins, whose example of philanthropic conscience is rare enough in our day and was virtually unknown in the Latin America of the 1950s. It was no wonder the Chileans were paranoid about him. If Tompkins had taken up a gun—or better yet, paid someone else to—the Chileans would have known what to do (shoot him or strike a deal, depending on how good his connections in Santiago were). But this way, he had them foxed. They'd never met a petulant, post-capitalist plutocrat before.

I never got my interview. Having eaten his food, caught his fish, and listened to his music, on the fourth morning I followed the Chileans down to the fjord and boarded the little green ketch again. We had all taken something we needed from him: the musicians were happy and well fed, and I'd rested my ribs and reached the point that I could get out of bed in the morning without yelping. We sailed up the narrow inlet for an hour together, as happy a band of mariners as there ever was. The sun even came out. The mountains were truly magnificent.

While we stood on deck, feeling the ocean drawing closer, one of the musicians told me that *el patrón* was "a nice man, but he's being very stubborn about the televisions." I asked what he meant. The villagers of Reñihué had, it turned out, petitioned Tompkins to get a satellite dish so they could see television. He had turned down their request.

Many of the musicians had left their instruments inside the

cabin and now sat on deck listening to portable cassette players with tiny headphones. As we pitched up the fjord toward Caleta Gonzalo, I went around the boat, peering surreptitiously at their musical choices. Most of them were listening to American rap.

I had to wonder if Che would be an environmentalist by now.

There is nothing so dispiriting on a long, difficult journey as being forced to backtrack. But now I waited in the cold at the ferry ramp at Caleta Gonzalo and contemplated a small retreat. The waves lapping on cement called me north—if I waited here I could eventually catch a ferry to Puerto Montt—but there was business behind me, back to the south. I didn't even know what day of the week it was anymore, but I knew I had to retrace my steps and recover what I could from the accident. When the *micro* arrived a dozen of us piled in and began bouncing south.

The road was paved with a mixture of gravel and ground seashells. There were a lot of potholes and gullies. The bridges were tiny and primitive—six logs bolted into a raft and thrown over a gully. The driver had an unlit cigarette sewn to his mustache, and the cigarette bobbed up and down and grew soggy with spittle as we rattled along. He drove too fast and informed us with studied cheer that two people had been killed on the road last night. They had driven off a bridge in the rain. The bridges were only about four feet off the ground, so I didn't see how fatal that could be, but maybe they were going fast.

After a while we pulled over to have a birthday party for someone on board the bus. The dozen of us dismounted, stood in the road, and passed a single large bottle of beer clockwise while singing "Happy Birthday" and a Chilean song I didn't recognize. Then we got back in the van. As we were starting up, a red pickup came along in the other direction. It had California plates. I leaned out the window, which put me right next to the driver, who was leaning out his window.

"You're a long way from home," I said to him.

"So are you," he said, and drove on.

Chaitén was such an important metropolis that it had pavement, although not much. Squeezed between a bay with a massive tidal swing and a range of steep hills, the town had a few thousand people and was a typical transit center, either full or empty depending on the movements of ferries and the migrations of fish and tourists arriving or departing, heading south toward Tierra del Fuego or east to Argentina. There were some half-decent restaurants, a dozen hotels, a supermarket, and a waterfront office full of blond wood and nature photography designed to draw visitors to Tompkins's park, just north.

The bus dropped me by an empty lot in the center of town, and I began walking toward a hostel called La Watson. I heard a distant beep and then a motor and turned to see the same bus coming back around the block in a hurry. The bus pulled to a halt, and a woman in the back passed a small camera through the window. It was my own; it had fallen on the floor as I dozed during the return trip. Those thieving Latins in action again.

This was not my first visit to La Watson. When I left the scene of my crash a week before, I had done so with paralyzing reluctance. My problem was not technical—to my amazement the bike sprang to life the instant I hit the starter button. I had let it idle for a while in that drizzle, and then turned it off. I sat under a bush for a bit, walked around, inspected the road for evidence of what made me crash (there was nothing, not even the pothole I thought I'd hit), and then sat under a bush again. My breathing was already painful, and my head still tasted of smoke, although I later realized there had been no smoke, only the bitter chemical backwash of the violent jolt spinning through my brain. I wiped the blood off my knuckles and forehead and waited a long time alone. Then I got on the bike, started it again, and drove on. There had been nothing else to do, no choice about it all. After the friendly trucker and his daughter left, I was alone in the wilderness in the rain. So I went on.

After a couple of hours I found a fancy inn beneath a glacier and ate an expensive meal while telling the waiter, the cook, and the innkeeper that I had just crashed. They said nothing and served me quickly, as if eager to get rid of me. I realized later that I was coated with mud.

By nightfall I staggered into a tiny village called Santa Lucia, rented a room behind the general store, and fell asleep. When I woke up a day later my left ribs were giving me a sharp pain at each inrush of breath. I kept my respiration shallow and asked the landlady about a doctor. She directed me to an army outpost three blocks away—that is, all the way on the other side of town. Only a few hundred people lived here in wet wood houses. Horses roamed loose in the gravel streets. The military base was a triangular stockade fresh-carved from the wilderness, with a guard tower at each corner. A Chilean soldier wearing a rain cape and cradling an automatic rifle stood at the front gate. The lieutenant came out and told me that there was no doctor in the town. He offered to radio for a truck that would arrive in the morning, take me up the coast to a doctor by afternoon, and then return me the next day. It was a generous offer considering the circumstances, but I decided to sleep it off. It rained for two days. Eventually, my saddlebags still held shut with duct tape, I struggled on toward Chaitén, where I took a room at La Watson and fell asleep.

Now the Kent family welcomed me back to the same bed in their son's old room. I called them the Kent family because their favorite show was a dubbed version of *Lois and Clark*, the Superman spinoff. The show came in only dimly, drifting at the edges of the frame and filled with snow by the long trip from a transmitter up the coast, but the Kents considered themselves lucky to have TV. When I'd been sitting around their house a few days before, wheezing and complaining, they had been glued to a telethon raising money for some illness. Telethons were a recent phenomenon in Chile, and there seemed to be a new one every week shilling for some cause, asking Chileans to solve a social problem by sending a small check. Their other favorite show was *Sábado Gigante*, an epic variety program broadcast from Miami and popular all over Latin America. The host, Don Francisco, was a right-wing Chilean Jew who could sing and dance, and if you were into leering at salsa starlets and watching housewives chase balloons for prizes it was pretty entertaining. I liked the commercials, which were built into the show. Don Francisco himself would stand there with a box of detergent, telling you how clean it would make your life.

"That's what America is like," Mr. Kent told me. He was pointing at the TV screen, at *Lois and Clark*. I peered through the static to check his bearings. Lois and Clark were both very beautiful and wore incredibly expensive clothes. Mr. Kent pointed out how short her skirts were. "You must have a good time in America," he said, wink wink, making sure his wife heard. I liked him, though. Now back from my healing sojourn at Reñihué, I set my bags down in La Watson and was greeted enthusiastically by Mr. Kent. He took me outside to the tool shed and threw open the door with ill-concealed satisfaction. There was La Cucaracha.

We had bonded, of course, in the grip of accident. The motorcycle was now covered with scars—streaks in the tank, dings on the handlebars, cracks in the orange turn signal lamps, and a whole set of vicious scabs on the front fender, which had twisted straight upward in the impact. The windshield was gone; its support bars and clamps sat empty and rigid on the front of the bike.

> *La cucaracha, la cucaracha*
> *ya no puede caminar*

But it actually *did* still run. La Cucaracha was uglier than ever but impossible to kill. From my lyrical obsession I had gradually begun, despite my efforts, to think of the bike as La Cucaracha. Inevitably the short form, just Kooky, took over in my mind. Kooky, as in nuts, which I was if I talked to my motorcycle. All my rationalizations about the cold nature of machines were forgotten during the terrifying four-second journey down that embankment.

"Hello, Kooky," I said, and stroked the tank softly, fawning over the machine turned companion. Mr. Kent had done everything he'd promised: the mirrors were welded back on, the mudguard bent back into place, the crack in the turn signal glued up. Most remarkably, he'd managed to fix the left saddlebag, which had been crushed by the impact. Mr. Kent had worked patiently with a rubber hammer, bending the aluminum hinges into alignment and fitting the two halves of the plastic clamshell against each other. It wasn't perfect—water would get into the case from now on—but I was out of duct tape and thought this was heaven. Mr. Kent refused any payment except for ten dollars to reimburse his neighbor, the welder. The banging and gluing were all free. He was retired and wanted to be useful.

The next night I ate an early dinner of fried eel along the waterfront, where I met a Chilean traveling south on a BMW motorcycle. He lived near Santiago and gave me his phone number with instructions to call when I needed a place to stay. After dinner, when it was just starting to get dark, I rode the fully loaded Cucaracha out past the end of town to the municipal wharf, where a long line of trucks was waiting for the tide to rise. When the water came in, the ferry to Puerto Montt came in, too: the short trucks growled and spewed black smoke as they pulled their heavy loads back and forth, inching their way onto the boat under the direction of a grimly competent load master. Fifty or sixty Chileans had gathered to watch the proceedings. This was the best entertainment going in Chaitén, and they cheered the truckers and hoped something would go wrong. I sat on the bike looking downhill at the proceedings. A policeman told me I would be the last one to board. The ferry was completely reserved by trucks and a few minivans, but there was usually room for a motorbike.

The tide kept rising, and the ferry filled, and the sun set. The last trucks were loaded at around 10 P.M. under a perfect black sky littered with crisp stars. When the ramp came flat with the dock there was no more time: the ferry master squeezed a minivan into the spot between two timber trucks, looked up the hill, and gave a final wave. The policeman blew his whistle, the entire crowd cheered, and I rolled down the hill, over the ramp, and into the ferry, slipping between a beer truck and a bulkhead. Hands from the darkness helped me tie down the bike.

It was difficult to see anything after the loading ramp came up. The ferry jolted and pulled back, and I could feel the great metal box begin to spin and slide forward over an unstable surface. I climbed up a gangway and watched the town and then the harbor shrink away. We headed out to sea at a tremendous clip. Down below a dozen trucks were cheek to jowl, the drivers already trying to sleep across their seats. The tiny lounge inside the superstructure smelled of metal, paint, and vomit, its few seats taken by screaming children. I went forward, climbed a ladder, and stood for a while examining the stars. Eventually I just lay down on the half-inch-thick steel plate and fell asleep under my leather jacket, my head braced on a coil of rope.

Five hours later the sun came up, Puerto Montt hauled over the horizon, we docked, the ramp went down, and the dozen truckers blew their horns while I heaved on the kick starter again and again. There was no green light at all. I rolled La Cucaracha down the ramp and, leaning into the weight, pushed the bike through the quiet, early-morning streets of Puerto Montt.

A cabdriver in a gas station gave the bike a jump start. I let the engine charge itself as I looked back over the port, drinking bad instant coffee—Chileans call all coffee "Nescafé"—and read a paper that I had bought in the gas station. Under the headline WHERE IS CHE GUEVARA? I learned the news from Bolivia:

> The whereabouts of the body of the elusive Argentine-Cuban guerrilla Ernesto "Che" Guevara has still not come to light seventy days after a search team started digging in Vallegrande, Bolivia, where he was allegedly buried in 1967. A team of Argentine, Cuban and Bolivian experts have wielded the pick and shovel relentlessly, but not a sign has been found of the revolutionary's remains.

The port was ringed with immense, sodden piles of wood chips bound for Japan. This wood pulp, once forests like those Tompkins hoped to protect, was going to be converted into specialty papers and rayon for clothes. The whole town stank of sawdust, and with the bike idling I felt an urge to leave right away.

I rolled over the narrow, flat green floor that was Chile's coastal plain and then up an increasingly twisty valley into the Andes. The road turned to dirt and a raging green river appeared alongside. I followed road and water upstream, eventually coming under the slopes of Mount Osorno, a perfectly shaped volcanic cone. Osorno was theoretically still active, but the tablecloth-white snowfields running upward at an even, 45-degree pitch showed that it was dormant and cold right now. The road ended on the far side of the volcano, overlooking a wide lake ringed with mountains. The lake was called Todos los Santos, or All the Saints, and from the spot where my kickstand landed there did seem to be as many visible peaks as there were saints in the Catholic panoply.

On the maps this spot was called Petrohué, but it was not a town, just a single hotel built for Queen Elizabeth when she visited the region and, across the river mouth, a handful of dilapidated huts occupied by the local ferry men and fishing guides. The volcano's snowfields glowed so brightly that it was painful to look that way. I stood a long time, examining the ring of peaks and overlapping arms of land that hinted of the passage to Argentina. It was the most beautiful view I had ever seen.

A fisherman was disrobing from his gear a few feet away, stuffing rod and vest into the trunk of a Saab. I made the usual inquiries and so did he. When he learned I was an American and a journalist he burst into an unprovoked tirade about General Augusto Pinochet. It was a pro-Pinochet tirade: the general was misunderstood by Americans; the general had saved Chile from communism; the general had built the very road we were standing on; the general had also built the magnificent Southern Highway; the general was the greatest leader in Chilean history; the general was very, very, underappreciated by Americans.

I found this argument hard to swallow, given how tightly America had worked with General Pinochet and other military men in the past. In 1973, Pinochet had overthrown the elected president of Chile, Salvador Allende, with the direct connivance and enthusiastic backing of the CIA, Henry Kissinger, and American corporations like ITT and Anaconda, the copper giant. Pinochet's supporters were only angry because the American public had renounced that official support as Pinochet spent the 1970s assembling a dictatorship, carrying out mass arrests, building an archipelago of prison camps, and torturing or "disappearing" thousands of his countrymen. The general then spent the 1980s beating back pro-democracy demonstrations and the 1990s retreating furiously from his image as a strongman, taking credit for civil works and standing punctiliously on points of law that had been denied his victims.

I doubted that the general had put one spade into the road we were standing on, or that this Saab-driving, fly-fishing, gear-encrusted, right-wing angler had ever actually traveled on the Carreterra Austral. But my new friend was already red in the face so I let these details slide and accepted his offer of a huge green woolly bugger fly that he had tied himself. It had a long hook shaft wrapped in tufts of green fur and thin copper wire that would sink it down deep. It looked like it would catch big fish, and a year later—on the Missouri River, in Montana—it would catch me the largest trout I had ever caught. I always thought of it as the Pinochet bugger. But neither of us knew that at the time. He was just an asshole standing by the side of a road, and he apparently had the same opinion about me. We all saw our own utopias in this landscape.

The two G's arrived at Petrohué by boat. Todos los Santos was the final link in the watery chain of the Seven Lakes route, the passage that had brought Alberto and Ernesto across from Bariloche. When the ferry landed at Petrohué, the boys wrestled La Poderosa onto solid ground, probably with very tired muscles. It had taken them days to make the transit, and they'd paid their way by working the bilge pumps. Between boats, they had gone wandering in the hills, but their blue-sky days were coming to an end.

At Petrohué, "Sniper" (one of Guevara's many nicknames, this one earned on the rugby field) took a long-overdue bath. Guevara was notorious for his indifference to filth, a habit that would annoy his comrades and fellow travelers for years to come and that even earned a special mention in his CIA file ("He is really outstandingly and spectacularly dirty," the agency warned). Now, as Che scrubbed himself in the lake, Granado wandered off and got laid, or at least implied that he did. Granado had spent the boat ride chatting up a pair of Brazilian girls, one of them a student of biochemistry. His subsequent diary entry played coy, noting that upon arrival in Petrohué, he and his new "colleague" went off to see the lake together: "After speaking of biochemistry we passed by mutual accord to topographical anatomy. . . . I hope not to have arrived at embryology."

With the motorbike on solid ground again, Guevara and Granado were able to move forward with what looked to be an easy trek up the densely settled, green flatlands of Chile. After camping a night on the far side of the lake and plucking a single long trout from a speedy run in the river, I followed their route back out into the plain and then turned north for the long run up the length of Chile. I quickly passed through the town of Osorno and made for Valdivia, a major port where I hoped to find a new battery and an end to my electrical problems.

The landscape was fat. Even Granado broke form by praising the beauty of the shade trees and the wheat fields. Soon he caught himself, however. The "exploited sharecroppers" tending the fields were victims of "usurious" and "parasitical" absentee owners.

I watched the fields rushing by, but these were planted with corn, not wheat. There was an optical illusion in the way the rows passed so quickly that you could never quite see down them. Instead of an aisle of space between the plants, there was a dark blur that was as fixed as the horizon. No matter how many times I looked away, I kept noticing that dark band again and twisting my head, sure that if I looked fast enough I would see through it.

CHAPTER FIVE

CHE AND THE ART OF
MOTORCYCLE MAINTENANCE

I bought 400 cc's of SA40 motor oil at a mechanic's workshop on the outskirts of Valdivia. The oil was measured from a barrel into a paper cone, which I clenched in my fist and carried back across the street as pinkish brown rivulets coated my hand. I fed the tip of the paper cone into a hole on the left side of the bike and then loosened my grip. When all the oil had disappeared down into the engine I dropped the dipstick back into place, then lifted it again and read the depth of the smear against the engraved advice to *"Nicht uber 'max' Auffullen!"*

It is a law of nature that old motorcycles lose a little oil from time to time. Nortons were famous for their oil leaks, and I had no doubt that La Poderosa left a stain behind every time it was parked. The thirteen-year-old Norton probably trailed blue smoke as it ran down the road, too. BMWs were supposed to be above this, but I'd been riding hard, so La Cucaracha's thirst was nothing to worry about.

The bike ran clean when it ran. The battery seemed to be dying, although I couldn't tell if this was caused by the battery itself, or the alternator, or a wiring problem somewhere. I checked the spark plugs from time to time but their tips were clean. There was something mysterious and frustrating in the way the bike would start only if it had been running recently. If the engine had time to cool down then the starter solenoid produced nothing but an unpleasant choking noise.

I'd stopped across from the workshop because of a little municipal museum I saw there. I'd only been inside long enough to learn
they didn't stock what I was looking for, the archives of Valdivia's old
newspaper, the *Correo del Austral*. During their visit, Guevara and
Granado had stopped around the office of the paper, which had then
published a "very nice" article about them. The *Correo* had gone bust
years before, but the museum staff told me the 1952 issues were
stored with the municipal archives in a building near the port. It was
already seven in the evening, still bright out but too late for work and
the end to a long day that had begun at the shores of Todos los Santos. To my surprise the road north—National Route 5, the central
highway of Chile and a crucial component of the Pan-American
Highway system—had been in poor shape, filled with potholes and
cuts. You could make good time but it took a lot of concentration to
avoid all the broken asphalt. You might be thrown off the bike at any
time if you didn't watch where you were going. Twice during the day
I passed concrete retaining walls decorated in black spray paint with
the phrase TOMPKINS OUT OF CHILE! My shoulder ached from the
strain and I needed a bed, a meal, and a mechanic.

I took what consolation I could from the predicament of the
Argentines. La Poderosa was falling apart beneath their butts. On
February 21, Granado wrote with heartfelt exaggeration that they
had crossed the "highest mountains in the world almost without
brakes." Aside from all the crashes, the alternator had given out and
the rear brake had grown so weak since Bahía Blanca that "we practically have to brake with our boots." Granado seemed to shiver with
dread as he wrote that there was "little possibility of continuing the
journey on the Powerful One."

As dilapidated as the Norton sounded, the alternative—traveling on to Peru without a bike—loomed like a thundercloud. With the
bike they could set their own itinerary, make plans, keep a schedule,
budget expenses, and depend only on themselves; without it, the trip
would take longer, cost more, and cover less ground. They would be
children of happenstance, with little hope of reaching the expedition's ultimate goal, the great land of the north.

The same unspoken question loomed over me as I remounted and drove around Valdivia looking for a guest house. If the bikes died—La Poderosa and La Cucaracha both—we travelers would be left in mid-journey, far from home and even farther from our goals. Sputtering along with a dying electrical system, the question of what to do if the bike failed at this early stage of the trip tickled at the edge of my conscience. Turn back or go on? It was a query I wasn't prepared to answer.

I found that bed, that meal, and that mechanic all under the same roof. The bed was in the front room of a rambling old wood house a half mile from the port of Valdivia. The meal was some rice with a can of Chilean mussels that I cooked on the kitchen stove. The mechanic was the old bald fellow who watched me eat and spent the whole meal describing what was happening on the television screen I was trying not to watch. It was an old American detective show, something from the '70s that I didn't recognize and didn't want to. I spooned rice and mussels off my plate and the husband sat there, reciting what he saw: "He's going inside . . . it's dark. . . . There's the lady. . . . They're talking. . . . It's a commercial now . . . another commercial . . . another commercial. . . . Wait, he's driving along now. . . ." His wife wore black and followed me around the house even though I was the only guest. When I went to sleep I could hear her checking the door to my room, to see if it was locked. Later, lying in the dark, I heard the couple arguing. Their words were indistinct, but it sounded like he was defending me. I don't know what I was accused of.

In the morning the husband listened attentively as I described Kooky's electrical problems. "I will help you," he said. His name was Don, so I called him Don Don out of respect. He was sixty-six and proud of the fact he had "a drop" of Mapuche blood in him. The Mapuche were tough warriors who had repeatedly driven the conquistadors out of this part of Chile. They'd learned to ride horses, mastered the ambush, and eventually captured and killed Pedro de Valdivia, the town's namesake. Legend had it that they poured molten gold down his throat, telling him he could finally have what he had come so far to find.

Don Don took me out the kitchen door and down a narrow path between the houses. The path cut through to the other side of the block, where it led to the back door of a large garage. This was a professional's workshop, a tin shed big enough for four cars and filled with power tools and dusty car parts. The old man had been a mechanic before he retired. His specialty was tractor repairs, but now he worked on cars to make ends meet. Currently he was working on a 1951 Vauxhall, a '61 Toyota Land Cruiser, a Ford Turino from the early '70s, and a Brazilian Chrysler of unknown vintage. He said we would fix the motorcycle together. I rolled it around the block and into the garage. He pulled out a volt meter and told me to come back later.

I walked into town. It was a beautiful Saturday morning in February, the height of summer. The air was always moist here in the south; the sun burned but everything felt crisp and cool. The harbor itself wasn't exactly busy, but there were a few small, colorfully painted wooden dories tied to the wharf and every now and then a launch would go by. The action was on land, where the walkway along the wharf was lined on both sides by vendors. They were selling seafood in riotous splendor: live blue crabs clattering in baskets; enormous and lethargic king crabs with foot-long legs; sea urchins; bundles of smoked clams, oysters, and mussels; glistening eels; blocks of pressed seaweed called *luche;* and salmon opened like butterflies to reveal red flesh and white ribs. Several vendors tried to interest me in an odd little crustacean that lay, red and quivering and alive, inside a polyp of a shell encrusted with dirt and slime. I had no idea what it was and refused to eat it when they waved samples at me on the end of a fork.

I settled into a stall instead and ate a slab of fried fish for lunch. The Chileans crowded all around me, reading newspapers and dressed in wool caps and jackets. Chileans were sometimes called "the sweater Latins" because it was cold here and they dressed like Norwegians.

It was impossible to miss the euphoria in Guevara's voice as he surveyed this scene in Valdivia:

> *The harbor, crammed full of goods we'd never seen before,*
> *the market where they sold different foods, the typically*
> *Chilean wooden houses, the clothes of the rustics, all felt totally*
> *different from what we knew back home; there was something*
> *indigenously American, untouched by the exoticism which*
> *invaded our pampas.*

Ernesto's meditation on newness expired on the familiar note of self-deprecation. Chile might seem different to a young Argentine who'd never been anywhere before, but the two countries did share some traits, as he discovered walking at the port. The tall Ernesto had been wearing a pair of hand-me-down pants that were too short for him. Here in Valdivia, just as in Argentina, the locals took one look at his ankles and cried out "Highwater!"

City Hall was only a couple of blocks from the harbor, in a square gray modern building. I found the archivist's office closed until Monday, but on the way out I noticed a book fair taking place on the ground floor, in a kind of interior courtyard. Booths ran around the edge of the space and I joined a dense crowd in working my way slowly along the rows. There were a lot of children's stories and poetry collections published in various parts of the Spanish-speaking world. At the back of the room I found a booth selling textbooks. One of them was called *The History of Chile.* I opened it at the back: the last entry covered the entire span of history from 1972 to today in two pages. It mentioned in passing that there had been a constitutional reform in 1982 and that the Carreterra Austral had been pushed into the south. There was no mention of the 1973 coup by the general, nor that thousands of people had been killed, nor that hideous concentration camps had been set up in the deserts of the far north and on islands in the subarctic ocean near Tierra del Fuego.

The last entry in this factless history book was a brief mention of the country's partial transition to democracy in 1989. Under pressure from mass demonstrations and foreign governments, the general had staged a yes-or-no vote on whether he should remain in power for another six years. To his amazement, he'd lost; to his enemies' amazement, he had accepted the verdict and beat a partial retreat from power. In the book, this was an electoral "reform." I quickly found another book on Chilean history, but the authors were perhaps too honest to rewrite history and simply stopped the book cold in 1972.

Here was a nation paralyzed: Chile was now a democracy in name, with a free press, elected legislature, and independent judiciary, but there were certain monumental subjects that could not be discussed. Around me, the browsers kept their eyes down as they moved past this booth with its unpleasant silences.

Two booths up I saw a couple of saggy, middle-aged men in berets. They both wore full beards and had cigarettes fuming from their lips. Their hair was disheveled, their eyes were afire, and their shirts were rumpled—the unmistakable plumage of the leftist intellectual. The berets alone drew me in, and I introduced myself. The one in suspenders was Ricardo. The one in a paisley shirt and ill-fitting trousers was Pedro. Respectively, they were editor and subeditor of a little magazine called *Caballo de Proa,* which is the Spanish phrase for the carved figure on the prow of a sailing ship.

When I say little, I mean little: their magazine was so small it almost disappeared among the assorted books of poetry they were also selling. I bought three back issues, which stacked together were the size and shape of a deck of cards without the aces. In Spanish this was called a "purse magazine," and Pedro and Ricardo crammed as many items into their purse as any grandmother. The problem with this format wasn't the number of articles—any given issue included three or four pieces of cultural criticism, music and book reviews, an essay on the esthetics of eating, a few cartoons, some appeals for environmental and human rights causes, a dispatch from Chiapas, a history of the cinema in Valdivia, some satire, an odd quote from

Kafka, and even an ad or two taken out by one of Ricardo's friends or by Pedro himself for one of his other ventures, like his Sunday morning radio show. No, the problem was length—the longest article in the bunch took ninety seconds to read, and most were only two or three paragraphs long. I read all three issues while standing in front of their booth, and we agreed to meet for coffee later. They named a café and a time.

We spent Sunday on our backs on the floor, on opposite sides of the bike. Don Don pressed the wires of the volt meter against various bits of Kooky's anatomy while I pretended to understand what he was doing. Once in a while I would jump up at his instruction and turn on the key or try the headlight and horn or press the starter button. Diagnostic work is slow and boring, requiring a passionless, methodical routine. After an hour we'd learned nothing.

With a pop, Don Don pulled the black spark-plug wire off the cylinder on his side of the engine. He inserted the tip of a screwdriver into the cap at the end of the wire, and then held a finger to the metal of the screwdriver.

"Start it," he said.

I refused, but he insisted. I gave a gentle kick on the starter.

"Harder," he said, and I did, and he winced and dropped the screwdriver and then said, "There is a spark."

We stopped working for a while, and while we stretched our legs Don Don told me the story of the four Americans he had met in his life. He'd learned to repair John Deeres from an American. In one six-month period he'd met two men, both from Livermore, California, who claimed not to know each other. I was the fourth. The mechanic had strong opinions about America, how Ohio was near Iowa, and how Illinois was the most powerful state because it had both Abraham Lincoln's birthplace and the Caterpillar factory.

"I know I will never go now," Don Don said without warning. "In this economy, never." I told him how back home all the papers said Chile was an economic success. They called it the "Chilean miracle." He thought I was joking. As people do, he cited his own situation: his pension covered little, and he was scrambling for body work on cars to make ends meet. In the old days, his skills as a tractor mechanic had been good enough for him to work on any car in Chile. But now, with the inrush of new products under the free-market system, everyone was buying complicated foreign cars. The pollution controls were too elaborate; the equipment to test electronic ignitions cost thousands of dollars, which he didn't have. You needed a college degree to fix those cars, he said.

The statistics robbed General Pinochet's economic miracle of much of its wonder. Pinochet had applied virtually every item on the checklist of free market reform, cutting subsidies, privatizing industries, liberalizing trade, and opening the country to foreign investment. But it wasn't until 1988—after fifteen years of shock therapy—that individual income reached the level last seen under Allende. Consumption hardly rose at all; the new wealth flowed to the top of the social pyramid, pushing Chile from a relatively middle-class society into one where the rich got richer (the top tenth of the population went from collecting 36.2 percent of national income in 1978 to 46.8 percent ten years later) but the poor either stayed the same or actually got poorer (the bottom half of the public went from 20.4 to 16.8 percent of income in the same period). And this was in Chile, the "miracle" and best case. Across the hemisphere the same neoliberal reforms were increasing inequality and widening income distribution. People like Don Don were moving out of the middle class, but not upward.

He didn't speak for a while and then asked me if Gary Hart supported expanding NAFTA to Chile.

Perdón? He repeated the question: Does Gary Hart support expanding NAFTA to Chile?

"Maybe," I said.

He turned away from me and fussed with something on the tool bench. "Boot ta tie 'em drugged," he said.

Perdón?

"Boot ta tie 'em drugged," he repeated, and then: "Esmall grope his beggin toe christ are under TV sex."

I looked over his shoulder. He was reading from an American magazine, rather tattered and dusty. He mouthed the words to show he spoke English, but I had to read over his shoulder to follow what he was saying:

> *But the time dragged. Small groups began to cluster around TV sets. Campaign workers whispered anxiously among themselves. Still no candidate, still no statement. Finally, a few minutes after 11 P.M., Walter Mondale waded slowly through the now diminished crowd, family and entourage in tow.*

It was a twelve-year-old copy of *Time* magazine. In the garage, I suddenly realized, time had come to a stop. As long as I relied on Don Don I would never leave Valdivia. The bike was not going to be fixed. In his Caterpillar dreams and John Deere reveries he did not want to admit it, but he really had no idea what was wrong with the electrical system. I had to move on. On Monday morning I charged the battery and rode into town to meet the intellectuals.

Pedro published dirty cartoons in his magazine from time to time, not because he thought they were profound but because he imagined that it annoyed the powers that be. The first Great Power in Chile was the Catholic Church—"a shadow over the nation," Pedro intoned sternly—and the Church owned one of two national television networks and tended to censor the naughty bits of various shows. So in one issue Pedro stuck in a drawing of Marilyn Monroe with her knickers around her ankles and her hands in a suspicious place. It was a blow for freedom disguised as a turn-on.

The other Big Power in Chile was the military. Ever since 1989, when the general began to yield power in bits and pieces, the military had been furiously working to avoid any prosecutions for crimes committed during and after the 1973 coup. A blanket pardon was thrown over the military; Pinochet appointed himself "Senator-for-life" with his immunity written into the new constitution. But there were small holes in the blanket: a few officers had been prosecuted and convicted for assassinations carried out abroad. The country had just survived a bitter constitutional crisis over refusal of one of these convicted men—General Manuel Contreras—to go to jail. The military had protected him, and Pinochet's own guards had ushered the balking Contreras to an isolated military hospital. From his sickbed, General Contreras demanded a jail "suitable to his rank" and reflecting his "long service to the nation." After much negotiation, the jittery civilians agreed and rapidly built a special jail that resembled a penthouse, with a multiroom cell outfitted with a gym and a cellular phone and a view of the ocean.

So Pedro published an essay—albeit a short one—demanding equal treatment for intellectuals. The author of the piece, a local painter, declared that he would never submit to jail unless he too had a special cell with an ocean view, a double bed, and the right to receive collect calls from his kids when they were on vacation. This jail for artists also had to be staffed only by women wearing bright colors ("Green is insupportable," the painter declared). And of course, he would never submit to jail until his rank in the local painters' club had been recognized.

Pedro expounded on these themes in the Café Paula, an orange linoleum dump whose twin virtues were that it had the local newspapers and that it let impoverished intellectuals loiter all afternoon over a single cup of coffee. The staff, contributors, friends, enemies, and sympathizers of *Caballo de Proa* gathered at the Paula after lunch on most days, and sometimes they even bought food. It was here that Pedro could rage against the fallen state of the world.

When the bill came it wasn't much, but I was trying to get inside Ernesto Guevara's head, and if there was one certain lesson of his 1952 journey it was the art of the mooch. With my funds dwindling, I'd been feeling an increasing pressure to do some serious sponging—

as the Cubans say, to "Be Like Che." A natural coward, I decided to start with Pedro and a cup of coffee. The bill was a couple of bucks, and I figured that the home team should pay.

So I sat there, waiting for him to offer. And I sat there. We finished our coffee. We stared at each other. We ran out of conversation. We cleared our throats. I ordered and slowly drank a glass of water.

Finally, I said, "Well, Pedro, I've got to go, but thanks a lot. It was nice of you to show me La Paula."

We got up, and I tried to move only very slowly in the general direction of the door. But this wasn't getting anywhere. If Pedro was going to cough up a couple of bucks for the coffee he would have offered by now. I caved in and decided, in an act of generosity, to pay for my half. I wearily shuffled through my pocket, counting out coins to the precise halfway mark. Then I turned to ask for Pedro's half.

He was gone. I never even heard the door swing. I noted this maneuver for future use.

I paid the bill and found Pedro outside, engaged in minute inspection of some faded For Sale notices in a storefront. He walked me back to the bike, smiling faintly.

The new issue of *Caballo de Proa* was being "presented" that night at a concert of folk music in the municipal theater. I wasn't sure what presenting a magazine actually entailed, but I went—and I went by foot. Despite the recharged battery Kooky's green light glowed only dimly, and kicking it over and over produced nothing. I had to walk and was a little late getting into the theater, where a crowd of about four hundred was staring at Ricardo and Pedro, who were staring back at them. Basically, presenting the magazine meant giving it some free publicity. The local literary establishment were all thick as La Paula thieves, and the emcee for the concert was up there quizzing the boys about their latest and greatest issue, asking them questions like "What is your opinion of the national culture today?"

Presumably, P. and R. were hitting these softballs over the plate.

I say presumably because like intellectuals everywhere they were standing too far from the microphone. Nobody could hear a word they were saying. The audience didn't mind: the Chileans just talked among themselves while the emcee boomed out his questions; and P. and R. stood there babbling away inaudibly, so that occasional words like "theme" and "fundamental debate" came across but no larger point was made.

The folksingers came on next, and they were pretty good. They were local heroes who'd been at it since the darkest days of the dictatorship. After a while they let a poet on stage, and he read some verse. That was the funny thing about a dictatorship: it was great for culture. If there was one sure way Pinochet could support poetry, it was by staging a military coup, shooting a bunch of people, and tossing some tear gas around once in a while. Literature became not some pointless abstraction, but a pointed one. The history books were empty but the poets spoke volumes. The dictatorship filled their readings, it put standing room crowds in theaters. Politics was banned, but culture was there, and the people of Chile used it like they used oxygen.

And then they unbanned politics. Democracy was restored in 1990. The good guys won, sort of. And suddenly the poets weren't needed anymore. Theaters were half full, the folk concerts were like fifteenth-year college reunions where people were going gray and starting to forget who everyone else was. The natural order had been restored: bookstores everywhere were going broke.

This upset Ricardo, and it drove Pedro crazy, but the poet, whose name was Clemente Riedemann, seemed to welcome any escape from those overly heroic times. He recited this free verse into the microphone; it was, he said, from a poem called "Regarding Cuba, the Sunrise":

> *When I was young and it was not possible to inhabit this world*
> *without a monthly quota of heroism, Cuba was a standard, a*
> *fire that took bearings on the future. What did Fidel think when*

*he rested, what did he sing under the shower? I put a poster of
Che in the dormitory, to see if he would collaborate in dreams
and give a hand with the student protest. . . . Thanks for the
sugar and the folk songs. Even more for the historical material,
even less, without doubt, for the dialectics, for living with an
honorable dream of the great revolution we owe ourselves.
What happiness does Fidel feel at this hour? Who accompanies
him in his sadness?*

People applauded all night, but in a halfhearted way.

There was plenty of news that day. A nineteen-year-old actress
named Elizabeth Taylor was getting married (her second time). An
entire family in Georgia, USA, had been electrocuted. France was
backing a pan-European army. Someone had jumped from the seventh floor of a building in Valdivia. The story I wanted was less
important than any of these, and was consequently buried on page 9,
in the middle of the sports section:

TWO VALIANT ARGENTINE RAIDERS ON
MOTORCYCLE PASS THROUGH VALDIVIA

*One Is Doctor and the Other Studies Medicine;
Specialists in Leprosy*

Currently found in our city are two Argentine raiders,
making a journey of great courage through the principal
countries of South America. They are the doctor of biochemistry, Mr. Alberto Granados, and the seventh year
student of medicine, Mr. Ernesto Guevara Serna, who are
making the raid on motorcycle. They left Córdoba the 29 of
December of last year and after traveling over the north and

south of that province and the principal cities and provinces
of the Atlantic of their homeland, they arrived in Chile by
Puella, Petrohué, heading for Osorno, but having passed
through Junín, San Martín, and Bariloche.

This was the "very nice" article the *Correo de Valdivia* had published on Monday, February 18, 1952. On a Monday morning forty-
four years later the archivist at the municipal building, a mousy man
with thick glasses and a sweater vest, had quickly located the volume,
and after much turning to and fro I'd found the clip. The paper had
stylized their trip as a "raid," a glamorous term for long-distance
racing that ill fit the supposed medical agenda of the two Argentines
but that pleased Guevara (upon his return home he insisted on
describing the trip as a "raid" to unimpressed friends).

When I showed the article to the archivist—pointing to the
name Ernesto Guevara—he looked slightly ill and backpedaled
toward his desk, where he buried his nose again in another book. The
novelist Isabel Allende—a niece of the deposed president—noted
acerbically that any discussion of the past here was "in really bad
taste."

I sought out one of the small number of people in Valdivia with
that kind of bad taste. Roberto Arroyo was the painter who had written the little satire about jail that I'd liked so much in *Caballo de Proa*.
Despite claiming in the piece that he could not abide green, Roberto,
a dapper, thick-haired young man who slept on the floor of his studio
in a sleeping bag, had filled the small space with big canvases of
swirling green scenes that evoked the local forests. The paintings
were built around traditional Mapuche imagery, particularly birds, but
updated with twists of barbed wire and swirls of pure primary colors.

"People have forgotten Che," he said when I showed him a photo-
copy of the 1952 article. Guevara's death in 1967 had made him a
martyr to Chileans on the left, and at age fourteen Roberto had joined
what he called a "Guevarist youth group." This was a bunch of students and left-wing activists who studied the life and teachings of

their hero. At that point, before the coup, there had been pictures of Che everywhere. "Che had an immense influence in the country," Roberto said. But after September 1973 his image was suppressed and his teachings largely surpassed or forgotten. Twenty-five free-market years later, the country was "surging in another direction. We've moved from social solidarity to commercial solidarity," Roberto said. Instead of government programs, "Now we have telethons."

Roberto kept a copy of the multivolume report by a Truth and Reconciliation Commission set up after the return to civilian government, and he began flipping through the pages of one binder, reading me details of the military repression in Valdivia. Statistically speaking, this southern region was the fourth worst site of repression in the country. This was a kind of perverse tribute to the local people, many of whom believed they had been forging a new era of electoral revolutions, of democratic "people's power." Scores of farms in the area had been occupied by peasants, who set up local parliaments and named their communes after Che Guevara. One of the local leaders put on a beret, styled himself as "Comandante Pepe," and gave suitably fevered statements about seizing power and establishing a dictatorship of the proletariat to any journalists who visited his "guerrilla base" (an idle farm decorated with slogans). Inevitably, the fantasies of the left and right began to meet, and Pepe was labeled the Che of Chile. On the day of the coup itself, September 11, 1973, battalion-sized units of soldiers and police instantly closed the mountain passes to Argentina and began rounding up all these left-wing activists. In Panguipulli, just across the flat valley, the military and police detained these peasants and anyone associated even vaguely with the left. Even the leaders of high school student councils were taken, as was the educational director of the region. In Puerto Montt, some people had been summarily executed simply because they were suspected thieves or were involved in personal disputes with military men.

The leftists had misread history, and badly. From the Truth and Reconciliation Commission report:

The 7th day of October, 1973, Andrés SILVA SILVA, 33 years old, logger, was executed by army personnel in the Panguipulli Forestry Complex. He was arrested in his parents' home on October 6, 1973, by a military contingent which took him to a farm in the Nilahue Sector. The next day, the same soldiers took him to his home which they searched. Later he was executed in the area called Sichahue and his lifeless body abandoned in a small wood in that place. . . . Andrés Silva was executed by state agents . . .

It went on and on. Two days after Silva was arrested, the military took seventeen loggers and unionists to a private farm a little higher in the hills and killed them all. The next day, using a list provided by civilian supporters, a combined unit of police and air force men in the same zone detained sixteen people. They were unionists or members of different peasant organizations. The sixteen were taken at night to a bridge over the Toltén River, which is about half an hour from Valdivia. They were shot in the head and dumped, one by one, into the water.

The justification for these acts was always the same: Chile was at war. The country was about to be taken over by communists, and the military had acted just in time to save the nation from a brutal Marxist regime loyal to Cuba and Moscow. It was the ghost of Che Guevara the military was fighting, not just implicitly but explicitly: before the coup the rightist newspaper *El Mercurio* (which was extensively funded by the CIA) portrayed the preposterous Comandante Pepe as an all-powerful KGB agent. Rumor, propaganda, and paranoia amplified Pepe's fifty hapless, pick-and-shovel followers into a crack squad of five thousand Cuban-trained guerrillas led by North Korean and North Vietnamese advisers. When the coup came, a few local communists did grab guns and head for the hills, hoping to escape to Argentina. But there was no doubt who had lost this Battle of Valdivia: one policeman and two soldiers died in shootouts, but in the end the regime took the lives of one hundred and twenty-eight local civilians. In a few months the leftist movements of Valdivia were extinguished, their dream of standing in the vanguard of history now washed away like detritus on one of the region's fast-moving rivers.

Once the immediate control of the countryside had been established, each of the armed forces contributed some four hundred or five hundred men to the joint operations of DINA, the military intelligence unit whose acronym became a synonym for murder in Latin America. Special military squads called "death caravans" were unleashed, rolling through the countryside to round up and "disappear" opponents of the new regime (one caravan in northern Chile eliminated seventy-six *subversivos* in two months). DINA targeted Chileans according to a strict list of priorities. During 1974 the main targets were the leadership of MIR (the Left Revolutionary Movement), the one small armed guerrilla group that tried, under the leadership of Salvador Allende's son, to resist the military coup. With MIR wiped out within the first year, the killing shifted to members of the Socialist Party, once an important legitimate member of the government coalition. By 1976 it was the small and bureaucratic Communist Party that DINA was wiping out. DINA and its successor agencies also attacked Chileans in exile: a general who had the courage to resist the coup and go abroad (killed in Buenos Aires in 1974); a moderate Christian Democratic leader and his wife (shot in Italy in 1975); and a former aide to Allende (blown up in Washington, D.C., in 1976).

Roberto and I bonded over this last case. Orlando Letelier was a charismatic aide to President Allende when the tanks rolled in 1973. He'd been imprisoned in a notorious concentration camp near the Antarctic Circle and finally sent into exile. In September 1976, he was heading to work at a Washington, D.C., think tank when a bomb planted in his car vaporized his legs and killed him immediately. His passenger, an American named Roni Moffit, wasn't as lucky. She took a sliver of metal through the neck and slowly choked to death on her own blood while passersby struggled to help. I explained to Roberto that I took this one personally: I'd grown up around Washington and had driven through that traffic circle a million times. I remembered the day the bomb went off, and the long, ponderous investigation that followed every clue but the obvious ones. Right-wing columnists, retired CIA officers, and American diplomats had spent years trying to blame the bombing on the left. Letelier had been blown up by his own supporters, they argued, as part of a clever, Moscow-Havana plot to smear General Pinochet. Unfortunately for this theory, the evidence was clear, down to the paper trail of receipts and airline tickets eventually uncovered by the FBI: the bomb had been planted by DINA agents dispatched from Santiago.

And this was where Roberto joined in my personal interest. The officer in charge of the operation was none other than General (then Colonel) Manuel Contreras, the subject of Roberto's mocking essay in *Caballo de Proa*. The civilian government finally got around to prosecuting Contreras in the 1990s; he had been convicted, had appealed, had lost his appeal, and was now, as we talked, cowering in his military hospital issuing demands. Like a good soldier, he was careful to cover his rear; Contreras filed an affidavit stating that "only [Pinochet] as supreme authority of DINA had the power to order the missions that were executed. Always in my capacity as delegate for the President, I carried out strictly what was ordered." This was an obvious threat. If Pinochet sacrificed Contreras to the civilians, Contreras would reveal who ordered the Letelier attack and DINA's many other murders. As a moral defense, this "just following orders" explanation would never clear Contreras, but as a political maneuver it was smart.

While Roberto showed me paperwork on all of these events, he emphasized the names, not the numbers. There was an individuality to the names that evaporated in the meaningless debate over statistics. The Truth and Reconciliation Commission had identified 2,279 people who died violently at the hands of the regime. The commission had been unable to resolve another 642 deaths for lack of evidence, leading to a round, consensus figure that 3,000 people had "disappeared." Like everyone I'd talked to who had been involved in the actual enumeration of the dead, however, Roberto found the official estimates absurdly low. He was convinced that about 6,000 had died across Chile. There were at least four more graves in the immediate Valdivia area that had never been opened, he said. I asked him why he didn't go out with some of the human rights people and dig them up. "I had to quit working in the graves," he replied. "Death has numbed me."

"Those involved are still prominent throughout government, business, every kind of commerce, the police, the landowners, and common citizens," Roberto added. "They don't want their past dug up." He spoke while staring out a little window of this top-floor room, watching the street below. This was Chile's sentence in history: the victims and the victimizers had to walk past each other on the street every day. Guilt could not be acknowledged because guilt calls for retribution, for punishment and perhaps even justice.

There was a little item Roberto had written and taped to the wall:

Don't remain in the past! Forget that your father, your mother,
your brother was murdered. Forget that you were tortured.
Forget that you cannot find your family member who
disappeared. Forget that the murderers were dressed in
green and gray. Look to the future, man!

Forget about the past. Think about foreign investment, the free market, globalization. Think about the future. Think about new times. In fact, that was the slogan of the national government: "We're living in new times."

Before I left Roberto gave me a book of poetry by Clemente Riedemann, the fellow who had been on-stage at the municipal theater reminiscing about Fidel Castro in the shower. Roberto had done the illustrations for Riedemann's collection of poems, called *Karra Maw'n,* which was the Mapuche Indian name for this land before the conquistadors like Pedro de Valdivia arrived. It means "land of rain."

"Ironic," Roberto said. "You've brought sunshine to the land of rain." It was true: the sun had come out and from his little window he could see over a sunlit downtown Valdivia.

"For Patricio," he wrote on the title page, "on the trail of Ernesto, past and present."

Kooky was running intermittently, and I pursued the rumor of a new battery up into the hills, climbing a long, well-maintained gravel road into a settlement that I'd call a slum except for the fact that the houses had running water and electricity. Give the devil his due: Pinochet had pushed basic sanitation services into the poorest neighborhoods, and people in Peru and Bolivia would have looked at these slums with envy.

I found the mechanic I'd been told about, a young fellow who ran a shop out of his garage. Unfortunately, he was out of batteries. He wrote down the address of a motorcycle shop in Osorno, but when I tried to leave Kooky just sat there. The mechanic—who'd never set eyes on me before—handed me the keys to his own 125 cc dirt bike, which I rode to Osorno. I strapped the new battery on the back and returned up the gravel road two hours later.

There were a couple of Chilean policemen waiting there when I returned. They were making cosmetic repairs to the dirt bikes they rode on patrol in the settlement, green Japanese bikes with the crossed rifles of the *carabineros* painted on the tanks. They asked me a million questions about my trip and helped me install the battery. They said the only problem in this poor settlement was a small influx of drugs. They like working in the area and said the people were first rate.

They were just like the lawmen who filled Che's diary: polite, generous, correct in all their behavior. This might have seemed obvious in 1952, but in retrospect—given what the *carabineros* had done in Chile—it was disconcerting.

I went around the Paula two days in a row, but I never saw Pedro or Ricardo again.

The poet Pablo Neruda grew up in Temuco, which is about all I knew of the place when I pulled into town just before noon after an easy ride up from Valdivia. I circled the large town plaza and parked Kooky on the sidewalk in front of the local newspaper, *El Diario Austral.* A gray-haired rental cop trundled out to shoo me away but his heart wasn't in it. When I said I was actually going into the newspaper on business he agreed to look after the machine and me. I left the luggage tied on, smoothed my clothes, and went inside. The elevator was sparkling, and I looked at myself in the reflective doors—greasy, dusty, and dubious. Six weeks of Patagonian austerity had shaken off the bloat of B.A. I was lean, sunburned, and needed a shave. The doors opened on the newsroom.

It was like newsrooms everywhere. Desks were scattered about in clumps and there was paper on every surface. Phones jangled incessantly. It looked like twenty or so people worked in the room, but only a few were present and none of them looked up when I came in.

A secretary told me to wait, and I set my helmet on the bench beside me. The archivist came out and listened to my request. He led me to the back of the room, to a reading table tall enough to stand at. In a moment he produced a heavy, bound volume of back issues from 1952. He was not interested in me and went away. Buried in the back pages, near a political gossip column and the news of an insecticide campaign, was a photograph of two Argentine motorcyclists who had just arrived in Temuco. With their disheveled hair and soiled jumpsuits even the short Granado looked rather dashing while Guevara resembled a movie star. Translated literally, which is how I was reading it, the article went like this:

TWO ARGENTINE LEPROLOGY EXPERTS
TOUR SOUTH AMERICA BY MOTORBIKE

They are in Temuco and want to visit Easter Island

Since yesterday has been found in Temuco the doctor of biochemistry, Mr. Alberto Granados and the student of the seventh year of medical studies in the University of Buenos Aires, Mr. Ernesto Guevara Serna, who are completing a

raid by motorcycle with the purpose of visiting the principal countries of Latin America.

The raiders left the province of Córdoba the 29th
of December. They are effecting the trip on an English
machine brand "Norton."

Specialists in Leprology

The visiting scientists are specialists in leprology and other
types of infirmities derived from this terrible illness. They
know amply the problem that in this aspect affected their
country: they have some three thousand patients that
are interned at the leprosariums of Cerritos, Diamantes,
General Rodríguez, Córdoba, and Posadas. Also they have
visited the centers of curing that exist in Brazil, one of the
countries that has a high percentage of the ill.

Interested in Knowing the Easter Island

Apart from the particular interest in coming to know the
reality of the health system in the diverse countries of
South America, Misters Granados and Guevara, who are
effecting the trip with their own economic means, have
special interest to know up close the Chilean leper colony
at Easter Island . . . the scientist raiders wish to end their
trip in Venezuela. Ending their visit of one day to Temuco,
Misters Granados and Guevara continue today in the
morning heading for Concepción.

Not quite. At the very moment they were supposed to be rattling
toward Concepción the "scientist raiders" were actually ensconced
safely at the breakfast table, engaged in Ernesto's favorite pastime:
eating.

The previous day had gone badly for the boys. Shortly after leaving the newspaper and Temuco, La Poderosa got a flat tire; then it

began to rain. Wet and miserable, they were rescued by a veterinary student named Raúl, who put La Poderosa on his truck and drove them back to town. The bike was left in a garage on the outskirts.

Raúl was their type of guy. He had a semblance of education (Raúl was "not a very serious" veterinary student, Guevara noted admiringly) and a fondness for food, drink, and chasing girls. Ernesto knew just how to play his new friend. Raúl was soon boasting about how much money he spent at the local "cabaret"; shortly thereafter he invited the Argentines to join him there, at his own expense. The cabaret, of course, was a whorehouse. Ernesto called it "that very interesting place of entertainment."

In the end, Raúl withdrew his financial backing, a move that only seemed to increase Ernesto's respect for him. Too broke to pay for their own sex, the boys accepted the lesser satisfaction of food. At one in the morning Raúl took them home, fed them everything they could eat, and put them both in one bed. It wasn't who they had wanted to sleep with, but they were old friends by now.

In the morning, Che put on his boots—the only things he had removed for sleep—and went to find the newspaper. He must have felt a growing tension as he flipped through the paper (he noted how many more pages there were than he expected) and then relief when he finally spotted the article about two Argentine raiders.

Just as he had hoped, the publicity changed everything. The family suddenly discovered that the motorcycle bums in their midst were actually famous medical authorities. The visitors were "no longer just a pair of reasonably likable bums with a bike in tow. No, we were now 'the experts,' and that's how we were treated." Everywhere they walked in town they were recognized and lauded, thanks to the article. They spent the rest of the day working on the bike while "a little dark maid" brought them snacks.

The publicity scam they had first attempted in Valdivia had now been perfected. Aside from having its desired effect—acting as a letter of introduction to the region's public—the article suffered from a few inaccuracies. Alberto Granado had gained an *s* while sitting in

someone's notebook, but such mistakes are virtually required in journalism. The real changes in the story were the work of Che, as he
boasted that morning in his diary. Here is my favorite entry of his
whole journal:

> *This was our audacity in a nutshell. We, the experts, key figures
> in the field of leprology in the Americas, with vast experience,
> having treated three thousand patients, familiar with all the
> important centers on the continent and their sanitary condi-
> tions, had deigned to visit this picturesque, melancholy little
> town. . . . Soon the whole family had gathered round the article
> and all the other items in the paper were treated with Olympian
> contempt. And so, basking in their admiration, we said goodbye
> to* these people of whom we remember nothing, not even their
> name.

Emphasis mine. It was impossible not to laugh the first time I
read this. Ernesto had inflated his résumé to a gullible local journalist, leavening the minor sin with acute self-mockery. In exchange he
got what he needed: a complimentary article that, displayed like a set
of credentials, led directly to a free meal or three.

I had to wonder what had happened to that self-mocking tone.
The young man had been skeptical of his own urges in a way the
older self would forget.

I stood around the *Diario Austral* newsroom for a while, left, came
back in, left again, went down in the elevator, went up again, went
down and across the street to eat lunch, and, fortified by a beer, went
back into the newsroom. I asked to speak to the editor. A heavy man
in a tie and sweater vest trundled into the room.

"I'm a famous American writer," I said, and when he didn't
blink I added that I was a special correspondent to *The New York
Times*, a columnist at *The Washington Post*, a contributor for various

magazines, and editorial director of the *Express,* which sounded like a good name for either a paper or a magazine.

I told him about the purpose of my trip, showed him Che's diary, and took him to the reading table, which was still open to the clip from 1952. "I want you to write an article about me," I said. He stared at me blankly and said nothing that I can remember, but gestured for me to wait in the conference room. A moment later a beautiful dark-haired reporter named Pilar and a photographer joined me. I answered all their questions, exaggerating wildly, and was careful to put the helmet where it would show in photographs. (If you want to Be Like Che, you really have to Be Like Che.)

I went downstairs, unsure what I had wrought, and prepared to ride away on Kooky.

"Good luck," the rent-a-cop at the entrance said.

I spent the night on a patch of dust beside the Bío Bío river. I'd pulled in just as it was getting dark. As a camping spot, the riverbank offered few amenities—a grove of fragrant conifers, water for cooking rice, and the softness of the powdery ground—but it had the advantage of being neither legal nor illegal. Late at night a Chilean family in an old station wagon pulled into the grove, spread out a few blankets, and went to sleep, too.

In the morning I brushed dust and a few loose feathers from the sleeping bag and looked at the river. It was broad and slow moving, shallow but with a few deep pools and undercut banks that might hold trout. I pulled the rod case from where it had been resting on the back of the bike and began jointing the four pieces together. Just then a group of four female Mapuche Indians—two women and two girls, in peasant dresses, with long braided hair—came wading down the river. They set up shop on a gravel bar in front of me and began scrubbing their laundry on rocks. They were the poorest people I had seen in Chile, and the darkest. I disassembled the rod, slipped the pieces back into their cloth sleeve, and tied the case back onto the side of my backpack. I knew it was the last time I would handle the rod. The road ran north now for thousands of miles, and the farther I went the worse things would be.

There were many reprieves between me and the desperate Latin America that loomed closer with each mile. A little town called Los Ángeles, just a half hour up the road, was the first. It was an unremarkable place with the low buildings that this earthquake-prone region demanded, but I bought a cup of Nescafé for breakfast and circled around town until I found the firehouse, the place where Ernesto became Che and Alberto inadvertently revealed something.

I had circled the name "Los Ángeles" on my map of Chile months before, because the two travelers had here what Granado called "one of the most unimaginable and most interesting adventures of the trip." Their second attempt to leave Temuco had ended even worse than the first. There was another flat tire, and then their spare went flat as well. They were saved from spending a night in the open by their newspaper fame: "We weren't just anybody now," Ernesto wrote, "we were the experts; we soon found a railway worker who took us to his house where we were treated like kings." They spent the next day fixing the tires and eating, finally departing at the crack of sunset. They spent that night with a forest warden and, early the next morning, set off for what should have been a long, easy day of travel. But after a few miles "the bike suddenly veered sideways and threw us off." It sounded just like my accident on the Carretera Austral—the unexpected twisting of the bike from side to side that motorcyclists call a "tank slapper."

The boys were unhurt, but La Poderosa was nearly ruined. The steering column and gearbox were both smashed. As they waited by the side of the road, more passersby recognized them from the newspaper. For a couple of days they exploited their media fame to cadge food and help with the bike. They slept in what Ernesto called the "local barracks," apparently the police station, possibly the jail cells in it. Overconfident, they got extremely drunk at a Chilean party and Ernesto made a forceful pass at the wife of one of the local mechanics. Since he did this in the middle of the dance floor, there was a fight.

The wife somehow ended up on the floor; Ernesto and Alberto ended up running for their lives, chased by a crowd of angry Chileans.

Fleeing the now-hostile village on La Poderosa, the pair made only a few kilometers before disaster struck. Ernesto was driving when, rounding a bend, the back brake came apart; seconds later, the front brake also snapped. It was the worst possible scenario: they were shooting down a steep hill, on a road blocked by a herd of cows, behind which was a river. Fighting for control, Ernesto struck one of the cows, then avoided the river by slamming up a two-meter embankment. Everything came to rest in a pile. They tried to continue, but the bike was ruined and gave out at once.

La Poderosa was dead. They hauled the Norton to the nearby town of Los Ángeles, stored it in the local firehouse, and sat back to consider the situation. Ernesto predicted trouble in his diary: "It was our last day as 'motorized bums,'" he said. The next stage "looked . . . more difficult."

I left Kooky on the sidewalk that had once hosted La Poderosa and scouted the building to make sure it was the same: there was the bell tower the boys mentioned, and the second story was home to the resident firemen, just as they described. A couple of old-fashioned pumpers with the rounded look of 1950s machines were parked outside the building, ready to roll, and there was a beautiful, new squared-off engine inside. The two G's had mentioned that one of the trucks of 1952 had been christened "Chile-España" but none of them had names now.

I found a back door open and wandered past a small kitchen, went upstairs, and stumbled directly into the fire chief, who had just arrived at work. In Chile, as Ernesto noted with admiration, the firemen are traditionally volunteers and the job is considered highly prestigious and attracts the best men in any town. The fire chief certainly seemed to fit this mold: he looked like a politician, conventionally handsome with a fierce helmet of gray hair topping a resolute chin and a compact, strong body. After he had taken care of some routine business—checking the roster to make sure duty assignments like cleaning the station and engines were under way—he invited me into his office. We sat down and, with several other firemen watching from the doorway, I told him that the famous revolutionary Che Guevara had once stayed in this very firehouse.

"Impossible," he said.

I pulled out the diaries. In a passage headlined "Los Ángeles, February 28 1952," Granado detailed how two women introduced the Argentines to the then-chief of the fire department. I explained to the current chief how his predecessor had first agreed to store the broken motorbike in the garage, then allowed the vagabonds to sleep next to the fire engines; how Granado had later climbed up-stairs to find more room, and had been awakened in the night by a head-splitting alarm (he had inadvertently gone to sleep in the sta-tion's cupola, a few feet beneath the alarm bell); and how the two new "volunteers" pleaded to attend that midnight fire. As the chief and the other men listened, I read Granado's account of what happened next:

> . . . the chief loaned us a pair of helmets and protective coats.
> After a moment we swept off on the fire engine Chile-España.
> . . . After a few kilometers the reflection of flames was visible,
> and soon the typical smell of burning pitch, the product of
> conifers. Despite the diligence with which we acted, almost the
> whole edifice constructed of pines and tacuara cane was
> destroyed. One group attacked the burning forest, the other the
> fire in the house and the shed. I worked with a hose and [Gue-
> vara] at removing the debris. When the fire was under control
> the cry of a trapped cat was heard in the smoking ruins of the
> roof of the house. [Guevara] went to search for it, despite the
> protest of the other firemen who wanted to return to their beds.
> But when [Guevara] returned with the kitten in his hands the
> whole world applauded, and it was decided to keep it as a mas-
> cot at the firehouse.

I also read them Guevara's account, which was the same but for one crucial detail: in his diary, it was Alberto Granado who had saved the cat and been cheered. According to Ernesto:

> *Alberto saw the danger, measured it at a glance and, with an agile leap, jumped the twenty centimeters of flames and saved the little endangered life for its owners. As he received effusive congratulations for his peerless courage, his eyes shone with pleasure behind the huge borrowed helmet.*

Simple error could not account for this rather striking misalignment between the diaries. After all, it's not as though you could forget whether you had rushed into a burning building to save a cat. Alone, the story of the kitten meant nothing—but I couldn't help but remember the different accounts of why they had set out on the trip, and who had gone fishing and caught how many, and whether the Von Puttkamers were friendly or Nazis. The discrepancies were sometimes of fact, sometimes of opinion, but they were beginning to seem less than coincidental. Guevara's diary was, as he stated in his introduction, not a true diary at all but a "random account" of the trip done for literary purposes shortly after he returned home. Granado's diary was much rougher and clearly contemporaneous: its long passages were filled with the unedited, unabridged details that seemed so important at the time (precise accounts of bedding, lists of repairs and expenses, and cryptic notes to himself on the types of medicines he found available along his route). But decades later this text had been edited for publishing in Cuba. Granado's unvarnished thinking and dependence on the hospitality of the Cuban regime could easily have persuaded him to "enhance" his portrait of the now-famous Che. It would have required only an hour's revision of his original road diary to make the young Ernesto look as cool in a 1952 house fire as El Che had supposedly been in a 1958 firefight.

There were other comments in the diary that stood out as disingenuously worshipful of Ernesto. Granado's rather straight account of the final crash of La Poderosa, for example, was introduced with this:

> *After a few kilometers we had another tumble in which I once more admired the serenity, cold blood, and quick reactions of Ernesto.*

This was a funny way to describe someone crashing and destroying your motorbike. Ernesto's own account of the crash emphasized not his "serenity" but his comic incompetence and remarkable luck ("By an absolute miracle, all we touched was the leg of the last cow").

The literary detective in me suspected that the Ernesto appearing in Granado's diaries had been polished and "cleaned up" for political reasons. The incentives for doing this were obvious: Granado was living in Cuba, where his status was derived entirely from his testimony about Che's life. If he made Che seem retroactively heroic, how would anyone know otherwise? The only witness to these incidents was Che himself, long dead, and there wasn't—in 1986—any inkling that a contradictory account by Che himself would emerge.

Admittedly, the reverse was also possible. Ernesto's own diary was full of literary embellishment and tale-telling, as he conceded in the opening. There was no definitive way to settle which man had really saved the cat and then tried to make the other look good. I was only sure of one thing: one of the two Argentines was fibbing.

Another curiosity from these same entries was the matter of names, for it was here in Los Ángeles that Che apparently became known as Che for the first time in his life. Like most Argentines, Guevara and Granado sprinkled "che" through their conversations. To the Chileans in the Los Ángeles firehouse, this odd habit of speech branded both travelers right away (indeed, a Chilean newspaper I'd seen the previous week had referred to the forest fires across the border with the headline CHE FIREFIGHTERS BATTLE BLAZES). In Los Ángeles, Ernesto proudly noted, the Chileans called them "Big Che" and "Little Che." Granado, who was the shorter of the two by far, might not have been as enchanted with his nickname; he didn't mention it in his diary. But apparently it struck the ears of his tall partner quite well, and he recorded the firemen calling out their farewells to "Big Che and Little Che" when the two finally left. As the man on the sidewalk in Córdoba had noted, it was upon his return from this trip that Ernestito had insisted on keeping at least half that nickname, styling himself a regular-size Che.

I explained all this to the fire chief as I showed him the diaries, spreading them out on his desk and pointing out the different passages. "This is impossible," he said again. "Che Guevara here? No. I was never told about this." He grew agitated when I suggested that the guru of Marxist guerrilla warfare had earned his signature nickname right in this very building. "Impossible," he kept sputtering. I countered by suggesting that the proof might lie in his own hands: the station caretaker, a kind of night watchman, kept a daily logbook of comings and goings. The old logbooks went back to the 1940s and might show entries referring to the presence of the boys, or at least to the storage of a motorcycle inside the station. I had the exact dates of their visit—

"The caretaker is on vacation," the chief interrupted. "I can't open his office without permission." There were three other firemen still watching the discussion from the doorway, and one of them burst out, "I have the keys!" The chief glowered at him and repeated, in three different formulations, that he absolutely could not under any circumstances pry into the old firehouse records without the caretaker's permission. The other firemen were visibly unimpressed with this argument—they were unpaid volunteers and didn't take the chief too seriously. They argued on my behalf and offered to search the old books themselves.

"Impossible," the chief kept muttering, and then, "Che Guevara? Impossible. Nobody told me about this. Impossible."

After an hour I left reluctantly, unsatisfied and frustrated. Of all the possible reactions denial had seemed the least likely, but there were obviously some things the chief—like a lot of Chileans—didn't want to consider.

I walked downstairs and turned a corner into the hallway that led toward the street and Kooky. My approach had been almost silent, so the two firemen standing in the hallway had not heard me coming. They were both very young.

"Is it true?" the shorter one asked his friend.

"Yes," the taller one replied. "El Che was here."

They were both beaming.

Two hundred and eight miles later, night caught me an hour short of Santiago, in a city called Rancagua. I don't know what Rancagua looks like, since I arrived after dark and left before sunrise. I'd been carrying the phone number of the Chilean motorcyclist I had met weeks before in Puerto Montt. He had offered to put me up when I reached Rancagua, but when I called the number his wife answered.

"Another motorcyclist." She sighed. "Well, I'm sorry, but he's in Argentina right now."

A friendly policeman suggested that I try camping in a certain park, which I could not find, and while lost, wandering from street to street, I stopped to chat with a motorcyclist at the entrance to an industrial area. No one helps out a stranger, so I made myself known. We fell into a now-practiced routine: I described the length of my trip, mentioned how fast Kooky went, and praised his battered dirt bike as a fine machine. I heaped praise on Chile until he started criticizing it, at which point I agreed the country was awful. The motorcyclist accepted our essential brotherhood and spoke to the guard at the industrial park on my behalf. They were friends, and after hearing the same story the guard made a phone call. The conversation went on a long time in rapid Chilean Spanish, which I could not follow. Finally he hung up and told me to go down the access road, past the construction, to the golf course, where I could stay with Carlos, the night watchman.

Carlos was an old man, more in body and mind than in years. Perhaps fifty, he had a broken life that required description, and he invited me to sleep in the toolshed if I promised to leave before six, when the construction crews began arriving. The shed had a ply-wood floor, was lined with power saws, levels, and hammers, and had the sawdust smell that I always associated with my father. I put my things inside, pushed the bike out of sight, and fell in with Carlos.

He was a Seventh-Day Adventist, he explained, and life was wonderful. His wife had left him, of course, but life was wonderful because he had Christ. He didn't know how to cook and hadn't had a hot meal in the weeks since she left, he said, but thank goodness he had Christ. The job didn't pay much, and his children never helped him at all, but there was always Jesus Christ.

"Salads and fruit." Carlos sighed. "I am almost one hundred percent vegetarian now. They say it is very healthy."

I knew a mooch when I heard it, and broke out the nesting alu-minum pots. I showed him how to boil water, pointed out the instruc-tions on the back of the noodles, and we cut up an onion. We talked about his wife while the stove whispered, and how good life was any-way thanks to Jesus Christ, and when the noodles were ready all Car-los said was "Hot food at last." Although we had only one set of utensils, he swore it was the best meal he had eaten in weeks.

While washing the dishes under a lawn spigot I asked him if he knew who this Che Guevara character in the papers was. "Yes, yes," he said, lifting his head enough to stare into the distance. "I know who he was. He was a guerrilla. Born in Bolivia. Some people say he was really a European or a North American, but I doubt it. He died in . . . oh, I don't remember. You know Noriega? General Manuel Noriega in Panama? He was just like that. A drug trafficker."

Later I was walking back to the toolshed alone when the entire golf course erupted. With a pop, automatic sprinklers shot out of their holes and blasted huge arcs of water in slow, stuttering swings across the night. It was a clear, moonless sky. The water caught the glow of a single distant arc light and spat high into the darkness.

I stood there a long time watching the water burn up into the night and then drop out of sight, disappearing into the black, heading forever beyond any place I would go.

CHAPTER SIX

THE MIRACLE

Like the boys, I passed through Santiago too quickly for it to leave much of an impression on me. Their diary entries were just a few paragraphs. Having hauled the corpse of La Poderosa all the way to the capital on a truck, they sold the remains for traveling money and walked the city for a few days. Ernesto described a chance encounter with some young men he knew from Córdoba, members of a water polo team who were touring the city in the company of Chilean society ladies. These were Ernesto's own people—gentlemen athletes and debutantes—and his finely tuned class instincts jumped to the ready. The young men were "embarrassed" by his ragged appearance, he said—one wonders if it was really they who were most embarrassed—but "were very friendly—as friendly as people could be from worlds as far apart as theirs and ours at that particular moment in our lives."

From worlds far apart, my girlfriend flew down from New York to join me for a week. We luxuriated in a clean hotel that served breakfast in bed, then went hiking in the Andes and saw a filthy glacier. At 10:40 on the morning of February 22 we were caught in a long, rattling earthquake that knocked me off the can while I was reading the paper. We spent a couple of days at the beach eating fish, drinking beer, and staring at the cold water. The bourgeois side of my universe was definitely under construction.

After she left, I drove Kooky over to the barracks of the Chilean presidential guard. Guevara had spent a lot of time hanging around police barracks like this, which had the feel of a military encampment with sweaty *carabineros* cleaning their gear and radios squawking. There were a lot of women *carabineros* now, and these Amazons strutted around confidently in their jackboots and jodhpurs, pistols dangling off their hips. The squad rode BMWs as it ushered the president on his rounds, almost the only BMW motorcycles in South America. A sergeant undertook to give Kooky a full tuneup and purge the electrical system using the squad's microfiche wiring diagrams. He showed me a few tricks about BMWs I'd never noticed before and told me not to remove the bash plate from the bottom of the oil pan. "Where you are going, the single biggest danger is breaking the oil pain open on a rock. I've seen foreigners go up into the Andes on motorcycles and come down again on foot."

The repairs would take a few days, so I walked the city with a guidebook, looking for signs of the past. The enormous presidential palace, La Moneda, was guarded by a legion of Chilean soldiers wearing gray uniforms with Nazi-style helmets. There were still bullet holes from the coup in a few side buildings, but the façade of the palace itself had been repaired.

Twenty-three years had passed, and just as the right tried to ignore or forget what it had done in Chile, so, in many ways, did the left. The reality of Salvador Allende's martyrdom was somewhat more complicated than his sympathizers cared to recall. Allende only looked good when compared to Pinochet. A career politician and bombastic Marxist, he was elected president in 1970 in a three-way race with only 36 percent of the vote. Despite this minority backing he immediately launched a program of nationalizing banks and large sectors of the economy, aiming for a legalistic and nonviolent version of the Cuban revolution. Although he disagreed sharply with Castro on several points, Allende's sympathies were clear. He liked to show off a copy of *Guerrilla Warfare*, autographed by the author to read, "To Salvador Allende, who is trying to obtain the same result by other means. Affectionately, Che."

Much of the resistance to Allende was genuine, but not all of it. The United States waged a staggeringly large campaign of economic sabotage, intimidation, propaganda, and covert action to destabilize his administration. With U.S. economic control of copper and other assets threatened, CIA director Richard M. Helms took notes on what President Nixon told him to do in a White House meeting: "save Chile"; "not acceptable"; "ten million dollars"; "make the economy scream." The CIA shipped submachine guns and ammunition to Chile, but the agency's most effective tool was propaganda. The agency paid the country's leading newspaper, *El Mercurio*, to report that Cuban submarines were circling offshore and that Marxists were feeding human flesh to Chilean families. *Time* magazine swallowed everything the CIA had to say in special "inside" briefings, and published a cover story virtually demanding an invasion of Chile. After the coup the propaganda mill announced that "one hundred thousand weapons" were seized from unionists and students, a pure fabrication that is nevertheless cited by rightists defending Pinochet to this day. (If Allende really had distributed a hundred thousand weapons the coup would never have succeeded and the tally of casualties would not have attained the lopsided margins of 128 to 3 that characterized places like Valdivia.)

When the military finally pounced, on the morning of September 11, 1973, Allende and his bodyguards made a brave stand in La Moneda, but they were surrounded and the air force's Hawker fighter-bombers repeatedly strafed and rocketed the building, setting it afire. General Pinochet offered Allende safe passage out of the country, but the president wisely declined the offer. Tapes of radio conversations that day show that Pinochet planned to murder Allende after putting him on a plane to exile. ("Kill the bitch," he said then, "and you eliminate the litter.") Rather than surrender a one-hundred-and-fifty-year democratic tradition in Chile, Allende took his own life with a submachine gun bearing a gold plaque reading "To my good friend Salvador Allende from Fidel Castro."

Both Allende and Pinochet were paradoxical men, one a duly elected revolutionary, the other a military dictator who bowed, in

1990, to an electoral verdict against him. Though Pinochet had stepped down from politics, he remained commander of the military through my visit to Santiago. When he finally retired from uniform the next year, to take up a self-designated position as an immunized "senator-for-life," Pinochet praised the military as "the savior of democracy" in Chile and called himself "the defender of Western Christian civilization." About twenty-five percent of the public—largely military families and the affluent—said they agreed.

I went to see a political scientist to fill in the blank spots in Chile's history. If a quarter of the population agreed that Pinochet had saved Chile, what had he saved it from? Francisco Rojas, a think-tank analyst, stopped me halfway through my first question about the various guerrilla groups that had threatened Chile. "The armed left never had a significant effect as a force in Chile," he said. I admitted some surprise at this claim: the military had always justified the coup as a necessary step to head off a civil war. There were Chilean Ches organizing guerrillas in the south, after all, and a great tidal wave of Marxism had been about to bury the country. Fidel Castro had personally presented a submachine gun to Salvador Allende, after all. Che Guevara pictures were everywhere, after all. Wasn't Che's doctrine of socialist revolution about to sweep over the land in 1973?

Rojas looked at me with pity. I had things backward, he explained: the rise of Marxism in Chile had been the *defeat* of Che Guevara's influence and doctrines. "Allende's electoral triumph was the triumph of a thesis opposed to Guevarism," Rojas said. "It proved that it was possible to a have a socialist government derived from elections, not from force. The weight of the Chilean democratic tradition was greater than the weight of Guevarism."

Stock in this violent Guevarism plummeted when Allende came to office. The usefulness of Che's image to folksingers and strike organizers exceeded his true influence by a vast measure. Most of the guerrilla groups in Chile were phantoms of collective imagination, a cooperative dream between a few delusional leftists and the repressive machinery of the state, which needed them to justify its own actions. A group called the Frente Armada Manuel Rodríguez took a few terrorist actions, but it really believed in "popular insurrection; that is, having the mass of people on its side, as opposed to Guevara's idea of five guerrillas on a mountain," Rojas said. (That said, the Frente did occasionally exploit the guerrilla-friendly mountains of Chile. In 1986 the group staged a spectacular ambush of Pinochet's motorcade in a tight mountain pass, killing many of his guards but narrowly missing the dictator.)

Although leftist Chileans revered El Che then and now, they tended to reject his doctrines, even in the hardest years of the dictatorship. "The idea of the New Man, the idea of a socialist utopia, was generally part of the thinking of the early 1970s," Rojas said. "After that, Guevarism disappeared as a school of thought. Today Cuba has no influence on South America. The other way around, in fact. Cuba only had importance in a bipolar world, during the Cold War."

Since Kooky was in the hands of the presidential guard I took a taxi back to my hotel. The traffic was awful. It was the last day of summer vacation for many Chileans; eighty thousand cars had returned to the city that week, according to the radio. A brown smog enveloped us, and there was no wind. The cabdriver explained that from April to November, when pollution is at its worst, you had to leave your car at home one day a week by law (unless you had the catalytic converter and elaborate pollution controls that Don Don had been complaining about). There were special "pollution emergencies" sometimes, when you couldn't drive for two days.

It was hard to see the gleam of the skyscrapers for all the smog. Pollution was one sign of Chile's bustling economy. General Pinochet had been an early proponent of American-style capitalism—his economists were known as "*los* Chicago boys" because they studied under Milton Friedman at the University of Chicago—and had reduced import tariffs, liberalized investment rules, and created some innovative programs like private pension funds that let Chilean workers choose where to invest their savings. It was easy to see—on nonsmoggy days—what Americans find so miraculous about Chile: shopping malls that take credit cards, pleasant vineyards, and a deregulated stock market go a long way with Americans. This was a swept corner of an unswept continent. But the results of this new economic deal were as obvious as they were mixed. Of course there was a Chilean miracle—Pinochet had flooded the country with consumer electronics and the new cars that were choking everything—but there was also a Chilean despair. One of the fuels for the new economy was easy credit; shop windows in Santiago were covered with flyers advertising the price of shoes in twelve easy payments of four dollars each. Personal debt was the new national curse, and although the investment dollars were flowing in, the profits were mostly flowing out. Personal income in Chile had still not recovered to the levels of 1972—when a Marxist was supposedly ruining the country. Chile had just now, after twenty years of free-market economics, tied the basic social indicators (literacy, longevity, nutrition, and inoculation rates) of Cuba, another supposedly failed Marxist regime. It seemed strange to pay for shoes four dollars at a time and call it a miracle.

Some Chileans did. On February 26 a group of upper-class women calling themselves the Friends of the Armed Forces assembled outside the Ministry of Defense with a boom box. In Argentina, the mothers of the disappeared paraded their grief; these Chilean matrons sang Mexican folk songs dedicated to General Pinochet's continued well-being. His birthday was marked with a set of parties around the country, all linked by live satellite feed.

On my last day in Santiago the fax machine at the hotel sputtered and ground out the article that Pilar had written about me in *El Diario Austral*. I was as nervous as Ernesto had been flipping through the pages of the paper forty-four years before. The photo made me look bald (then again, I am), and under a banner headline (ON THE TRAIL OF CHE) the piece described some guy who was traveling South America in search of "the spirit of Che." It was amazing how much my Spanish had improved under Pilar's hand. There were verbs in some of my quotes that I'd never conjugated in my life. I carefully preserved the shiny paper in one of my saddlebags. I liked the piece, and it had me crossing a lot of mountains and doing other heroic-sounding things, but it also frightened me. Before, it had been only a

promise to myself that pushed me up the road each morning, heading for some final accounting. Now my fate was as plain as the ther-
mofax paper.

"For Symmes," the piece concluded,

> *there remains a long voyage through the Chilean desert. From
> there, with his notes and memories, with the diary of the guer-
> rilla as his most valuable treasure, he will continue to Peru and
> Bolivia . . . always on the same trail.*

The desert could be put off for a moment more. The road north
jogged west, and I followed Big and Little Che down from Santiago
to the port city of Valparaíso in search of a bar called La Gioconda.

From now on, our experiences of the road could only grow more
different. Kooky emerged from Santiago with a change of oil, a valve
job, clutch and throttle cables adjusted, and, the sergeant from
the presidential guard claimed, a problem with the alternator's
ground now fixed. La Poderosa did not emerge from Santiago at all.
Wrapped in a tarp, the ruined Norton resembled "a cadaver,"
Granado wrote. They waited four hours for their first hitchhiking
lift, and in the end the short trip to Valparaíso, on the coast—just
over an hour for me on the bike—took them until well after nightfall.

Up to now, the pair had been "gentlemen of the road. We'd
belonged to a time-honored aristocracy of wayfarers," Ernesto
wrote. Now they were dismounted, "just two tramps with packs on
our backs, and the grime of the road encrusted in our overalls, shadows of our former aristocratic selves." He noted how those packs—
the converted cloth saddlebags from the bike—weighed heavily on
them as they finally marched down into Valparaíso late that night.

Seeking rest and refuge, they boys stumbled into La Gioconda,
a seedy café that would be their home for several days. The owner
was unaccountably generous and fed the Argentines lunch and din-

ner for three days without charging them a penny. They spent some time in a futile effort to arrange a trip to Easter Island, where they were supposedly going to do medical research (in fact, they simply wanted to see the South Pacific, eat lobster, and seduce maidens, as Ernesto emphasized in his diary).

The atmosphere of La Gioconda seemed to awake something in Ernesto. He befriended other customers, and through them was introduced to the lower orders of life in Valparaíso. In place of the natural beauty of the south, there was now the horror of modern urban poverty to gaze on:

> As if patiently dissecting, we pry into dirty stairways and dark recesses, talking to the swarms of beggars; we plumb the city's depths, the miasmas to which we are drawn. Our dilated nostrils inhale the poverty with sadistic intensity.

One afternoon Ernesto went alone to see a customer of the café, an old woman suffering from the asthma that he knew only too well. After recounting the fetid conditions in her humble house, he noted the emotional costs of poverty and illness, the way they alienate the sick from the healthy, the hungry from the fed. This was, he said, making a leap from the emotional to the political, the result of an unjust economic system and an "absurd" social order. In the first explicitly political declaration in the diary, he wrote that governments should spend more money—"much more money"—on social programs.

In retrospect, this was a tepid statement from the man who would later imagine worldwide guerrilla warfare as the solution to social problems. In La Gioconda, Ernesto still had confidence in the system.

I pulled into town only for a few hours. The descriptions of the café were vague—it was next to a truck stop and on a road leading down into the city. I circled the steep hills, which were fitted with little funicular railways to carry pedestrians up to their homes, for a while. After a half hour I found a place that looked suspiciously possible—a dank little café just uphill from a big gas station. It was just called Bar *y* Restaurant and had the permanent special painted on the window (fried fish and a side dish, 950 pesos). Five people were inside eating soup, but when I sat down at the five-foot-long bar and asked for food, a fat woman told me there was none. I waited a while, watching the others eat the nonexistent soup.

"Is this place called La Gioconda?" I asked the room.

"No," the fat woman said.

One of the lessons I had learned from newspaper reporting was that sooner or later, if you said nothing, someone else would speak. It took a lifetime, but eventually, from the darkest corner of the bar, I heard the sound of a chair shifting.

"La Gioconda?" said a voice that was attached to a man in a green acrylic sweater. He clutched at a memory in the darkness, and eventually grabbed it.

"It's up there," he said, dragging a finger toward the uphill wall of the bar. "It's a business. They sell children's clothing." This didn't sound like the right place at all. I was after . . .

"*Antiguamente*," he said (or, in old times), "*antiguamente* it was a restaurant." When I prompted him, he said the old place was "two turns up." In a city full of switchbacks, you gave directions by saying how many times the road doubled back.

He put his right hand over his face and fell permanently silent. I followed his pointed finger up the hill but found nothing at the first, second, or third turns that resembled a bar, a former bar, or even a children's clothing store. There were a lot of shuttered, unmarked buildings. Any one of them could have been the place.

Daylight was burning up fast, and I had a long, very long, way to go. I went back to the bar, but the old man in green was gone. I gave up after a while. I wasn't sure what I had hoped to see in the wreck of the old café anyway.

CHAPTER SEVEN

JUBILATION

The road became unbearably straight. The Pan-American Highway—a grand name for two half-decent lanes of blacktop—uncoiled itself from the horizon in endless monotony, and I rolled steadily north at seventy miles an hour, leaning into the wind hour after hour, day after day. The landscape began to atrophy and desiccate. Scrub brush faded and then disappeared. I ate lunch in a whorehouse while an Argentine trucker shagged the waitress in his cab. Late in the afternoon of the second day the first cactuses shot by, but these were rare. There was sheer desert by dusk, a wasteland of red rock and dust devils. I kept moving into dusk with nothing to see but the occasional dirt road splitting off toward the horizon and a plume of dust that marked a mining operation. It grew dark, but there was no place to stop, no towns or motels or campgrounds or houses or inviting copses or anything but nothing, and so I kept moving. It grew black. Oncoming trucks were visible from miles away. My own headlight carved a fixed oasis of light around me, while the vibration of the motor, the battering of the wind, and the endless pain of clutching the throttle ten and eleven hours a day lulled me into a neurological daze.

Around ten at night I saw a tiny orange glow far off the road, and pulled over. A dirt driveway led up to a tiny settlement of houses. Most of them were made of wood from packing crates, and the tallest building was a one-and-a-half-story evangelical church. The orange light (the only light in the entire hamlet) came from a gas lantern sitting in the general store, which was also the living room of someone's house. The front door was open, and I could see a family of three dining around a battered wood table. The shelves were lined with eggs, rice, bouillon cubes, and candy. I knocked on the door frame just to be polite, and the father came forward. I asked him if there was any place around the town where I could spend the night.

He looked briefly over his shoulder at his wife, then said, "Here."

Helped by his son, the man moved the table aside. I slept on the floorboards. At dawn, as I was preparing to ride away, they gave me a pineapple. I tried to pay for it, but they would not accept my money because the whole point for this transaction was in the gesture of sharing.

The poor are no more noble at heart than the rich, I suppose, but they certainly look that way. Their generosity is deeper precisely because it is so constricted by circumstance and so necessary to their collective survival. To give is to live.

I strapped the pineapple onto the back of the bike and drove out into the desert again, worried that I was slowly turning into a commie.

Twelve hours later I pulled off the road and slept in a cave over a beach. The ocean reeked of rotten shellfish and seaweed. To Guevara's horror, Granado had insisted on eating raw shellfish from the rocks somewhere along this coastline; the food must have been really terrible if the ever-famished Guevara had been repulsed. Someone had painted CAVE OF THE GRINGOS on a rock. Apparently we were drawn to this bleak spot like kitchen knives to a magnet.

There was no more landscape after this, just desert. The Atacama is said to be the driest place on earth: some scientific sources claim that no rain has ever been recorded here. The cold current of the South Pacific yielded an occasional fog but no refreshment. By the end of the fourth day I came to Antofagasta, where I could once again pick up the trail of the Argentines.

Ernesto and Alberto had done everything in their power to avoid traveling the route I had just crossed. As hitchhikers, they knew enough to avoid such a relentlessly long, lightly traveled route. They left Valparaíso by hitching, but hitching a boat. A friendly sailor snuck them onto a cargo ship headed for Antofagasta, and they hid in a bathroom until the boat was at sea, then presented themselves as stowaways and volunteered to work their passage. Ernesto didn't regret this trick for a moment, and the feeling of being carried over the limitless sea awoke a flight of "sentimental nonsense" in him:

> *At night . . . we'd lean on the rail and look out over the vast*
> *sea, gleaming greeny-white, side by side but each lost in his own*
> *thoughts, on his own flight towards the stratosphere of dreams.*
> *There we discovered that our vocation, our true vocation, was*
> *to roam the highways and waterways of the world for ever.*
> *Always curious, investigating everything we set eyes on, sniffing*
> *into nooks and crannies; but always detached, not putting down*
> *roots anywhere, not staying long enough to discover what lay*
> *beneath things; the surface was enough.*

The surface was enough. At least for now.

Antofagasta was a mean town, dirty, colorless, rumbling with trucks. The municipal motto could be "Looks good after two hundred miles of desert." The city was dominated by the military and a few big mining companies, which created sympathies not found everywhere in Chile. A monument at the harbor celebrated the military coup of 1973 on an equal footing with the 1810 War of Independence against Spain. The only explanation for Antofagasta—for the streets, the colorless apartment blocks, the military barracks, the port, the railway—lay out in the hard soil of the Atacama. The desert was full of minerals, nitrate (for fertilizer and explosives), and copper (for wiring the information age). Between war and gossip there was a heavy demand for the products of Antofagasta, and Chile had seized these lucrative northern territories from Bolivia and Peru in a war before the turn of the century. The Peruvians were still sore about their defeat—the Chileans had even occupied Lima at one point—but the Bolivians were truly traumatized. They'd lost their coastline and now huddled in isolation in the mountains, blaming their poverty on their lack of access to the sea. They were serious about this: Bolivia still had a navy department, just in case, and its army kept rumbling about reconquering the lost lands. The Chilean military relished the challenge, and I would sometimes see army troops moving through the far desert, training or digging emplacements. I watched three Jaguar jet fighters leap off the local runway and smear the sky with black exhaust. Despite the pressure of an arms embargo and the poverty of everyone involved, the Pinochet regime had promoted an arms race with its neighbors. The Jaguars could be equipped with cluster bombs and even fuel-air explosives, an obscure technology so powerful it was sometimes called the poor man's atomic bomb.

I spent a few days interviewing people around Antofagasta. An environmentalist told me that the main problem at the copper mines was the ignorance of the workers. The corporations had adopted fairly responsible environmental policies, he explained, which the older workers routinely ignored. They wouldn't wear their safety masks and were used to dumping anything from trash to oil to chemical leaching agents into the thirsty ground.

A new mine had opened in the area five and a half years ago, and I went to see a display on copper production. Chilean copper ore is of low grade, but since the Atacama holds the largest deposits in the world, quantity makes up for quality. The ore was crushed into a fine grit and then sprayed into "concentrators," huge tanks where a chemically induced reaction allowed the stone to sink and the copper to rise. A thick scum of bluish slurry was visible across the top of the tank, and that contained the copper. Almost all the copper left Chile by boat and was then made into useful things, many of which were sold back to Chile at a huge markup (Chile still imports copper telephone wire, for example). The public relations officer balked when I asked him how many men had died at the mine. "To ask how many died, that is a very hard question," he said. "Explosives, trucks that weighs many tons, heavy machinery; it's always possible to have accidents."

I asked again how many had died. "Two," he said. "That's how many workers have died in five and a half years of operation. Two." It sounded like a statistic the way he said it, and I suppose it was.

Roaming the waterways of the world for ever proved impossible, of course. The boys couldn't even get out of Antofagasta. They tried their stowaway trick once more but were discovered and angrily tossed off a ship before it left the harbor. They set out the hard way for the north, spending most of the first day lying by the side of the road hoping for a lift. Finally a van carried them as far as a little town called Banquedano, which wasn't far at all. Because of the important commerce in the area—the copper industry provides forty percent of Chile's export earnings—the state invested heavily in the local roads, and a smooth, fresh blacktop swept me to Banquedano in thirty minutes.

Ernesto and Alberto spent a freezing night here covered by a single thin blanket. They had two, but loaned the second to a couple they met in the railway station who were in even worse shape. The man had just spent three months in jail on suspicion of communist activities; his wife was now loyally following him as he searched for work in the mines, where the conditions were so dangerous that they would hire anyone, regardless of politics. Both of the boys noted in their diaries the powerful effect this encounter had on them. Granado was struck by the wife, who endured desperate circumstances without complaint, but Ernesto—perhaps because he had

spent less time thinking about it than his friend—was fascinated by
the man's communist beliefs, by his purposeful dedication to an
abstract ideology that seemed to be breaking over the world. In 1952
the Soviet Union was a rising power and Mao's Red Army had seized
control of China, but communism was still a remote notion in Latin
America, a strange doctrine that had yet to be tested in practice in the
region. Ernesto noted rumors that some Chilean communists were
being abducted by the military, killed, and dumped into the sea. This
seemed so obviously impossible in a civilized country like Chile that
he discounted it as a rumor. Still, the communist under his blanket
awoke Ernesto's sympathy:

> *It's really upsetting to think they use repressive measures against
> people like these. Leaving aside the question of whether or not
> "Communist vermin" are dangerous for a society's health,
> what had burgeoned in him was nothing more than the natural
> desire for a better life, a protest against persistent hunger trans-
> formed into a love for this strange doctrine, whose real meaning
> he could never grasp but, translated into "bread for the poor,"
> was something he understood and, more importantly, that filled
> him with hope.*

Obviously, this was not Cuban Comandante Che Guevara writing, but an uncommitted observer, inspired more by basic hopes of
justice and dignity—bread for the poor—than by specific plans for
realizing them. The benefits or costs of communism had not been
calculated yet. Ernesto was still not Che.

They watched the sun rise over the desert, one of those
moments when the earth seems revealed for the first time and all life
is compressed into a transient instant. The spectacle moved Ernesto
to quietly recite several Pablo Neruda poems that he had memorized.

Alberto countered by reciting the only Neruda poem he knew,
one that the poet, a dedicated communist, had written during the
dark days of World War II when his usual subjects, love and nature,
seemed too frivolous:

> *I wrote of the weather and about the water*
> *I described sorrow and its purple metal*
> *I wrote of the sky and the apple*
> *now I write about Stalingrad*

For Alberto, the sunrise was red in more than one sense.

I rode on toward the next stop on our mutual itinerary—the great mine at Chuquicamata.

Kooky was equipped with an adjustable throttle screw on the right handle grip that you could tighten down to keep the motor racing as you warmed it up on cold mornings in Bavaria. I had always resisted the temptation of using this screw as a poor man's cruise control—until now. The desert was so immensely boring, and I had been holding the throttle with my hand for so long—two months now—that I couldn't resist. Flying down the road at seventy miles an hour, I twisted the screw inward until it pushed hard on the throttle and locked the speed in place. Then I let go.

I went along like this for quite a while, steering with my left hand while my right rested comfortably on my lap. The screw worked well as long as I didn't need to slow down, which I didn't. Chuquicamata was somewhere up ahead, but I figured on plenty of warning before hitting it.

After a few minutes I decided that using one hand to ride a motorcycle was one hand too many. The road was straight and in beautiful condition, and as long as I didn't move suddenly, hit anything, or miscalculate how smart I was, I would be able to steer by balance alone. I took my left hand off the handlebar, tentatively at first, but then with confidence. I put both hands in the pockets of my black leather jacket. I thought I might be able to do it for a mile, and a mile went by.

Then another, and another. Occasionally a car would pass in the other direction, the drivers invariably staring at me with concern. After five miles I got out my camera and took some blurry pictures. After ten miles I saw a long, slow curve to the left, and swung gently through it without a hitch.

After thirteen miles, it started to rain. I put my hands back where they belonged, loosed the throttle screw, pulled over, took off my helmet, and let the warm drizzle wet my upturned face.

They said it never rained in the Atacama, ever, but obviously they were wrong. The fact was, there had never been any *recorded* rain in the Atacama. It did rain there, as the canyon washes coming out of the hills showed. The rain was simply in short and rare bursts that tended, in a big world, to miss the few measuring instruments of scientists and government monitors. That didn't rob the Atacama of its arid beauty or its title as driest desert in the world. It did, however, make me wonder if I was getting stupider with every mile. I stood there, wet, looking at the handlebars. I was starting to do things that made no sense. The drizzle stopped after a few minutes, and when the air cleared I looked up toward the horizon and there, visible through the washed air like a dark mountain, was the mine.

At last, a hero I could believe in. At the firehouse in Chuquicamata I deployed the exact script that Ernesto had proudly outlined in his diary for cadging free room and board. First, I talked my way inside ("I just need a place to change my clothes," I told the lonely eighteen-year-old caretaker), and soon enough I casually began entertaining this innocent young man with stories of my world travels. We discussed all his important questions: Was China a good place to find a job? Was America founded before Christ? Eventually he provided a glass of Chilean red to accompany such talk, but I steadfastly refused to touch the wine until he grew concerned and even insulted. "Well," I said, having memorized Ernesto's own line, "no offense, but in my country we're not used to drinking without some food to wash it down." In no time at all the caretaker had whipped up a vast meal. He threw in a free bed for the night. Guevara knew so many ways to lead men.

In the morning I stood, slightly hung over, at the lip of the Chuquicamata copper mine. It is an astoundingly large hole in the desert, two miles long, a mile and a half wide, almost two thousand feet deep. All of this had been dug out by the ten thousand men who have labored here over the course of the century. The pit has hardly changed since 1952—it was the largest open-pit mine in the world then, and it still is—but the political terrain had shifted around it. When Ernesto stood here the mine belonged to Anaconda, the Montana copper giant. The miners were paid a dismal wage and lived in shacks.

Ernesto and Alberto toured the facilities on the strength of their medical credentials, and the former noted that while health care for the miners was bad, it would prove much better than what he would see later in the trip. The hospitals were dirty and their rates were "monuments to legalized robbery." Much had changed since that conversation, but the realities of mining were constant and the political climate, after shifting back and forth around the mine, was now heading again toward what it had been. In 1964 the mine was partly nationalized, and not by a Marxist like Salvador Allende but by President Eduardo Frei, a centrist. During the early 1970s Allende expanded state control and gave the miners a social contract unprecedented in Latin America: housing allowances, a subsidized canteen, free medical care, and guaranteed employment for life. Chuquicamata was an immense national treasure. Even General Pinochet, the laissez-faire dictator, was careful to preserve this public ownership of the means of production. This is why some Chileans called his economic policy "right-wing socialism."

Now President Frei—that is, the son of the earlier President Frei—was talking about "efficiency" and "new times" for Chile, which the miners interpreted to mean selling the mine back to the gringos. The men Ernesto called the "blond, efficient, arrogant managers" were already back in the desert: Australian, South African, and American firms were behind the new, highly automated mine whose settling ponds I had visited near Antofagasta.

From the lip of the pit I could see trucks working in every direction. There were a hundred and five of them in the fleet; one of the smaller ones, parked behind me, had tires so big I could not touch their tops even with my fingertips. It took them two hours to drive from the bottom up to the rim where I stood.

Perched high above the money, I was not alone. A single miner stood nearby, gazing over the works. He was a short fellow in a dusty orange jumpsuit and a blue hard hat. From time to time a little Motorola radio in his hand cackled and he muttered something in reply. He was studiously ignoring a suitcase at his feet from which two wires ran to a disk resembling a Frisbee on a stick.

"G.P.S.," he said when I asked, referring to the Global Positioning System. He worked for the mine's surveying office, which tracked on a daily basis the constantly changing shape of the hole. They were testing the new GPS technology. If it worked, the surveying office would be reduced from ten men to five.

"They will find a job for me somewhere else," he said. It might be with one of the new private subcontractors the mine has relied on more and more to cut costs. The pay was guaranteed the same, but the safety standards were much lower. "They care only for this," he said, rubbing two fingers together. He thought Codelco—the Chilean state's copper company—was well run. The health insurance was very good, he said, and after thirty years you could retire with a pension and a gold watch. That was the dangerous moment, he explained; after a lifetime in the desert, miners who left the region were vulnerable to humidity and would grow sick and die within five years. It sounded like silicosis was a more likely culprit than moist air. The disease finally caught up with retired miners just when they lost their health coverage.

The Spanish word for *retirement* is *jubilación*. "It's called jubilation," he said, "but few survive long to enjoy it."

He'd worked here for sixteen years. One way or another, he doubted that he would make it to the gold watch. While I looked at the tiny trucks crawling slowly up from the seventh circle, he discoursed with casual familiarity on the challenges of globalization, the benefits of added-value production, the latest rumors about privatization, and the price of Indonesian copper. The union kept them informed about these things in a newsletter.

Ernesto recounted a disturbing conversation here with a miner he called the "foreman-poet" due to his eloquence. Guevara asked how many men had died working the mine, and the man's only reply was gratitude for Guevara's concern in asking; no one knew how many had died at Chuqi. This was the bedrock reality beneath all ideologies and outcomes. No matter what happened, the work would still be harsh, the life of the miner squalid. Although Ernesto indirectly criticized the gringos running the mine, he did not blame the lack of hope on capitalism. Granado did, and liked to cite the glories of communism and Joseph Stalin that were rising in the East with all the historical certainty of the morning sun. But for Ernesto, this "red blaze" looked like nothing more than another false hope. He closed the chapter on Chuqi with a prescient observation:

> . . . *maybe one day, some miner will joyfully take up his pick and go and poison his lungs with a smile. They say that's what it's like over there, where the red blaze dazzling the world comes from. So they say. I don't know.*

A great cloud of dust floated up from the left, where the digging was close to some buildings that my new friend from the surveying office pointed out. "*El pueblo norteamericano,*" he said: "The American town." The little village of white clapboard houses had been constructed long ago for the Anaconda engineers and their families. The digging had to follow the copper vein wherever it went, and right now that was toward the *pueblo norteamericano*. It would take years to cover the last few hundred yards, according to the surveyors' calculations, but eventually the iron rule of profit meant that the copper must be taken out and the town must fall. "In 2005," the miner said, undercutting the white houses with a swift slice of his hand, "pfft."

Back in town, I ate lunch in the mine workers' social club. Off-duty machine operators and electricians were drinking orange soda and watching blondes sing on television. I pestered those at tables near me about when there had last been a strike at the mine. The response from each was the same: "A strike? I don't know . . . no, I can't remember one, ever. . . . A strike?"

They mouthed the word as if they had never heard it before.

Out in the desert again, there was so little to look at that I began gazing far off the roadside and finally noticed a low brown smudge of buildings in the distance. I took a side road and then bounced down a dirt path the last few hundred yards before pulling up at the gate of a "nitrate office," as the old mining camps were known in Chile. Like most of the nitrate mines, this one had closed decades ago. There were several dozen low barracks buildings and a couple of three-story offices. The whole place was surrounded by a wall, and on top of the wall was rusting barbed wire.

The sound of my engine roused the caretaker from his siesta. He was unshaven and seemed drunk, but agreed to show me around. A small construction crew was "restoring" one of the biggest buildings, a plan that seemed to require dismantling it.

In the mid-1970s Chacabuco had been a concentration camp in the most literal sense. A small number of high-ranking Allende aides had been concentrated here from other prisons. The old nitrate offices made useful little jails: they were far from public scrutiny, already had the ideal infrastructure of spartan barracks, and, surrounded by barbed wire and relentless desert, were essentially escape-proof. The prisoners suffered from a blazing sun by day and freezing temperatures by night. In the metaphoric eloquence of Castilian, Chileans referred to this gulag archipelago as "the red desert."

The signs of prison life were still everywhere: a jury-rigged basketball hoop for exercise, a pile of cafeteria-style trays used during feeding hour, a cross roughly gouged into the plaster high on one wall, making a chapel out of a small dank room. This sad little house of improvised worship with its roof falling in was the one place where Allende's aides could escape their fate, however briefly.

There was graffiti in a couple of places, mostly just names ("Alex Acuna 10-12-76") but also a few longer messages ("Here were tortured Chaparrón, Chacay and his loyal friend Buco González and the Doctor Dulit"). There were also fresh Nazi swastikas penned on several walls alongside cryptic initials. The keeper explained that they were made by right-wing extremist groups who considered the camp a shrine, not a shame. They were proud of what Chile had done here.

"Here Endures the Memory of the Wounded Public," someone responded in a broad, angry hand on one wall, right above the swastikas. "Not Even Fascist Graffiti Can Erase the Red Desert." A sign near the entrance said that this mine had been a "Patrimony of Mankind" since 1971, but the sign mentioned nothing about the red desert. As usual in Chile, official accounts of history suffered a bout of amnesia around 1973.

Power tools growled in the background, gnawing away at the buildings. The historical audit—the final accounting of what had really happened in Chile during the time of blooding—was only just beginning.

Back on the road, I again saw a low brown wall in the distance and bounced over the broken ground toward what proved to be a lonely cemetery. A sign identified it as the Rica Aventura nitrate mine. Rich Adventure; the name rang a bell, and digging in Granado's diary—Big Che hadn't mentioned it—I found that the boys had spent a couple of nights in the workers' dormitory, observing some of the same miners now buried in front of me. I counted two hundred graves and then stopped, overwhelmed by how many yet remained. Entire rows were set aside for infants who had lived only a few days, they or their mothers unable to endure the poisoned mining environment. There were a few wooden crosses, their words worn away by the wind ("inconsolable parents . . . dust and forgetting"), but since even plastic flowers wilt in such severe heat most of the tombs were decorated only with scraps of iron—wreaths made from barrel hoops, metal flowers blooming with rust, and vines of barbed wire. The whole boneyard rattled with the wind like an untuned orchestra.

Back on the road, a few hours of emptiness passed with monotonous speed. In a sandstorm an isolated gas station fed my tank. Moments after pulling out, I spotted what at first seemed a mirage: a lone figure walking by the side of the road in this vast emptiness. The man proved corporeal, yet unreal: he was sunburned and utterly mad, his brain baked by the heat. In a great rush of words he explained that he was patrolling the desert with ten liters of water in his backpack, speaking the secret language of trees and mountains. I tape-recorded him as he babbled about Masonic conspiracies and a Japanese/Nazi/Jewish/communist plot to wreck the world. Looking about us, I could see only hills and sand and red rock. The road was already nearly ruined, so there was little the secret masters of his world could do to make things worse. I gave the madman some bread.

"In Chile, there are only two kinds of people," he said by way of thanks. "The innocent and the living."

I did not have to struggle now to Be Like Che. His lust for self-invention had seeped from the surface of my skin deep into my bones, and I had slowly come to accept that on the road we were beyond all consequence. The childish appeal of military code names and clandestine operations had a clear prologue in the glancing, slightly criminal life of the traveler.

In Arica, just before the Peruvian border, I stopped at the local newspaper in my most ragged clothes, introduced myself—or a version of myself—and wove an elaborate tale about my literary adventures in South America. I posed for a photo while trying to look dashing on the motorbike, and stole some office supplies on the way out. I'd been particularly careful to downplay the whole Che Guevara angle to my trip; I was tired of living in his shadow, and dammit *my own trip should be good enough for these rubes*.

When the paper came out the next morning I grabbed a copy and began flipping through it eagerly. Page after page went by with no sign of me. All sorts of stuff was judged more newsworthy than my arrival in Arica: Mia Farrow had lost the rent control on her New York apartment, and down in Valdivia a Socialist member of Parliament had been thrown into jail (admittedly, only for half an hour) for "insults to the commander in chief Augusto Pinochet."

Finally I found it, buried on the very last page. ERNESTO GUEVARA WAS IN ARICA IN MARCH 1952, the headline roared. The article barely mentioned me.

The bulk of the text simply repeated *his* comments on Arica, described *his* adventures, and quoted *his* delight at meeting a border guard who liked the foul *yerba mate*. The piece even detailed how Che had taken one of his rare baths in the ocean, "with soap and everything."

The photo made me look preppy, not dashing. I wandered around town for a couple of days, but no one recognized me or paid the slightest attention.

CHAPTER EIGHT

THE RED BLAZE

The night before Lima I slept in a field of bones and dreamed of a motorcycle shop full of spare parts. Because it was a dream, the glass counters in the store held only the things that I needed: a new tail-light to replace the one that had broken somewhere in the desert; the odd little screw that held the seat lock together; brake pads fresh from Bavaria. When I woke up, what I remembered was that the staff in this dream store all spoke English. That was it. That was the whole dream: a parts store with an English-speaking staff.

The dream came to me while I slept atop a mass grave in the sandy coastal desert three hundred miles south of Lima. Called Chauchilla, the cemetery was an ancient repository of bones about twenty miles from the famous "lines" of Nazca, those giant drawings of abstract geometry and dogs, birds, trees, and monkeys that had been etched in the desert floor more than a thousand years ago. There were a hundred or more old cemeteries in the same area, filled with the remains of the Paracas and the Nazcas, people who had once held sway in this region and now dwelled under its soil. All you had to do to find them was pull off the freshly paved Pan-American Highway of southern Peru—a two-lane paradise of black asphalt, the single best road I saw in all South America—and bounce over the desert for a few hundred yards. The valley floor at Chauchilla was dotted with bleached femurs and bits of smashed skulls sitting in plain sight. The dry climate had preserved an extraordinary array of burial cloths and scraps of tapestries—even mummies. Looters both ancient and modern had worked over the graves many times, plundering everything of value, but there was something moving in the ordinary bits of twine and tattered bundles that you could uncover here just by kicking a little sand aside.

I pitched my tent, which promptly blew away. I sprinted over the dunes to catch it and reset it in the lee of the motorcycle with the belly of the shelter filled with my saddlebags and other gear to keep it rooted. I wandered the bones for a while, watered at the nearby creek that ran out of the brown hills, and after sunset went to my disturbed sleep. Normally, I was too tired to dream. I'd wake up where I had lain down, in the same position, each night a long black nothing—sometimes ten or twelve hours—undisturbed by motions, images, or needs. I'd close my eyes and the blackness would come and stay.

Before the dream there had been other signs. On the first night after crossing the border into Peru I had found myself weeping uncontrollably and without explanation. My mouth was often dry now. I fell in love with almost every woman I met, and got drunk one afternoon with a couple of Peruvians and shot holes in things with an air rifle.

The border crossing had been slow and complex, requiring trips back and forth, hour after hour of waiting in the hot sun, and an enormous amount of paperwork. I sat on the curb for a while with a Peruvian customs broker named Pato, who specialized in moving stolen cars from Chile into Peru. We talked about women until that was exhausted and then about Che Guevara. Pato said they were still looking for Che's bones in Vallegrande, which was "some place up there," he said, pointing toward the Andes. They still couldn't find the body. I feigned ignorance, and Pato said he knew all about it and would fill me in. His Life of Guevara went like this:

> *Well, they say he was an Argentine, but really he was from*
> *Uruguay. He was a student of medicine in Buenos Aires, but he*
> *quit medicine and started to read. A light switched on. He*
> *became leader of a socialist group, and got to know Fidel Cas-*

*tro, and when the revolution began in Cuba, he joined it. But
afterwards he and Castro couldn't agree on anything. When
Castro saw white, Che saw black. So what did he do? He came
to Peru. This was around 1974. Che came down through
Nicaragua, all of Central America, Colombia, to Peru, to find
the guerrillas here and give them help. He began arming them.
But the Peruvian army discovered him while he still had only a
small force. So that's why he went to Bolivia. My brother knew
him personally, that's how I know so much.*

Nearly every fact in this biography was wrong, which made me
like Pato even more. They were all nice guys at the border. A Peruvian supervisor named Mr. Rojo was supposed to take the day off, but
he spent an entire afternoon filling out paperwork for me. He com-
pleted the *Relación del Vehículo y Pasajeros* in triplicate, and typed the
green *Permiso de Circulación No. 4186* and filled in the date (*Marzo 8,
1996*), and even got down on his knees in the parking lot to search out
the engine number on Kooky's left cylinder head. When we were
finally done with the paperwork it was dark and I realized that Mr.
Rojo had spent almost six hours of his day off smoothing my way
through customs, through the police, through the agricultural
inspection, and through immigration. When I was finally in Peru, we
said good-bye in the parking lot and I tried to hand him a ten-dollar
tip for all he had done. Mr. Rojo blanched, waved away the money,
and then spoke the cruelest words I had heard in months: "*Te equivocaste, Patricio, te equivocaste*"—"You were mistaken."

The bones in the graveyard where I slept the next and last night
before Lima had been tossed about by all the looters that the centuries could provide, and lay in disordered heaps and random collections. Only one or two intact skeletons were visible, and these
featured bits of dried, leathery flesh still attached to the forearms and
shins and ribs. Natural cotton bolls, stuffed into the body cavities to
absorb fluid and therefore aid mummification, now tumbled loose in
the shallow depressions of sand. There were bits of woven fabric, but
the burial bundles had all been plundered long ago of the tools, jew-

elry, and personal items these small people had expected to need in the next world. They hadn't understood that the next world was simply this same world, only without them.

These people had died long before the violent struggles between the twentieth century's left and right; I suspected that they would still recognize Peru, however. If they were to wake up from their graves and shake off the sand they would see the same broad valley, the same stony hills, the same neighbors in the village across the creek, still tilling fields of irrigated potatoes. Even the chaos of modern Peru would seem familiar. War changed its shape and donned costumes of ambition and ideology, but the basic human urge to dispute was eternal.

The bones were nothing to take too seriously. The dead deserved and received no respect: some kids who had played in the valley before me had used twenty-three femurs and three skulls to spell out the word *Buzz* on the ground. This was probably the name of their favorite heavy metal band.

In the morning, with the wind drumming sand against my tent, the spare parts dream sat there in my mind, pathetically unremarkable but for the fact that I couldn't think of another dream I'd had on the entire trip. I waved it off and rode furiously toward Lima all day.

The Scorch. I had always called Lima by that bitter, blackened name. It was a foul metropolis of dusty brown buildings and clogged streets and cold hills that had chilled my heart since the first day I had seen it. It was my least favorite place in the hemisphere, a burden of sorrow on the ground, and when the desert began to give way to the edges of the city, to its ring of hills and its outer badges of poverty, I rode Kooky with slow care and felt an emotional paralysis overwhelm me. I realized, as I rolled up a highway into the suburb of Miraflores, what was driving my strange visions and violent impulses of recent days: It was this.

Peru was what made Chile look good. The measly numbers that were death in slim, sophisticated Chile could never measure against the mass of suffering that was Peru. Sixty thousand children died here every year before the age of one, mostly for lack of clean water. Cholera raged through the land. Poverty was endemic. A fifth of the 22 million people had never seen a school. Seventy percent of children under five were malnourished. Suffering was like a tax on the living, with collections that rolled over year after year, sapping the lives of millions upon millions, steadily laying Peruvians into the ground. The uprisings against one form of oppression or another were just as routine and constant: there had been guerrillas in the mountains here almost continuously for the last seven hundred years, culminating in the psychopathic Shining Path movement and a savage civil war that had killed perhaps thirty thousand people since 1980.

Scorch was where I had first set foot in Peru. The plane arrived at dawn, and I remember the swirling dust storms that cleared just enough on our approach to show some Mi-6 attack helicopters sitting limply on the tarmac, itself half-buried under shifting drifts. On the cab ride into the city I passed through the first shantytown I had seen. I'd viewed Soweto and the *favelas* of Rio de Janeiro on television, of course, and had assumed that shanties in Peru would look pretty much the same. That wasn't the case: since it never rains in Lima, adobe bricks, loose-fitting stones, and roofs of thatch or even cardboard were the building materials of choice. Corrugated tin was rare. Later, when I'd been out in the real shantytowns, I would learn that the places near the airport were practically middle class. There were shantytowns and then there were shantytowns, with gradations of desperation and success, each with its own character and qualities.

Miraflores was the best that the Scorch had to offer, and it wasn't much, just a modest suburb along the sea with a few tall buildings and some roast chicken restaurants and pizza joints. There was a triangular park at the center that they nonetheless called "*el ovalo*," and as I drove around it and over the bridge into neighboring San Isidro I saw that things had improved somewhat since my previous visits.

There was less broken glass around, and the buildings that the guerrillas had once turned into empty eye sockets with their car bombs were now glazed again into mirrored privacy. Miraflores was filled with business. There was a new Blockbuster Video wrapped in its own parking lot like a bunker with a clear field of fire.

The owner of a guest house let me bring Kooky inside, then closed the wrought iron gates behind me and double-locked the front doors. The outer wall was topped with broken glass. Every house was still a fortress here.

I took a long shower and washed the desert from my skin for the last time. From here I would turn inland and climb up into the mountains, leaving the dry coast behind. The mountains were dangerous. Peruvians called them "the Red Zone" because of all the guerrillas. I'd already met the guerrillas of Peru once, five years before, and once was more than enough.

That day had started with a long wait in yet another dusty field of rocks on the outskirts of Lima. It was visiting day, and two hundred women and perhaps a hundred men stood with Incan patience in the heat, slowly inching forward as each person and her or his paperwork was inspected, handled, stamped, and inked by teams of soldiers. The line began out in the street and ran in fits and busts through the stony parking lot and toward the great fortress wall of the Canto Grande prison. Soldiers with automatic rifles strolled around the scene, pestering vendors, kicking dogs, and "borrowing" newspapers from the people in line. A tiny door in the wall opened from time to time and admitted a few supplicants or expelled a few more soldiers. You were only admitted to the prison on visiting day if you had the name of a specific someone to visit: I wrote "Juan Valdez" on the little form handed to me at the first checkpoint.

At six-two, I towered over these four-foot-tall women, and inevitably the soldiers grew nervous and began watching me. A private raced off but nothing happened for a long time, and I made it to the second checkpoint before they pulled me out of line. A Chinese-Peruvian captain appeared (there were many Asian immigrants to

Peru; President Alberto Fujimori's parents were from Japan, and his nickname was El Chino). The captain listened to the explanation for my mission—to interview the guerrillas imprisoned here—and nodded curtly. A sergeant then led me straight to the head of the line. I rolled my right sleeve up and a series of corporals applied seven different purple stamps to my arms, beginning at the wrist and working up to the biceps by the seventh seal. A soldier cheerfully wrote the number "150" on my other arm in ballpoint. This, he explained, was to help identify bodies.

In 1986 the Shining Path prisoners had staged a coordinated uprising in three Lima prisons, using dynamite and small arms they had smuggled inside. In the counterattack Peruvian troops had killed one hundred and twenty-four prisoners at Canto Grande; one hundred of them were shot in the head after surrendering. A hundred and thirty-five were killed at another prison, apparently in the same way. Both sides were expecting a repeat (which has since happened, twice).

The corporals ordered me to stand in the sun until the purple ink dried, which I did, and then I was pushed through the door into the pitch-black interior of the prison. A fat, sweaty sergeant fingerprinted me and ordered me to surrender my wallet, which went into a drawer. I assumed I would never see it again. The sergeant then gingerly felt me up, checking my ankles, thighs, scrotum, and armpits through my clothes. When he was done he pushed me through a confusing maze of iron bars into the inner courtyard of the prison, a sun-baked expanse that reeked of urine and sweat. The cell blocks rose up around the outside in oddly modernist shapes, rounded and swooping. It was a prison by Gaudí.

There were several hundred starving men dressed in rags in the courtyard. "Which one?" I asked the sergeant, who was safe behind his iron gate again. He pointed to the right, and I walked through the crowd trying to look like I did this all the time. The arms and legs of prisoners dangled from windows above, and the men up there hurled abuse and trash down on my head. Wires and laundry lines and

improvised TV antennas tangled the sky overhead. Within seconds I
was confronted by a half-naked, shivering man demanding money. I
pushed him aside and threaded my way through the rest of these living dead as quickly as possible. Several men in nothing but tattered
shorts chased after me, one of them carrying an enormous ship made
of matchsticks and shouting prices. I hustled up the first few feet of a
cement ramp, made a right where the sergeant had indicated, and
came face-to-face with a closed iron grate. A dispassionate woman
sat in a chair on the other side of the gate. She betrayed neither surprise nor interest as I let myself in. I had to duck my head beneath an
arch of red hammer and sickle flags to enter, and when I stood up
again a greeting committee of bright-faced young women in flowery
blouses and slacks burst into applause and called out "Welcome,
comrade!" They all shook my hand firmly, one after another, and
then began to sing:

> *President Gonzalo, we advance with you*
> *To final victory in the popular war!*
> *The Peruvian Communist Party*
> *Army of the new state!*

They finished with a two-line chant:

> *Militarize the party for a world revolution!*
> *Maoism in the world!*

The room was clean. Red banners declared LONG LIVE THE
PEOPLE'S WAR. Portraits of Marx, Mao, and Lenin were posted on the
walls beside quotes from each. More slogans urged me to remember
the Four Phases of Struggle, to Build World Maoism, and to Boil All
Drinking Water.

Because of threats to their families, the prison guards had long
ago ceded control of the block to Shining Path, and the guerrilla girls
now lived independently. They cooked their own food, even raising

rabbits, and days in A-1 were tightly scheduled around exercise, ideology classes, singing, mural painting, and military drills.

I borrowed a pen from a cooperative young woman and dug some paper out of my sock, where I had hidden it from the sergeant. A tall woman led me to a table in the main common room of the cell block. She had straight dark hair, Caucasian features, and an air of elegance. While attendants buzzed about her, bringing tea and bowls of fruit, she insisted in a clear, educated Spanish that she was "just an ordinary prisoner, someone with knowledge of the situation." I asked how was she chosen as a leader.

"There are no leaders in the Shining Path," she replied, fingering her glass of tea. "We are all equal." Looking at the attendants hovering over her, I pointed out that she had some kind of authority. Was she elected democratically to her position? She glared at me. "The best are chosen," she said.

Over lunch of rice and an oily stew in plastic bowls she quizzed me in detail about my politics and recent events. What was the attitude of Americans toward the Shining Path? Was the IRA a revolutionary organization or "merely" democratic? Was the Gulf War directed by American oil companies? Was the Chinese economy growing or collapsing? In exchange for my vague answers, she explained that Shining Path was the last bastion of true communism in the world, of course: Fidel Castro was a lackey of the United States; China was run by capitalist-imperialist dogs; communism collapsed not in 1989 but in 1975, when Mao died. From Tiananmen Square to the capitals of Eastern Europe, she explained, the masses were ready for a violent revolution. Peru's other major guerrilla group, the MRTA, were not the Marxists they claimed but in fact a group of capitalists. "We have no relations with them," she said. "They get support from Cuba. We consider the Cubans revisionists."

As I picked at the small bones in my stew—rabbit, I hoped—the torrent of dogma continued in a vocabulary that I could hear but not comprehend. Che Guevara was a revisionist because he compromised with the retrograde forces of class domination, whatever that meant. He was a tepid captive of his own upbringing, this woman told me, a "bourgeois revisionist" and "servant of capitalism." Her words followed a rigid internal logic that could not be translated to the world beyond these walls except through the blazing purity of violent action. Whether this logic made any sense or not was irrelevant: the language itself was the point. Revolutionary consciousness preempted and surpassed reality. In Peru, theory was fact.

Lunch came to an abrupt end when a pair of antennae emerged from my rice. Wriggling legs soon followed, property of a small cockroach who had apparently been waiting in my bowl when the rice arrived. My guide apologized and suggested a walk.

It was a prisoner's stroll, up and down the ample courtyard attached to A-1. The walls were twenty-five feet high, providing just enough room for the huge murals of the revolution and its patron saints that the women painted. An enormous picture of Chairman Mao held pride of place behind a basketball hoop, the great helmsman beaming down benignly with his usual Cheshire cat smile. At another spot he was shown towering over a tiny column of Chinese peasants. FORWARD TO VICTORY IN THE PEOPLE'S WAR, read the slogan at his feet. Another mural showed the Shining Path's leader, known as President Gonzalo or the Fourth Sword. He was sitting at a desk, a pudgy figure with thick glasses. Behind him were portraits of the previous three swords, Marx, Lenin, and Mao. There were six rabbit hutches under the murals.

A basketball game took over the courtyard. The women formed into two loose teams of about a dozen each, and ran up and down the yard tossing the ball haplessly and missing basket after basket. Chairman Mao watched from right behind the far hoop, and sometimes the ball would bounce off his chin. After half an hour there was still no apparent score. While my guide dutifully cheered the players I slipped out of sight, ducking through the lunch room and ascending the first set of stairs I saw. I crept down a corridor, peering into empty cell after empty cell. There were bunk beds and quilts, and the moist walls were decorated with family photographs and magazine pictures of Swiss mountains and Chinese maidens. I quickly checked under the thin mattresses for weapons or any other secrets, but there was nothing. I went up another flight silently and eavesdropped on a conversation among three women guerrillas. They were discussing sewing.

Soon I heard the heavy trod of my guide's feet on the stairs, and she found me staring innocently from the top floor over the courtyard. She was angry that I had slipped off, but I blabbered about needing a fresh breeze and followed her downstairs. She ushered me across the main prison courtyard and handed me off to a greeter in cell block B-4, where the three hundred male Shining Path prisoners lived. It proved to be simply a larger slice of liberated territory, run on the same principles as the women's section. The courtyard was bigger but also decorated with murals. In place of a basketball court there was an open-air bedroom, and about fifty men dozed or idled on cots in the shade of sheets strung overhead. I walked down the aisles, feeling the prisoners carefully avoiding my gaze. Eventually I spotted two young men who acknowledged my presence. They were César, nineteen, and Javier, twenty-two, both serving long sentences for terrorism. César was handsome and shy, but Javier recited doctrine aggressively. "Of course we know we are going to win. The masses reject the government," he said. He spoke easily of feudalism, mobilization, and the means of production. Marxist logic explained everything: "You are either for the revolution or you are against it. If you are against exploitation, you are for violent revolution. When I realized that point, I joined the party." He went on to explain the Four Phases of Struggle: (1) violent revolution, (2) class struggle, (3) the dictatorship of the proletariat, and (4) the struggle against revisionism. Javier and César immediately fell into an argument about whether we were in stage one or two, which just proved we were in stage four. We talked for a while about the Two Antagonistic Paths and the struggle against "parliamentary cretinism," known elsewhere as elections.

Then Javier leaned in close and lowered his voice. "Just tell me this," he said to me. "Who has the nicer murals, us or the women?"

On the way out, the tall woman reappeared and suggested

strongly that a stop at the guerrilla gift shop would be appropriate. It was in the stairwell, with the gifts spread over a small table. There were various handicrafts made by the prisoners; the money went "to further the revolution," the man running the table explained. I looked at some hairbands for women, made of leather and wood. The leather was carved with a scene of the globe exploding, with tooled flames shooting out of the various continents. There were earrings, made from coins stamped with a portrait of President Gonzalo and then decorated with microscopic slogans (LONG LIVE WORLD MAO-ISM!). I narrowly resisted buying a cloth shopping bag embroidered with a hammer and sickle (not the kind of item you wanted to carry around Lima) and instead bought two small paintings. The first showed Shining Path guerrillas wiping out an army garrison. The guerrillas were shooting some of the soldiers and then lecturing the survivors with clenched fists (in fact, the Shining Path almost never took prisoners). In the second painting, the glorious future had arrived. The sun set on an idealized Andean village, and happy peasants were cooking and raising their clenched fists in the air. A few of them carried rifles on their backs or large communist banners in their hands, but it was otherwise a peaceful scene, as simple as the childish hopes behind it.

The guerrilla running the stand wanted four dollars for a miniature diorama. As the tall woman looked on disapprovingly, I bargained him down to three and took it. The model was about four inches by four inches, made of cloth and painted paper in a folk-art style. It was a street scene, and showed three guerrillas machine-gunning somebody as he stepped out of his limousine. The limo was beautifully done. It was made entirely of carefully folded and glued paper. It even had tinted windows. The dolls were made of thread wrapped around wire and painted. The guns were wire.

The tall woman lowered a finger right in among the figures to show me the poor sucker who dared to thwart the Shining Path. He was bald and wore a gray suit, and his body was tumbling out the open door of the car. Lovingly painted rivulets of blood ran down the two-centimeter body. "This is a member of the reaction," she said.

"He is now a victim of the people's war." Then she pointed to a tiny doll on the fringe of the scene, its fist raised in the air. "This is a member of the public," she said. "He is shown supporting us." This was the only time I saw her smile.

We parted with an egalitarian handshake, and at the exit to B-4, I paused to watch the main courtyard, looking for a chance to cross. César appeared and offered to walk me to safety. We strolled out into the sun together, given a wide berth by the regular prisoners. César told me that before prison he had been a student at San Marcos University in Lima, a notorious recruiting ground for the Shining Path. He was arrested for bombing a store, and he hoped to go back to school after the revolution. With his slim good looks and stylish clothes, he looked as though he could be out on the street chasing girls. With a touch of shyness, he mentioned the "immense love" of the people for the revolution. "They love us very much," he said dreamily. *"Muchísimo."*

I asked him if his bomb had killed anyone. He shrugged his shoulders. "It was a capitalist store," he said.

Back inside the fortified guardhouse the darkness enfolded me again, welcome this time. The fat sergeant reappeared and handed me everything I had given him, including the watch and my money down to the dollar. A handful of young guards gathered around to look at my souvenirs. The Chinese captain came over and put on a broad smile. "Men, look how childish it is," he said. He held up the tiny diorama, and the guards ran their eyes over the little figures with machine guns and the street covered with blood. I showed them the painting of Peruvian soldiers being shot and blown up by heroic guerrillas. The soldiers laughed at first, but not as much as the captain wanted.

In five years some things had changed in Lima—but others had not, like the traffic. When I rode Kooky up the street named for Felipe Guamán Poma de Ayala a few days after my arrival it was clogged with sputtering vehicles. Guamán Poma was a sad historical figure known as "the Chronicler." Part of the very first mestizo generation, he was born (he claimed) to a Spanish conquistador and an Inca noblewoman. He wandered Peru for most of his life, composing a massive letter to the king of Spain that detailed the economic and political construction of Inca society, the founding myths and the glorious lessons that the Andes could teach Spain. Guamán Poma was utterly loyal to the Spanish Crown and believed with a touching innocence that His Majesty would end all the suffering and violence of the conquest if only it were drawn to his attention. Guamán Poma even illustrated the book himself; the final sad drawing showed Guamán Poma as an old man, trudging along with his book and his loyal dog following behind. He looked like Peru's first travel writer. In the end the king never saw the chronicle; it was discovered only centuries later, too late to rescue the world it described.

The old city center lay at the far end of Guamán Poma's name-sake avenue, and I wove in and out of the gridlocked microbuses and picked my way between Volkswagen beetles spewing black smoke, the inescapable taste of Lima. The microbuses were *colectivo* taxis that cost a few pennies and ran on fixed routes around the city. Each one featured a surly, macho driver and a "door boy," a young teenager charged with collecting fares and opening and closing doors. They were a particular hazard in my narrow maneuvers because the door boys delighted in hanging far out into traffic, shouting destinations. The competition among the *colectivos* was intense and profit margins were razor thin, so the drivers fought a kind of war against one another, furiously swerving toward any potential passenger, cutting each other off, and flinging their battered vehicles into any open space that appeared in the roadway, including oncoming lanes where possible. The Peruvian papers were delighting in the story of a local soccer team called Sporting Cristál that had been en route to practice when a microbus cut them off. The team jumped out and beat the opposition driver senseless. Attendance at their games immediately went up.

There were soldiers everywhere. Brown-skinned draftees from highland villages clouded sidewalks outside important buildings, dwarfed by their German automatic rifles. They looked nervous, which made me nervous. Armored cars were parked in the traffic medians, green and glowering with frightful intent. Peruvians were used to the heavy military presence and went about their business normally. Vendors flooded the stalled traffic at every intersection selling lottery tickets, cigarettes, gum, windshield wipers (I no longer had a windshield to wipe), key chains, old magazines, statuettes of Jesus Christ, and soccer balls.

In 1952, Lima was still the "city of the viceroys," as Ernesto wrote in his diary. The old city center was a sleepy gem filled with Spanish architecture, elaborate plazas, and arcaded galleries. The manner of the city was exclusively Spanish, the residents part of the white elite who had preserved their way of life without incorporating the rest of Peru. Ernesto called this Lima "the perfect example of a Peru which has never emerged from its feudal, colonial state. It is still waiting for the blood of a truly liberating revolution."

The *R* word at last. It was only here, in the obsolete seat of the Spanish empire in the Americas, that Ernesto Guevara de la Serna finally had a vision of a "truly liberating" revolution. The vision was not articulated—that would come years later—but the instinct was now present. The social vistas opened by months of travel now gnawed at Ernesto and opened a gap in his life. Something would have to bridge the chasm between what was and what should be. In 1952, the word *revolution* was itself enough.

In the years after Ernesto passed through, the revolution had indeed come to Peru, over and over again, in every imaginable guise. The greatest of the revolutions came into sight after I swept past the presidential palace and up onto the bridge over the filthy Río Rímac; there, as far as the eye could see, were the shantytowns. They were filled with the poor who were driven from their old lives during the course of the intervening decades, pushed out of mountain villages and provincial towns by poverty, by innumerable attempts at leftist revolutions, by the military's brutal counterrevolutionary sweeps, and by drug traffickers. There was also a pull in the simple lure of city lights, which plucked Peruvians from their devalued mountain lives as quickly as any other people who felt left behind by history.

There was no Doug Tompkins to shield them from the global economy when highland agriculture collapsed under the pressure of cheap imports. Beginning in the 1950s the poor and the ambitious and the lonely and the hungry had flooded down from the hills of Peru, an army of peasant millions who built their shanties in rings around the city, each wave adding another settlement that climbed a notch higher up the slopes of the surrounding hills. The newest immigrants lived in the worst terrain, sometimes the flatlands of the coast but more often the steep slopes of the rocky, useless hills. The wealthy had fled to the suburbs, where they sneered at the *cholos*, and Ernesto's city of viceroys was now dusty and neglected and ringed by the gaze of its own mestizo bastards.

I crossed the bridge and headed out into this, the true Lima. These communities were called *pueblos jóvenes*, or "young towns," and it was impossible for a stranger to navigate them. Only the oldest neighborhoods from way back in the 1950s had named streets, and the farther I rode out from the bridge the younger the community, the lower the buildings, the worse the materials, the fewer the landmarks and street signs. A blue VW Beetle rocketed from behind a bus and nearly crushed me. I asked directions continually and followed vague instructions to "go past the tower" and "make a left in five minutes" and "look for the restaurant." After half an hour of circling I finally stumbled onto the gate in a tall wall that I had been seeking, drove straight in, and killed the engine. There were a dozen buildings inside the wall, mostly small cabins and a few barracks-style buildings that were empty. Old medical supplies and rusting equipment were scattered around. Dogs wandered in profusion.

I had not even dismounted in the dusty courtyard before I was surrounded by children shouting questions. Their faces were bright and they wanted to know where I was from, and then if America was "the last country." They wiggled their thumbs and asked if I had a Nintendo set on board; was it true that in my country you could rent Nintendo? What kind of cargo was I carrying? And would I like to see where Che Guevara had lived?

The children were the offspring of the lepers Guevara had come to see. The two Argentines arrived here at the Hospital Guía leper colony in 1952, eager to touch the untouchables. Although they had exaggerated wildly in telling the Chilean newspapers that they were international experts with "three thousand patients" in five different leper hospitals, the truth was impressive enough. Granado had worked for years in various leper colonies, and Guevara genuinely intended to do likewise when he graduated from medical school.

Guevara's interest in medicine was a chronicle of lost hope. He'd been chasing cures since his own asthma kicked in at the age of four. The first cures were, like those he came to at the end of his life, driven by force of will. The constant sensation of suffocation drives many young asthmatics to develop an almost violent urge to live; according to Dolores Moyano, one of Ernesto's childhood friends, this explained the young man's ferocious determination in all physical pursuits. Little Ernesto loved dangerous stunts like walking along fence posts, and had taken up rugby, a British imperial sport, where he earned another of his innumerable nicknames, the Sniper. He was known for playing to the point of collapse, as if willing his body to fail. The psychological effect was the reverse of the physiological one: constantly pushing the limits imposed by his lungs, Ernesto overcame the crippling fear of death that accompanies near suffocation. Testing himself became a habit; pushing back against death a means of validating life. This aggressive response is so common among sufferers that it is sometimes called the asthmatic personality.

His own suffering informed Ernesto's decision to enter medical school, but it was not the only factor. There was his mother's cancer, which had prompted him to those gruesome basement experiments on guinea pigs. But he had also inherited an aristocratic idealism from her, a kind of noblesse oblige that required him to address injustice. He enrolled in medical school in Buenos Aires at the age of eighteen, which is normal in Argentina, and raced through his studies with precocious speed, which is not. He made and kept a public promise that he would return from the motorcycle trip and finish his medical degree.

But his rolling research had awoken something in Guevara that doomed the pursuit of medicine. He never practiced after graduation, except informally. He later said that the leper colonies of Peru had taught him that "the highest forms of human solidarity and loyalty arise among lonely and desperate men," but his search for that very loyalty led him away from medicine, toward the desperate solidarity of combat. Although he had joined Castro's invasion of Cuba as the team doctor, he trained with rifles, was a superb shot, and abandoned medicine as soon as he could. On their very first day of battle the rebels were routed and had to run for it. Guevara had to choose in that moment between carrying the medicine or carrying the ammunition, and he chose the latter. He mentioned this anecdote often in speeches to make sure everyone understood what he was saying: he had put down the bandages and picked up the bullets. Violent revolution was just as noble as the healing art—indeed, it *was* a form of healing if it was administered to a sick society by a trained specialist. This was Guevara's own Life of Guevara.

In a letter home from Lima, Little Ernesto was still recommending less rigorous cures. Writing to his father, he explained that one of the most powerful treatments for leprosy was a firm handshake. He sat with the lepers, took their hands confidently, and played soccer and ate with them. They saw that he had no fear. "This may seem pointless bravado," he wrote, "but the psychological benefit to these poor people—usually treated like animals—of being treated as normal human beings is incalculable. . . . "

The same courage was hard for me to summon. The first adult I met was named Serafino, and when we shook hands I blanched visibly at his thumbless grip. He'd lost only the tips of his other fingers to the disease. Like many lepers, Serafino also had a slightly "crazy" expression, the result of nerve degeneration in his face. His eyes were frozen in a permanent squint, and his mouth was locked in a half smile, as if he was letting me in on a joke that I couldn't get.

Even when Ernesto came here there were medicines to arrest the disease, but poverty is its own illness, and Serafino had grown up untreated. Born in the high sierra sometime in the 1950s—he didn't know when—he was first exiled to the San Pablo leper colony in 1961, when he was "the same size as them," he said, pointing at the cloud of little boys surrounding us. In 1968 he was transferred to Lima to live in the Hospital Guía colony. Although leprosy is not a particularly contagious disease—only a tiny portion of people are susceptible to it—fear, rumor, and a long tradition of discrimination surrounded the lepers as surely as any wall. Leprosy was a life sentence to prison back then.

In 1976 a military government had breached the walls and allowed the lepers to leave if they wanted. There were still eighteen families here. They remained victims of popular loathing outside and knew little of making their way in the world. Here they had a doctor on call, some free food, and no rent for shanties that were as good as most outside the walls.

Despite missing both thumbs and the rest of his fingers past the knuckles, Serafino wielded a mean rake and had a stunning garden to prove it. He grew tomatoes and Chinese onions, and showed me a high sierra corn strain that he was experimenting with. "You have to work or you go crazy," he said, picking at weeds with his rake. "That's a big problem here. Not many work. Some go outside to work but most just stay here. I was a carpenter until someone stole my tools, my saw and hammer and so on. That was four years ago, the sons of bitches. Since then I just work on the garden and with my birds."

There were a half dozen hens, some ducks, and several caged fighting cocks. The cock of the walk was an immense *macho* of Spanish-Chilean stock with black feathers tinged in iridescent green. He had survived six fights to the death and retired to father almost all the other chickens in the little cluster of wire-and-scrap hutches that Serafino tended.

"El Che was here," Serafino suddenly said. "He slept right over there." He pointed a half-formed digit toward a blue shack, solidly built but tiny, just a plain square of four walls. I told Serafino that yes, I had heard that Che had spent a week or two here.

"Longer than that," he replied. "He was here for months, at

least three. He lived right over there in that blue house. He worked in the hospital all day, in the lab, doing research. He only went out at night to meet with people. You know what kind of people. He was organizing his groups for Bolivia. Meetings."

Every detail of this story was wrong: Ernesto was in Lima for only a couple of weeks; he spent his days touring museums; he wasn't a guerrilla strategist yet; and he only visited the Hospital Guía briefly as a medical tourist, not a researcher. In the mind of Serafino, however, the story was true because it had to be true. For millions of the dispossessed all over Latin America, there were no other heroes. Che was a necessity, not a possibility; if he hadn't existed, they would have invented him anyway, and often did. The point of the legend was always the same, and as powerful as it was simple: Che lived and died for us.

We marched over, Serafino trailing his rake in the dust. He opened the front door of the shed, which proved to be empty and clean. It was the size of a cargo elevator. "There was a photo of him on the wall for years, but they took it down in '72 or '74," he said. Yes, I replied, it certainly wasn't safe to keep a photo of Che on display during those reactionary times. "No," Serafino countered, "they had to paint the place." With his frozen expression it was impossible to tell if he was kidding or not.

Dusk had fallen and I thanked the lepers and left in a hurry. I didn't want to pick my way back through the twisted streets in the dark. On the way to the motorcycle, kicking up clouds of dust with my boots, I looked up. There, gleaming on a hillside in neon splendor, was a statue of Jesus of Nazareth, arms outstretched, gazing down upon the city as champion of the humble.

After my prison visit I had to know if the Shining Path would win its battle. The future of Lima lay in the shantytowns, and I spent two days riding through them with a young leftist who agreed to show me his own revolution in the making. Our vehicle was less heroic than the motorcycle-Rocinante: David Medianero picked me up at the guest house in a dented blue Volkswagen Beetle belching smoke and lacking a speedometer, gas gauge, or radio, although it did have a tape deck on which he played Zamfir. Medianero was a lapsed communist who had found employment as a field worker for a Peruvian think tank called the Institute for Liberty and Democracy, which is where I had met him while researching an article. I liked the ILD because it was adept at siphoning the coffers of conservative American foundations by talking about free enterprise, then turning around and spending the money on Marxists. On our way out of the city that first morning we stopped at a market long enough to fill the back seat with bananas and the tank with gasoline.

Medianero was in his thirties, a man of the streets who had a poor person's obsession with neatness and wore a short-sleeved polyester shirt. We headed out toward a rural zone on the far outskirts of Lima, where he was negotiating with some farming cooperatives. The road went out of the city center, passing a thousand more old Volkswagens exactly like our own. We kept the Río Rímac on our left and rode out a highway named for Tupac Amaru, an eighteenth-century rebel who resisted the Spanish. The Movimiento Revolucinario Tupac Amaru, or MRTA, had taken his name, but few spoke it anymore. Following Guevarist tactics, the group was steadily burning out in a series of spectacular defeats. The last of these was a 1996 attack on the Japanese ambassador's residence during a Christmas party, where the guerrillas slipped into the event disguised as waiters carrying canapés and took more than four hundred hostages. During the long siege the guerrillas issued statements via their web page and spent most of their time watching soap operas. They allowed the hostages to conduct self-improvement seminars on topics like the benefits of kidnapping insurance, and even permitted a noted pollster—himself a captive—to survey the hostages on the first floor (surprisingly, only 87 percent felt that security at the party was "inadequate"). Their postmodern tactics collided with Peru's premodern realities: one morning the army burst into the building and killed every single guerrilla. Their leader's immortal last words— "We're screwed!"—accurately described MRTA's prospect these days. The siege eliminated the bulk of their military force, and MRTA took a back seat to the Shining Path, the Maoists who ridiculed Guevarism from the safety of their jail cells.

The slums were, along with San Marcos University, the Shining Path's recruiting ground, the sea in which the fish swam. In 1992 their insurgency controlled perhaps a third of Peru, including many of the young towns ringing Lima. I spent a month in Lima then, and there was bomb attack almost every day I was there. That sounds worse than it really was, because many of the attacks were surprisingly pathetic: one night the guerrillas tied a stick of dynamite to a statue of John F. Kennedy and decapitated it; they launched homemade rockets at the U.S. Embassy but the missiles fizzled and crashed onto the front lawn; and they blew up power pylons, plunging the poor parts of the city into darkness. The *limeños* were somewhat inured to these matters, and wandered the streets full of broken glass, keeping a watchful eye on any Volkswagen Beetle that appeared abandoned—the bug was the car bomb of choice. Not all the attacks on American symbols were so ineffective: near the end of my stay the Kentucky Fried Chicken in Miramar was gutted by a lunchtime car bomb that killed several people. The quiet, personal violence was in many ways more devastating than the splashy propaganda assaults. The Shining Path specialized in assassinating activists who offered the poor an alternative to Maoism—agricultural extension experts in the countryside, priests in the small towns, and, in the city, activists like David Medianero.

Now Medianero cut off the highway and through a series of the increasingly desperate slums. There were piles of garbage in the streets, some of them burning with a greasy stink. Mangy dogs lingered on the corners. The towns piled up the increasingly steep, stony hillsides, with improvised lanes separating insubstantial shacks. Everything—roads, people, clothing, dogs, houses—was coated in a fine tan dust, a khaki powder so thick that Medianero occasionally ran the bug's wipers in a vain effort to scrape the windshield clean.

We stopped at the farthest edge of the city. This area was once all farmland, but new slums were springing up, along with a few light manufacturing plants. The local farmers were feeling under pressure, and Medianeros's first stop was a farm building with a dusty court-yard surrounded by narrow fields of corn that ran between the new strips of shacks. Women worked the maize in traditional felt hats that showed they had not been out of the hills long. Medianero told me to pose as a European if anyone asked. In the same breath he said that there was no danger but that "anti-imperialist" feelings were common-place. Medianero was trying to convince these semiurban farmers to disband the co-ops and turn their land into private parcels.

Most of the farms and houses in the slums were sitting on seized land, often government land but sometimes private farmland. Fami-lies would pour their resources into building a small home, but since they did not legally own the land their lives remained precarious. When some of the older and better organized shantytowns put polit-ical pressure on the government, they were successful in getting titles. The result was a kind of economic enfranchisement as the owners poured effort into expanding their crude shacks into two-and even three-story houses. With title, you could demand social ser-vices like any other reputable homeowner. Bank loans against the title made it possible to finance repairs or a new business. Homes that were legally owned could be legally sold. An actual real estate market appeared in the slums where people had titles, and a few communi-ties were so developed they looked like lush islands in the sea of shanties.

Medianero dropped off some sample land titles with the co-op leader and then we remounted and went farther afield, a long drive up and over steep hills that had been covered with graffiti made by piling rocks into big letters. There was supposed to be an assembly for three hundred people at another cooperative, but we sat around for two hours and no one came. Then we drove to a roadside stand

and sat in the shade drinking Inca Cola, a neon-yellow soda that tastes like bubble gum and is Peru's national drink. Medianero sulked for a while.

"Most of the young towns are aligned with political parties of the left," he said, "like the Revolutionary Block, or the APRA, or the PUM." Some parties were just organized around a single leader, like the former president, Velasquez. The acronyms and affiliations formed a dizzying political landscape, but Medianero knew the map intimately. For many years he had been an activist in PUM, which stood for United Party of Mariátegui. Mariátegui was an early communist leader in Peru, and his name kept coming up. In 1952 Ernesto had befriended a Lima doctor who was both a noted researcher on leprosy and a friend of Mariátegui, and they had talked about Marxism late into the night (Ernesto apparently remained skeptical). The Shining Path was actually known (to itself) as "the Communist Party of Peru for the Shining Path of José Carlos Mariátegui."

Medianero had gotten his start in activism by organizing a grand, model land invasion. He still glowed with pride as he waved his yellow cola in the air and described the way he assembled the best, handpicked comrades—"We called everyone, even the women, comrade"—late one night. Armed with tools, ropes, building materials, and small wooden stakes, they snuck onto a piece of idle farmland in the darkness and spread out. The plan had been worked out in its smallest details, even to who would be mayor of the new settlement and where the soccer field would go. They drove stakes into the ground to mark where the streets would be, and each comrade claimed a piece of land and built a tiny lean-to out of thatched palm fronds stretched over a simple frame. By dawn there was a town—a somewhat theoretical one, but in Peru theory was fact.

Later, Medianero left the party. I asked him why. "Politics," he replied. Even the smallest parties were afflicted with endless schisms and feuds. Factionalism simply wore him out. He kept his friends on the left, however, and observed that they were slowly drifting away from radical activism. He'd recently attended the baptism of a child born to a friend who had been a fierce communist. Medianero was surprised to hear his friend had quit the party, and asked why. "I have a child," the man replied. "I need a cement floor in my house. I don't have time for politics."

After telling me this story, Medianero took a swig of his drink. "It's too easy to blame the imperialists," he said. "If a man needs a cement floor, he doesn't care where it comes from." The founders of the young towns had always been common laborers, he said, but their children were growing up as small entrepreneurs. This was a grand title for someone who sold things on the street or ran a business out of his shack, but it was a marked change in how people expected to live. Medianero said that life in Peru had changed faster than the vocabulary of politics.

"The farmers are used to old-fashioned ideological talk," he said. "You have to speak to them in the language of the left. I can talk to them in those terms, but then we make a pilot project to show them that private property is neither leftist nor rightist, just a good idea. You give them examples. People are slow to change their minds."

The second day was more urban than the first. We stopped at mid-morning at one of the model soup kitchens, called *comedores populares*. This was in Villa Salvador, itself a model slum where people were organized and had elected a local mayor and even a community assembly to speak for them. Two shy women dressed in the multiple petticoats of the Andean native showed me an empty larder. The building was adobe, about twenty feet wide and thirty feet long. It was decorated on one wall with Villa Salvador's municipal symbol, a picture of two arms crossed, one holding a rifle and the other a shovel. There were a few wobbly benches inside, and three tables. They were hoping that some food donations from the Catholic charity Caritas (which distributes about a million rations a day in Lima) would arrive soon. When they had food, they made a watery soup and charged about twenty cents a bowl. They sat, passive, patient, and hopeful, cleaning the few pots and pans they had. Sometimes they were instructed to read aloud from a pro–Shining Path pamphlet—and they did it, because the penalty for resisting the revolution was death.

A senile beggar woman approached me outside the *comedor*, fetid with poverty and dressed in rags. Medianero spoke to her quietly and led her to a bench. We climbed into the car but he did not start the engine. He waited, looking at the helpless old woman. "There is always this," he said. "Always."

We drove farther south, down across a huge flat expanse of shanties, a disorganized and truly new young town that extended for miles. We passed two hundred women waiting in line at the community water tap. They held bright plastic buckets and shuffled slowly up the line, past the usual burning garbage and stray dogs. Still moving south, we passed a soccer field, just a rectangle of rocks lying in the brown dust. Eventually we came to where the slums began to peter out in the sand dunes along the ocean. The last outposts of Lima were those decrepit sheds with no roofs and woven mats for walls. I could crane my neck right over these feeble homes and peer inside like a giraffe. Often, there wasn't even a cup inside. We climbed the highest dune and surveyed the slums as they ran up the coast toward central Lima. The cold blue ocean seemed impossibly beautiful.

The Uruguayan historian Eduardo Galeano had met Che during the heady, early years of the Cuban revolution, and he recounted Guevara's intimate familiarity with the details of poverty like this. Guevara could recite statistics on illiteracy, on infant mortality, on inoculation rates. Galeano had reverently placed Guevara's 1952 motorcycle journey in this context: "On this journey of journeys," he wrote in a review of Guevara's diary, "solitude found solidarity, *I* turned into *we*." The emotional basis for Guevara's politics, then, was here in the slums he had seen, among the untouchables that he had touched. This was where an individual had surrendered himself to the necessity of the plural, a noble vision of solidarity that had produced some very dubious results in practice, whether here or in Havana.

On the surface David Medianero had done the opposite—he had turned from the "we" of group action and party politics to the "I" of ownership and individual struggle. Perhaps the truly revolutionary act was to discard the cloak of doctrinal certainty and dare to accept the individuality of human beings again.

The battle of these slums was a struggle between paradigms—one dedicated to Marx, the other to markets. Yet both sides were on the left. The only idea coming from the right was austerity in one guise or another, which always means less for the poor. Only the left cared enough to come into the townships at all.

You could see all the way to Miraflores from on top of the dunes. Whichever way things were going, it was still a very long way.

I fell profoundly ill, as much from my hatred of Scorch as from the pathogens that inevitably crept up my intestinal tract. Lima could fell anyone. I sent my brake pads out for a recoating and spent four days lying in the guest house evacuating my innards into the toilet, first from the top and then from the bottom. I sipped rehydration solution (water, sugar, and salt) and read a book I'd found lying around, *The Secret Life of Alejandro Mayta*. It was by Peru's most famous author, Mario Vargas Llosa. Mayta was a fictional revolutionary, less charismatic and decisive than Che Guevara but similar in his faith that a tiny vanguard of guerrillas could change the world. The book's narrator was a contemporary writer, an obvious stand-in for Vargas Llosa himself, who was digging through the 1950s, looking up old revolutionaries and conspirators, interviewing fellow travelers and old friends, all in the search for Mayta's "precursory character." Back then Mayta sounded a lot like the young Ernesto Guevara of the 1950s, an unsullied intellectual still dwelling in "that adolescence in which politics consists exclusively of feelings, moral indignation, rebellion, idealism, dreams, generosity, disinterestedness, mysticism."

> *There he was, young, slim, handsome, smiling, talkative, with his invisible wings, believing that the revolution was a question of honesty, bravery, disinterestedness, daring. He didn't suspect and would perhaps never know that the revolution was a long*

act of patience, an infinite routine, a terribly sordid thing, a
thousand and one wants, a thousand and one vile deeds . . .

While I malingered in the bathroom, turning the pages, Mayta
went to his death in a small town in the Andes, leading a failed insurgency and followed only by a blind man. Che was less naïve, but
knowing the sordid nature of revolutions did not protect him from
the same fate in the end.

There were two Australians in the guest house who spent a lot of
time watching satellite television in the little corridor outside my
room. They were a cute, perky couple with a manic need to change
channels every few seconds. I sat with them one night, watching the
rest of the world flick by in two-second bursts of comedy, tragedy,
and spectacle.

"Stop!" I burst out. I made them back up and saw that I was not
having visions: there was Che on television. It was a show broadcast
live from Buenos Aires on the twentieth anniversary of the military
coup that had initiated the Dirty War. A vast public square was filled
with tens of thousands of people chanting "Never again!" Rock
bands played, and in between songs old ladies dressed in black took to
the microphone to urge their children to disobey authority. These
had to be the Mothers of the Plaza de Mayo, the only mothers who
considered rebellion the highest virtue.

While the crowd sang along with an anthem by Charlie García, a
South American Bob Dylan, huge banners of Che were brought forward through the crowd, tall red flags that swung over the sea of
heads. There were a dozen of them, each sporting the same image of
Che as always. It was the black-and-red iconic portrait, eyes fierce
and uncompromising, blazing into the future—this future.

An hour later the Australian couple knocked on my door. They
didn't speak Spanish and wanted help arranging a taxi for the airport, so I placed the call. Out of gratitude they handed me a little
paper bag containing all their leftover cocaine. After they were gone I
flushed it down the toilet. I needed to test the new brake pads, so
around midnight I rode Kooky into town—without a helmet, for

some reason—and circled the *ovalo*. Scorch didn't look so bad now that I was leaving. I kept driving, a final tour that lasted an hour, and for once all the avenues were clear.

I ended up circling the new Blockbuster endlessly, going round and round, wondering why the guerrillas always demolished the wrong symbols of American imperialism.

CHAPTER NINE

THE ROAD TO ROME

For the first time in almost three thousand miles, I turned my back on the left coast of South America. The narrow, flat strip of alluvial land that I had first glimpsed the day of my crash in southern Chile now dropped behind. A smooth divided highway ran east from Lima, out through yet more shantytowns, and then gradually began to rise. The Andes stood like a black thundercloud. In my rearview mirrors I could see the smudge of Lima and behind it the blue ocean.

After half an hour I came to a checkpoint. This was the only all-weather road connecting Lima to the sierra, and everything from potatoes to cocaine to guerrillas to tourists had to pass along this route. A somber officer inspected my papers and then asked me to dismount and bring my saddlebags inside. He was going to search me. In all the dozens of checkpoints I had passed through so far in Argentina, Chile, and Peru, no one had ever inspected my bags. Even the Chilean *carabineros* had done nothing more than confiscate the bread and cheese from a plastic bag shock-corded to the outside of my luggage. But for the Peruvian police this was a crucial frontier, a border between two worlds. The coast was a modernized wreck, where ruin and prosperity baked together under the sun. Above us were the cold and wild mountains, where Peru was more a notion than a nation.

I wanted a witness but couldn't find one, so I went into the little room with the officer and watched his hands closely. He opened the black plastic cases and slowly, professionally, worked his fingers through the clothing, reaching inside the plastic bags I used to keep things dry. He examined the spare clutch and brake cables; he opened the box containing my one spare inner tube; he passed over the diaries of Guevara and Granado without a glance. He closed the cases again. "Sorry," he said. "We have to do this."

He cleared me, but the search, the inspection of my paperwork, and the waiting still consumed an hour, and I was already behind schedule. I was determined to reach Huancayo, in the high Andes, by lunch, and I pulled out the cheap paper map of Peru that I kept folded in the inner breast pocket of my leather jacket. According to the map the pavement ended there in Huancayo, but the road south and east toward Cuzco was listed as a main component of the Pan-American Highway system, so I figured I could still make good time. I planned to be in Ayacucho by nightfall, since it was only two hundred miles from Lima. I'd allowed a generous two days to cover the last half of the distance to Cuzco. I ran my fingernail down the twisty length of the road, past names I couldn't pronounce. I'd underlined some of the places Guevara had stayed: Huancayo, Huanta, Ayacucho, Andahuaylas, Huancarama. I'd spent an afternoon at the South American Explorer's Club in Lima poring over its maps and the latest reports on roads and guerrillas. The club was a slightly doddery institution in an old Lima house where mountain climbers could store gear and backpackers exchanged information regarding everything from petty crime to hotel rates to the depth of the snowpack. The news wasn't all good, and I'd added annotations to my own map of Peru: "50 in column" referred to a company of Shining Path guerrillas spotted outside Chiclayo. I'd inked the whole region behind Huancayo with frantic black lines, indicating the presence of guerrillas there. There had been an attack at Huancavelica; another near Colcabamba; south of Ayacucho was particularly bad; everything south of Cuzco was dubious. Most of the reports were quite old. The Shining Path was on the run, its leaders arrested, its rank and file decimated. The MRTA was down to a few score combatants, most of them in the coca-growing valleys around Tingo

María, where I had no intention of setting foot. Plenty of people had gone up this road. I met an American woman in the club who'd just come through on a bus. There was nothing to be afraid of.

I was surprised when I got most of the way down the map and saw, in my own handwriting, the scribbled remark "Here be dragons." It sprawled over a swath of Peru, black ink on the page. I didn't remember writing that, but there it was in my own hand.

*U*p now, and yet farther up. The road slimmed to a humble two-lane blacktop, twisting in and out of the folds of the Andes, the steepest mountains in the world. This was Kooky's natural terrain, and we ate up the altitude, passing hesitant cars and staggering trucks, roaring lightly upward and upward and upward. With each thousand feet of altitude the temperature dropped three degrees, and eventually a mild fog closed in. There was nothing to see but steep walls of green vegetation on my right and a depthless expanse of white vapor on my left. A flock of excited bicyclists shot past in the other direction, tears streaming from their eyes.

At around nine thousand feet the engine finally gave out. It happened slowly, just a gradual decrease in power, until I had downshifted into second gear and Kooky was clawing upward with reluctance. I pulled into the parking lot of a small police post and drew my tool roll from beneath the seat. Two officers in insulated green coats came over to watch.

The best thing to be said about the R80 G/S is that it is simple. The bike was built to be rugged, not pretty, and sacrificed some of the tweakier high-performance characteristics of a street bike for raw torque. There were no pollution controls or catalytic converters to be destroyed by leaded South American gasoline; there was no chain to catch and break in some remote place, but a solid driveshaft that would last as long as the bike. The engine was cooled by the breeze rather than a fussy radiator that could puncture easily, leaving me stranded with a pool of coolant on the ground. The front wheel was bigger than the rear one to climb over logs, curbs, and rocks. The tool roll held an oddly incomplete set of metric crescent wrenches and just a few delicate Allen keys; these were exactly the tools needed to disassemble every part of the bike, and not one thing more.

Simplicity in engine design was admirable, but it was the streamlining of life itself that I craved. Travel was a constant act of reduction, of eliminating minutiae layer by layer until a substrate of hard reality emerged, welcome and fair, from beneath so many illusions. There were no office politics on the mountain, no ringing telephones or incessant advertising pitches, no cloying waiters or whining yuppies or monthly dunning notices. It seemed obvious from the perspective of a motorcycle seat what linked Guevara's ramblings to his revolutionary urges: the need for the extraordinary. Travel was a series of exceptional moments, a template for the heroic life Che would later seek. Stripped of the ordinary and stuffed with adventure and longing, life on the road imitated one of the heroic quests—*gestas*—so fundamental to Spanish legends and literature.

Now entering my third month on the road, I had steadily reduced my travel kit, shedding things deliberately or by accident. My camping gear grew scant. My fishing equipment had long ago gone back to America. I threw out the necktie that I had carried through three countries just in case someone invited me to dinner, and also the old pair of sneakers I that had torn up while fishing. "Our life is frittered away by detail," Thoreau wrote, "simplify, simplify." This imperative had slowly shaped my saddlebags; now it seeped into my bones. I lived within myself, both emotionally and practically ("You carry your house with you, like a snail," a Chilean policemen had informed me). The stop-and-go life of a thousand glancing friendships and the permanent instant had come to seem normal. A sense of disorientation—not knowing what day it was— yielded to a sense of reorientation—not caring what month it was. My muscles had become attuned to the long days. I was lean and hardened by the road. When Lima dropped into those rearview mirrors I recovered a serene, even smug, self-confidence.

"Galloping" Head, the English engineer who had ridden across the pampas a century and a half before, had traveled without luggage, living exposed to the elements and sleeping on the ground for months at a time. He described the improbable result of this regimen:

> [A]fter I had been riding for three or four months, and had
> lived upon beef and water, I found myself in a condition which I
> can only describe by saying that I felt no exertion could kill
> me. . . . At first, the constant galloping confuses the head, and
> I have often been so giddy when I dismounted that I could
> scarcely stand; but the system, by degrees, gets accustomed
> to it, and it then becomes the most delightful life which one
> can possibly enjoy.

Among my debits, I was behind schedule, over budget, and had so far covered eight thousand miles on a trip that I had guessed would total only seventy-five hundred. In the positive column, I had already suffered through a bout of illness in Lima, and that tended to harden my stomach against further assaults.

As I climbed up from the ruin of the capital I knew I was entering a long but final stretch, turning down the length of the Andes toward Bolivia and Che's resting place. The papers in Lima were silent about doings there; apparently they just couldn't find his body. I knew they would, sooner or later, but I wanted it to be later. Inevitably there would be a moment of forced answers in Bolivia, an end to all these questions.

Further progress, however, depended on the motorcycle, which lay powerless by the side of the road. The engine had simply run out of oxygen at this height. I lay down on the ground and stared up at the bottom of the machine, its two "boxer" cylinders sticking out to the sides like gull wings in classic BMW fashion. There were two carburetors, one behind each cylinder of the motor. I clicked off the small retaining clip that held the carb on the left side together. The metal underside dropped free; it was a steel bowl, filled with gasoline that spilled over my hands. Now visible inside the carb were a pair of foam blocks the size of matchbooks. These were floats, which bobbed on the pool of gasoline inside the carb. The whole system worked on gravity. As fuel dropped into the engine, the floats fell with the level in the carburetor, pulling open a tiny jet that then fed more gasoline into the chamber, raising the floats and cutting off the jets. Now, with the floats dangling free in the mountain air, gasoline shot out and sprayed over me. I pushed the float up, cutting off the spill, and then reached up with my opposite hand and twisted the petcock beneath the fuel tank to "Zu."

Those fuel jets were the source of what Guevara called in his diary "some carburetor problem which afflicts all engines at this altitude." At nine thousand feet there was too little oxygen in the air to burn fuel properly, and the engine began to drown in its own fuel. The three possible solutions to this problem were to increase the amount of oxygen (by descending to lower altitudes), to "advance the spark" (I had no idea what this meant), or to decrease the amount of fuel, and it was the last course that I now took. I had been carrying two replacement jets for the carbs, tiny brass bolts with finer openings than those in the bike now. Using the smallest wrench in the tool kit, I twisted the large jet out and then put a small one in. Then I held the foam floats back in place, put the metal cover on, and clipped the whole thing shut. I went over to the other side and repeated the process.

The two policemen watched this event with verbose curiosity. They saw people fiddling with carburetors all the time, but not gringo motorcyclists. They began by asking all the usual questions about the motorcycle ("a hundred and thirty kilometers an hour . . . eight hundred cubic centimeters . . . German") and then asked if it was true there were jobs in *los Estados Unidos*. They kept telling me how intrepid I was, and the more they said it the more nervous it made me. While I cleaned my hands and put the tool roll away, they talked about how nice it would be to drive a motorcycle across America someday, just to see it, and I nodded, hating these moments. We all knew that they would spend the rest of their lives in these cold mountains. Only a few nations are allowed to dream.

I bent the petcock back to "Auf," checked the green light, and touched the starter button. Clutch in, click down with left toe, throttle up, clutch out, left foot up, right foot up. I gave a final wave to the two cops and then fled higher, the engine once again growling in contentment.

The pass was at 15,400 feet. The road curled up and gently topped a rise, but there was little to be impressed about. The first and most striking sight was another mountain rising right ahead of me, far higher than this one. Some of the peaks in this region topped 20,000 feet. The landscape was lunar and volcanic, a barren plain of rocks and pockets of snow running to the south between lines of yet higher peaks that vanished into the clouds. Two and a half hours and almost three vertical miles of climbing had served only to deliver me to the floor of a new world.

This was the *altiplano*, a word that means nothing but "high plain" yet holds profound connotations in the Peruvian mind. The *altiplano* was an alien world of ancient Incas, llamas, and lost fortresses, of guerrillas and drug traffickers, of inscrutable peasants and isolated lives. The thin wedge of flat soil that opened in front of me would steadily widen as I moved south, the ground pushing back the Andes until, by the time the *altiplano* reached Bolivia, it had become a vast commons framed by distant peaks. In places it was fertile ground, and the great population of the Inca empire had lived here and been fed by the potato and other native miracle crops—corn, sweet potatoes, yams, squash, peanuts, pineapples, tomatoes, and peppers—that the Spaniards would later spread to the rest of the world.

I paused at 15,400 feet, but not long. The wind was howling and icy. A few Peruvians jumped from their cars, ran up a little hill, and placed another stone on top of a cairn marking the pass. "Apparently," Guevara wrote on observing this custom, "Indians deposit all their sorrows in the form of a symbolic stone in Pachamama, or Mother Earth, when they reach the top of a mountain; these gradually accumulate to form a cairn like the one we saw." He noted that the Spanish had tried and failed to wipe out this pagan ritual. I was equally disrespectful in all faiths, and moved on without leaving anything for Pachamama.

The road dropped, but only slightly, and then it began to snow. It had been eighty degrees when I left Lima at breakfast, two and a half hours before. At three degrees per thousand feet, at least forty-five degrees of warmth had fallen behind. Given the way the snow was already sticking to the ground, it was close to freezing here.

The snow was a surprise and a problem, though it shouldn't have been a surprise, since snow was right there in Ernesto's notes on his own first ascent into high Peru:

> The truck continued climbing through a landscape of utter desolation where only a few straggling thorn bushes gave any semblance of life. Then, suddenly, the truck's agonized whine as it trundled its way up hill gave way to a sigh of relief as we leveled out on to the plateau. . . . Ahead of us, low clouds covered the mountain peaks, but through gaps here and there you could see snow falling on the highest mountains, gradually turning them white.

My gloves were one of the things that had fallen by the wayside, a month ago in some desert canteen. I rode on, hopeful that the snow was just a momentary squall, as my fingers turned cold, then icy, and finally to ice. The road was now white and slick, and I was busy cursing that idiot Thoreau when a truck coming the other way around a curve lost control and slid wide, turning sideways as it came toward me. There was plenty of time to consider this event—I was riding slowly as a precaution—but none to act, since a quick turn or hard braking was out of the question on the iced pavement. I remember thinking how ridiculous it would be to end up splashed like a bug across the side of the only perfectly white truck in South America. At the last moment the truck's tires bit again on a patch of clear pavement and the whole vehicle shot past me, dousing me in slush.

I pulled over, but there was no point to it. There was not a single tree to shelter me, nor any building. There wasn't even a rock large enough to sit behind. I stood there for a while, beaten by the snow as it turned slowly to hail and began drumming on the gas tank. It was pointless to stay, so I went on again, and gradually the road descended and the air warmed and the hail turned back to rain and then stopped and the sun uncoiled its rays and touched the floor of the long valley. There was corn as far as the eye could see, and the road dried to black and I picked up speed. I passed a farm cooperative whose tall front gate was emblazoned with a slogan:

> AMA SUA
> AMA LLULLA
> AMA CHECKLA

This was the law of the Incas, the moral code they had exported up and down the Andes during their five hundred years of conquest. It was virtually their entire legal structure, and all it said was "DO NOT STEAL; DO NOT LIE; DO NOT BE LAZY."

With these three rules the Incas had become the Romans of South America. Like the Romans, they were predominantly interested in power and had a strong pragmatic streak. The wealth of the empire was its people, who belonged to the Inca (as the supreme ruler was known) himself. The various tribes of the Andes were subdued and then integrated into an utterly authoritarian system of communal property and group identity. Princes of a defeated people were sometimes taken to Cuzco, the capital and "navel of the world," to serve as hostages and be coopted by Quechua culture. They built a network of roads from Colombia to Chile and from the Pacific coast to the Amazon jungle (an area equivalent to Italy, Switzerland, France, Belgium, and Holland combined); they developed practical engineering and abstract mathematics; they built fortresses and temples; and they created a vast network of storehouses for surplus weapons, clothing, and food. Although they lacked writing and found no use for the wheel, their roads and irrigation systems were proof of their sophisticated civilization, especially given that they had to overcome the most seismically active region in the world. Built to standardized widths, with regulated post houses along the routes and engineered bridges and supports where necessary, the 12,000-mile road network was the basis of their empire and connected the four quarters of the known world to the imperial seat. The roads sped messengers across their realm so quickly that the Inca Atahuallpa, ruler of the north, could eat fish fresh from the ocean. When strange, pale-faced men with beards landed on his coast in 1532, Atahuallpa learned of it almost immediately.

The strange men were a tiny band of impoverished noblemen and mercenary adventurers led by an illegitimate swineherd named Francisco Pizarro. The Spaniards encountered an empire of great wealth, but one also divided and weakened by a recent civil war between half brothers who each aspired to the throne. The runners told Atahuallpa, who was winning this civil war from a base in the north, that the odd foreigners carried magic "fire sticks" that could kill a man from a great distance, but the invaders were so small in number—just 179 men—that Atahuallpa felt they could not possibly threaten his kingdom of millions. Eager for allies in war against his half brother's army in the south, and perhaps hoping that Pizarro was the god Viracocha predicted in Inca legends, Atahuallpa agreed to meet the newcomers. Pizarro and his men approached on foot, feigning fear, and then ripped the ruler of the known world from his bier. In the hands of 179 men, Toledo steel, gunpowder, and horses were more than enough to overcome thousands of Inca soldiers who had left their spears and war clubs behind as a gesture of peace. In a moment, the supreme ruler was a hostage and the Spanish seed had been planted in the Andes. The catalog of cruelties and injustices and plunderings, of battles, murders, feuds, reprisals, betrayals, and rapes that flowed from this conquest was so extensive it defeated even a lifelong chronicler like the itinerant Guamán Poma. The results of this forced marriage of cultures—Andean and Iberian, polytheistic and Christian, static and dynamic—were all around me, the aftershocks still rippling through the mountains like a buried temblor.

It was Ernesto, of course, who conceived a plan right here in these mountains for putting an end, once and for all, to the world that had been born that day in 1532. But I had not yet come to that chapter in his diary. There were still a few hills between me and his revelation.

The day ran out before the pavement did. I reached Huancayo not by lunch but well after nightfall, some eight hours behind schedule and only halfway to Ayacucho. The town was dark but lively, the streets full of people buying and selling beneath unlit street lamps. The crowds were a sign that the guerrillas were weak or entirely absent from the zone now. I found a room in a cheap guest house and pushed the motorbike through the front door and into the interior courtyard. Although I'd been reluctant to do this at first, South American hotel keepers considered it the most normal thing in the world. They often insisted that I store the bike at night in the lobby, or the courtyard, or even my bedroom if it would fit, which it usually wouldn't. Certainly nothing as valuable as a motorcycle—"And what a motorcycle, *Señor*, we have never seen anything like it!"—should be left on the street.

Over dinner I read in the local paper that thirty terrorists had been transferred yesterday to the prison here in Huancayo. They were a mix of Senderistas and members of MRTA, twenty-seven men and three women. Their trials would be in a secret military court where the judges wore wool ski masks to conceal their identities. I had a brief heart attack when I saw a headline on a back page of the newspaper, TOMB OF FIGHTER DISCOVERED, but it turned out to be a seventeen-hundred-year-old tomb, containing the mummy of a warrior from the Moche culture of northern Peru.

I slept lightly in the thin mountain air, and when I woke up

Kooky was waiting loyally in the courtyard just outside my door. I stared for a while at the bike, wondering how far we could go. I was turning south now, away from home. There was always the temptation of the road north, of the long trip through Central America and Texas and then the speedy highways of the East Coast. Guevara and Granado had gone north after they were done with Peru; nearing the end of the trip, Che was so exhausted that he wrote only a few pages of notes on their final two weeks in South America as the pair flew from a small Amazonian town to Colombia and then ventured into Venezuela. Granado found a job at a hospital there; they said goodbye, and Che flew home on a plane belonging to someone he knew in Argentina. One of the oddest details of this trip was not even mentioned in the diaries. The plane developed engine trouble during a stopover in Miami; instead of a few hours, the young Guevara was forced to spend a month in Florida, living on credit at a cheap hotel owned by an Argentine. There wasn't a single entry about this part of his trip; he'd recorded no impressions of the country that would come to dominate his thinking. It was a lost episode—and a tantalizing mystery. According to friends, he'd spent the time going to the beach. What else had Guevara seen and done for a month? Did he go to the track, or flirt with girls, or consider the implications of the American way of life? Did he hate the swampy heat and the low-slung architecture of pre-Cuban Miami? He'd said at the start of the trip that he was heading for North America, but having reached his goal he was silent. Whatever had happened to him during that last month was lost, and deliberately. When the plane was repaired he flew home to Argentina and the future course he had mapped in South America. It was as if the United States did not—could not— exist in any actual state for him. America was a state of mind.

In the early morning in Huancayo I missed all the things he might have hated about us—the wide highways lined with doughnut shops, the fat cars, the endless entertainment, the unspectacular, unheroic, grandly petty life of prosperity and wraparound comfort. Life on the road was spare and beautiful, full of clarity and delight, but when I roused myself at dawn in Huancayo I could not help but consider the last chance I would have to turn away from all this. I inserted the key in the dashboard and turned it to the right. The green light glowed, and I tried not to think too much as I headed south toward Ayacucho.

A police officer flagged me down on the outskirts of town and explained that for reasons of national security I had to give him a lift. He had a gun and a badge, so I lowered the rear foot pegs and let him climb on board. We rode south, and the pavement ended abruptly after a mile. It was all dirt from there on. The bike felt heavy with a passenger, and we bounced up and down on the dusty track that my map called the Pan-American Highway. After a while we came to the police barracks, a one-story house. The cop got down and stood there in his baggy, worn-out uniform, watching me drive away.

Ayacucho was about a hundred miles southeast of me, the same distance I had planned to cover yesterday afternoon. The country here was dry and fairly flat, but as the morning wore on the road grew twistier and the valleys tighter. The traffic declined to a few short trucks per hour, with the occasional microbus loaded with peasants. There were no villages for a long time, but you could tell there were people about because of the neatly cultivated plots of potatoes on the hillsides. The climate changed every few miles, dry and hot in one valley, foggy in the next, then dry, then rain. If I killed the engine and listened carefully I could hear goats and sheep up higher somewhere, and once I passed a dead horse rotting on the roadside and later a single, live llama chewing a mouthful of grass with dromedarian dignity. The herders of these animals were startled children of seven or nine years standing barefoot in the potato fields, their heads wrapped in pointed wool caps and their eyes fixed on the motorcycle as it passed.

The Andes are young mountains and have not had time to melt into the gentle valleys and smooth slopes that made my beloved Blue Ridge of Virginia seem so welcoming. The heavens worked on the Andes as fast as they could, however, and now the river on the valley floor was wild and red with earth. The narrow plain around it was heavily cultivated.

I was nearly run off the road by a truck whose bumper declared, in florid colors, YOU CAN LOOK BUT YOU CAN'T TOUCH.

I was trying to make good time and raced through a series of villages, but I skidded to a stop in one called Acostambo. My map showed the road going to the right when clearly it went to the left. I forged out of town to investigate and immediately came up behind a patrol of Peruvian soldiers dressed in black uniforms of a type I had never seen before. These were not the same ill-equipped, half-trained troops I had seen in Lima. The patrol was spread out in two columns on each side of the road, with enough space between the men to keep casualties down in an ambush. Each man carried a shiny automatic rifle. The young lieutenant was leading sensibly from the rear. He ran a cold eye over my papers.

"We're looking for a few bandits," he said.

"Where?"

"Just up ahead."

I turned around and rode back into the village. The people wore a mixture of traditional and Western clothes, and many were barefoot. At the general store, I bought some gasoline, which was measured out in an old coffee cup and poured sloppily over my bike by a girl of about twelve. The engine was very hot, and when the gas ran down the outside of the tank and dripped onto the cylinders I expected an explosion, but nothing happened, just like the previous forty or fifty times I'd spilled gasoline onto the hot engine. I took over from the twelve-year-old and finished spooning the gas myself, and once Kooky was fed I ate a lunch of soup in a canteen buzzing with flies. I was stalling.

The town mechanic came around to look at the motorbike, and then another group of soldiers in the odd black uniforms pulled up in a jeep. They were young and enthusiastic and wanted to know all about the bike and where I'd been and where I was going. They told me not to worry about the *bandidos*, who hadn't killed anyone in over a week. The last incident had been on the high road, and all I had to do was stick to the low road. Their sergeant examined my map with growing curiosity—"This is all wrong," he said—and then took a piece of paper from the canteen and drew me a beautiful map of where the road really went. The high road, which ran at thirteen thousand feet, was sometimes preferable, he said, because it was drier, but last week a bus driver had been pulled off his vehicle and shot. It was probably just robbery, he explained, not guerrillas, although the two ways of life were so intermingled now—as the final, desperate columns of Shining Path robbed to stay alive and the robbers pretended to be guerrillas to deflect blame—that who could tell anyway. The important thing was to stay off the high road.

But there was a problem with the low road, too. First of all, it wasn't on the west side of the Mantaro River, as my map claimed, but on the east. Second of all, it wasn't a road anymore because a big section had washed out two days ago. He filled in the names of the little towns along the low road with the lovely, illegible handwriting of an architect. Next to the town of Izcsomethingorother he wrote "BRIDGE." He didn't know exactly where the landslide was, but it was probably before Ancon or Anro or Acpau or whatever he'd written. None of these places was mentioned on the map, of course—although it was the most recent version available, the mapmakers had somehow not managed to locate these four- and six-hundred-year-old villages. My guidebook offered helpfully that "the military seem to have established control over this route after years of terrorist disruption."

I folded the sergeant's little handmade map into a square and carried it in my breast pocket as I set out again from town. It seemed like too sunny a day for anything to go wrong.

At least thirty thousand people had died during the most recent of Peru's bloody guerrilla wars, although the statistics were only guesses. It was a toss-up as to who had done the majority of the killing. The only thing that was clear was that the dead were rarely soldiers for either side. A guerrilla group was, like an official army, supposed to distinguish between combatants and civilians. Shining Path ignored this distinction and relied on terror tactics that lumped government soldiers and civilians together. The group's indiscriminant cruelty would have been a weakness, except that the Peruvian army had responded to Shining Path with a perfect illustration of how not to run a counterinsurgency campaign. To begin with, the army was profoundly corrupt. Peru produces the majority of the world's coca, the leafy plant that is typically refined into a paste and then shipped elsewhere for final processing into cocaine. The lucrative drug trade and the war in the highlands were intertwined at every level. Army privates receiving ten dollars a month in pay and twenty cents a day in ration allowance (enough to buy a bun) turned a blind eye when traffickers paid with loose change from the roughly billion dollars a year their business brought into Peru. Generals who were paid three hundred dollars a month lived in lush houses and kept foreign bank accounts. President Fujimori's top adviser, a shadowy former army captain named Vladímir Montesinos, managed to have close relations with the CIA, the Cubans, the big cocaine traffickers, and the army leadership all at once. The Shining Path and MRTA were also mixed up in the drug trade, extracting "taxes" per kilo of coca paste that moved through areas under their control. The army spent most of its time sitting in barracks, not out on patrol. Skirmishes between government soldiers and the guerrillas were sometimes just turf fights over particularly lucrative franchises like the landing strip at Tingo María.

When the fighting did get serious, it was not a good idea to be caught in the middle. Shining Path guerrillas typically entered a highland village in this region at night, chasing out any feeble police or "civil defense patrols" who tried to resist (the latter were just local farmers press-ganged by the army and given rifles and one day of training). They would hold a meeting in the schoolhouse or plaza, instructing people about the two antagonistic paths, and then they would slit the throats of the mayor, his assistant, any priests they could catch, and the local teacher if the village was lucky enough to have one. They would even kill the old fellow who held the keys to the cemetery, because he was obviously a collaborator with the imperialists. The Shining Path would also sometimes massacre an entire village or order children to kill their parents. Blood was the fertilizer of their revolution. Maoists also believe in deepening the contradictions.

After they left, the army would come in and do much the same. Often they would begin with random strafing from a helicopter, followed by daylight infantry sweeps that made no distinction between civilians and enemies. In 1988 the army retaliated for a Shining Path ambush by raiding the town of Cayara, in Ayacucho Department, killing or disappearing thirty-two civilians who appeared to be chosen at random. Peasants consequently deserted the highlands for the shanties of Lima—many villages had lost 50 percent of their populations during the war. The United States fed this cauldron with financial aid, helicopters, light attack aircraft, rifles, uniforms, mortars, and training for the Peruvian army. The CIA began training Peru's counterintelligence apparatus, too. The war was spiraling beyond control. In 1982 there were five provinces under emergency rule; in 1991 there were eighty-seven. The Shining Path began moving company-size units of troops through the countryside, men equipped with machine guns and rocket grenades. The movement released statements saying that it supported "polarization" and "clarification" of the situation in Peru, which was understood to mean there was going to be another Final Offensive.

In April 1992 President Fujimori responded by throwing what the Peruvians called an *autogolpe*, or a "self-coup," tossing his own administration out of power. Soldiers took over the streets of Lima; the parliament was disbanded; opposition politicians were jailed, the press muzzled; the judiciary was purged of perceived enemies; death squads began to appear. The Shining Path and the government started sounding the same in the early 1990s: both were against "fictitious forms of democracy" and felt threatened by what was called the "popular sector," or anybody who got organized for themselves. The prisons in Lima exploded in violence; more than fifty Senderistas were massacred after an escape attempt at Canto Grande, while another forty mysteriously disappeared from the jail, either dead or free. Two policemen died retaking the Shining Path cell blocks. Almost the entire leadership within B-4 and A-1 was killed.

But poor Peruvians, it turned out, welcomed Fujimori's dictatorial streak. His popularity skyrocketed after the self-coup, and he easily won an unfair election to another term. He rode around the country opening water taps in slums and handing out tractors. His new nickname, which he adored, was "Chinochet," the Asian Pinochet. He promised an aggressive fight against the guerrillas and Asian-style free-market authoritarianism. Using wiretaps and careful stakeouts, the counterintelligence men trained by the CIA began rolling up the MRTA and the Shining Path leadership in Lima. The army wiped out MRTA first, and now the Shining Path was taking it on the chin. From a peak of twenty-five thousand fighters in the late '80s the group was now down to a few thousand by the mid-'90s, mostly in remote provinces or the shantytowns of Lima. Even President Gonzalo had been busted since my earlier prison visit, and he now rotted in a special island jail off the coast of Lima. The truth was that the whole upper zone of the Andes was getting safer every month. It had been several years since a foreigner had been killed up here. Peruvians traveled this route all the time—already today I'd nearly been run off the road by several buses and half a dozen trucks carrying people on top of their cargoes. The towns looked bustling. The mechanic had told me he was getting rich fixing flat tires.

I caught the patrol a mile down the road and they waved, perhaps relieved that I was clearing their way but also fairly relaxed despite their arms. I suppose it was better that these soldiers in black were winning their war than losing it, but I wouldn't want to be between them and the guerrillas. I'd been thinking about what the madman in the desert had said about Chile—that there were only two categories of people there, the innocent and the living. Here in the Red Zone, even the dead were judged retroactively guilty.

Wherever the road cut into a hillside—which was almost every-where—there was erosion. The worst spots were the inside bends where the road undulated with the ridges. Streams gathered natu-rally at the bends, and if there was a drainage ditch or a culvert under the road it was almost always inadequate, but there was rarely either of those. The little streams simply ran down onto the road, across it, and then down the mountain again. They took much of the road with them as they went. Time and again I had to push through a deep mud that had been ground up by the trucks roaring up and down the route. There was only one dirt lane to begin with, and the erosion often cut it to a half lane with a steep drop on one side. The trucks would come barging down a mountain and wheel around the blind outside curves at ludicrous speeds. The curves were so sharp that only short-bed trucks could even fit around them—there were no eighteen-wheelers here—and as I followed one along I watched it repeatedly scrape against the hillsides. The rule of the road here was that might made right, and the trucks did not yield to anyone. This left me at the absolute bottom of the pecking order, where even bus drivers felt free to wing around an oncoming curve, pushing me to the extreme outside edge, where I could watch a shower of rocks slide down a steep hillside into the dusty valley scattered with cactus plants.

At mid-morning I passed through a narrow gorge where the river was spanned by an extraordinary stone bridge, just as the sergeant's map said ("Izcuchaca" turned out to be what he had written, which is Quechua for "stone bridge"). Built by the Incas and rebuilt by the Spanish in the eighteenth century, the bridge still arched over the water, but traffic now flowed on an ugly steel structure laid alongside it. I paused for a while to watch the river and admire the bridge. Some old men in fedoras wandered over and looked at the bike and asked if I had ever been to Lima. After they left a bus driver waiting for passen-gers scoffed at their ignorance and turned to me for sympathy. I rode away immediately.

The truckers and bus drivers were a special class of people in Peruvian society. They always carried more passengers than they were allowed, and they decorated their vehicles on the inside with pictures of naked women and the Madonna. On the outside they covered everything in bright colors and slogans (LOVE IS BLIND or HERE I COME GIRLS or GOD PROTECTS ME). Since these vehicles were usually the only communication with remote towns in the mountains, the drivers held positions of great prestige. Among the poor peasants, they seemed like astronauts. Nobody at NASA ever got drunk on the way to the moon, however, and it was a plain fact that many professional drivers did drink. Liquor was not considered an impediment to their work—in fact, it was a sign of your machismo and skill to navigate the road after a good bout with the bottle. Between the bad roads; the overloaded, undermaintained vehicles; and the custom of drinking on the job, the accident rate was tremendous. Peasants crossed themselves with gratitude when they debarked successfully.

Guevara had his own startling encounter with this phenomenon. Hitching through the mountains he discovered that the driver of the truck in whose cab he and Granado were riding was not drunk, as they routinely assumed, but legally *blind*. The man had suffered an accident that hurt his eyes; as long as he kept driving the same route that he knew, he could remember where the turns were. As he failed to see and then struck one object after another in the middle of the road, the two Argentines protested that this was insanely dangerous for both the driver and his passengers, but the man replied that it was the only job he could get, that he was paid well, and that he had invested too large a bribe in his driving license to give it up now.

One after another I forded seven rivers that day. The Peruvians called them rivers, but they were really creeks, shallow but sometimes hundreds of yards across. The water was silty and difficult to read. A few times I watched others cross—a truck smashing confidently toward me or a pair of Peruvian peasants wading barefoot—and at other points I simply barged in. The bike slipped and slid and nearly dumped me, and the hot engine yelped and threw off clouds of rusty steam when it was dunked in the deeper parts. My boots filled with water twice, but it was a beautiful day.

Whenever I could I asked about the landslide, and I was told that the road was completely blocked, that it was open again, that it was buried by rocks, that it was washed away by rain, that it would be reopened in a week or a day, that a person could get across on foot, that a motorcycle could get across, that it had been cut for two days or three, that it would be easy to bypass or impossible. At another police checkpoint an officer patted the bike's gas tank and asked, in broken Spanish, "Many fast is?" He ordered me to go back and take the high road, and I said yes, and then when he wasn't looking I continued on the low road.

The seventh ford was narrow but muddy, hiding its depth and bottom. I dismounted. To the left, across a thousand yards of muddy flat, a pair of mountain flanks squeezed close together with only enough room left for the stream. The muddy water swirled out of this gap, braided down through the mudflats, and came together again just in time to hit the road at its weakest point, the elbow of a deep bend. The road was being eaten away as I watched. The downstream end of the ford was a waterfall dropping several feet down to the eroding hillside. Someone had attempted to contain the damage with a dose of cement ten feet wide, but this infrastructure was no more than a gesture by now. The water gushed over the broken paving, carved under it, and simply melted it away. In a month there would be nothing left of this section. The mountains always won their struggle with the roads.

A sagging hut with balding thatch stood by the spot, as if guarding the crossing. Four other low adobe buildings were scattered within sight, all of them in various stages of wattled collapse. A cargo truck covered with tarpaulins sat by the hut, and behind the truck were a pair of brightly colored bicycles with panniers. The Peruvian trucker and two young Austrians were inside the hut, eating soup.

One of the bicyclists was too bowel-sick to talk, and lay in his sleeping bag moaning. The other was named Franz. His legs poked like tree trunks from padded Spandex shorts and he had a bad sunburn. Franz talked plainly, with the resigned tone of a man sentenced to labor he could not escape. A few days before, he had dallied in a mountain town while having a "romance" with a Peruvian woman. This had put the Austrians behind schedule and exposed Franz to dangerous levels of pleasure. Now he had hundreds of miles of cruel road to pedal in a hurry, and he resented it. Later, when the road had beaten the last reserves of generosity out of me, and I grew angry and sullen with the mountains, then I would feel more sympathy for Franz. But at the moment I thought he was ungrateful for the rare place we inhabited.

Franz and his buddy were heading for Lima. He asked about the road north, and I asked about the road south. I described the 15,400-foot pass and the glorious downhill ride into Lima awaiting him. He described the cut in the road a mile ahead. As usual, the road had given out at its weakest point, a steep cliff face. Rains had weakened the rocky soil, and a broad section had simply slid down the mountain. Although vehicles could not pass, some people were walking across the loose scree left behind by the collapse. The Austrians had carried their bikes over that way this morning, stepping gingerly in their biking slippers while trying not to look a thousand feet down into the valley floor. Franz said the road would be fixed tomorrow.

The trucker had been watching our conversation and now asked for a translation. He insisted it would be two days until the road was open. He was a skinny man of Andean origins, but dressed in the unremarkable uniform of the "civilized" Peruvian male—machine-made wool sweater, slacks, and thin black loafers that he shined ostentatiously from time to time with a small cloth from his breast pocket. It was dark and eerie in the hut with dusk falling. The ill Austrian lay in his doss bag, immobile, while three Indian women tended the fire that warmed the soup. They sold us the soup for pennies a bowl and peered in shock at our faces, our strange way of talking, and the bright Spandex uniforms of the Austrians. The trucker didn't want to admit it at first but he spoke a little Quechua and brokered the soup purchases. He came this way every week, he said, carrying beer to Ayacucho. The trip was always delayed by something, he said: weather, police operations, road problems, mechanical breakdown, illness, accidents, what have you. He looked at my map with the road on the wrong side of the river and said that was why he didn't use maps.

Franz and the trucker disagreed on the speed of repairs but were in accord on the scene at the cut. Twenty trucks and as many buses were waiting there, as well as private cars. The repair crews were working at a snail's pace while the drivers got drunk and howled over campfires. A steady stream of bus passengers on foot picked their way across the cliff face, hoping to find a lift among the vehicles on the far side. Stuck on the mountain face, people were pissing by the side of the road, cooking meals, fighting, and generally displaying the full splendor of human spirit. I decided to spend the night right here at the ford, rather than move up to the cut. The Austrians were relieved. This was bandit country, and their guidebook probably gave the same useless advice as mine: "Travel by day," "Do not display your wealth or eat in public," and "It is still not very safe to travel this route." We were zero for three.

Three women clucked outside the hut, staring at the fortunes embodied in our two-wheeled vehicles. I went out and they addressed me in Quechua with great gales of laugher. They did not speak Spanish—not even a word, it seemed. Their dress was as traditional as I had seen yet. From their jaunty bowler hats through their homespun sweaters and skirts to their seven layers of petticoats they were straight from an ancient time. They rubbed their bellies and pleaded in sounds that bounced off my eardrums. I gave them a bag of rice, which pleased them so much they asked for my watch and, when that didn't work, some money. They were very happy with the rice, however, and scampered up the road chatting and waving polite good-byes.

The tropics are mercilessly consistent in the measure of days and nights. It grew equatorially dark by 6:30, and there was, of course, no electricity here. On foot I splashed through the ford, wandered a hundred yards up the road, and found the three women in another collapsed hut, sharing the rice I had given them with a half-dozen filthy, shoeless children and an old man. One of the youngest children spoke a little Spanish: in baby talk, I learned that they came from a village that was "a day" up the creek. They had walked out of that narrow cut between hills and had been waiting three days now with no food, hoping for a lift to a place whose name I didn't recognize.

Ernesto wrote with plain delight of seeing the descendants of the Incas: "We were in an enchanted valley where time had stopped several centuries ago, and which we lucky mortals, until then stuck in the twentieth century, had been given the good fortune to see." Watching this clan gather around the fire and eat my rice, I was overwhelmed with a similar joy, but also despair. They were the most pure example of untrammeled indigenous life I had ever seen, but this essentially meant they were extremely poor: Their clothes were homemade, their feet bare, and they owned none of the necessities of life as I knew it. My wristwatch was to them a sign of enormous wealth. Yet for all their muddy deprivation, they were living lives determined by their own culture and history. They had none of the deadly anomie that plagued the shantytowns of Lima, or the psychotic alienation that fed the Shining Path. These were people living in their own time, speaking their own language, not yet ripped from the womb of their own world. For them, the stars still marched in order through the cosmos.

They fed me spoonfuls of plain boiled rice and stared at me with an artless gaze that quickly grew unbearable. I was used to doing the staring, and travel unwrapped an endless vista for me to appreciate. My all-consuming curiosity was a luxurious First World habit—the rudeness of a people used to evaluating everything with a distancing eye. Now the tables had turned; the traveler become the travel. This was fair, but it also grew old quickly, and I returned across the ford, where Franz and I decided to go to sleep on top of the truck. The driver agreed this was a good idea—we would be safer there if someone came during the night, he said, and none of us wanted to discuss who that might be. The sick Austrian did not want to move. I told him in the goriest possible detail about the *vinchuca* beetles that live in thatched roofs; how they crawl down at night and bite you, infecting you with Chagas disease, which eats away at the walls of your heart for years without any symptoms, until one day you drop dead while eating a pastry in Vienna. He rolled over and went to sleep. The driver locked himself in his cab and went to sleep, too. Franz and I scaled the side of the truck with our most valuable possessions and sleeping bags.

The canvas on top was stretched tight as a cot. Beneath us were 1,200 cases of pilsner. We settled down and said good-night like an old married couple. Slowly, under the pressure of our combined weight, the canvas began to stretch. Every few minutes I noticed that I had sunk lower. Eventually I was touching the beer; after a bit longer I was lying on a bed of beer caps. At twelve bottles a case that made 14,400 bottles, not one of them soft enough to sleep on. Franz had an air mattress and by 7:40 was snoring away. I lay awake on this bed of metal dimples and imagined Shining Path guerrillas sneaking into the settlement, intent on stealing Kooky. In my fantasies I routed the Western Hemisphere's most fanatical guerrilla force with a rain of beer bottles. The stars were spectacular. I sang under my breath:

> *Fourteen thousand four hundred bottles of beer on the*
> *   wall*
> *fourteen thousand four hundred bottles of beer,*
> *you take one down, pass it around,*
> *fourteen thousand three hundred and ninety-nine bottles*
> *   of beer on the wall.*
>
> *Fourteen thousand three hundred and ninety-nine bottles*
> *   of beer on the wall . . .*

I woke up at 5:45 with rain on my face. My back was buttoned with the indentations of beer caps. I looked around. It was still dark, but I was glad to be awake because I saw through the rain that I was now in Washington, D.C. I woke Franz up and explained where we were. He climbed down to the cab with me and I drove the beer truck down Massachusetts Avenue (we were about half a mile below the traffic circle where Letelier, the Chilean exile, was blown up), clattering the

stick shift while looking for an all-night coffee shop. That's the problem with Washington: no all-night coffee shops.

Somehow, despite the windshield, rain was blowing onto my face
as I drove around pointing out Congress and various monuments to
Franz. I turned on the wipers, but the rain kept coming. I had to
reach up and wipe the rain off my face. . . .

I woke up rubbing my face. It was still 5:45, it was still dark, and
it was still Peru. It was raining on my face—real rain, not dream rain.
I climbed down without waking Franz and went to boil some water.
In the lifting gray I set up my little camping stove on the bank of the
stream above the ford, where it braided in rivulets. I laid out my
instant coffee, my red plastic cup, my spoon, and my cigarette lighter.
The water boiled but was not hot, so I kept cooking it. Franz soon
joined me, rubbing sleep from his eyes, and laid out his cup, his
spoon, and his instant coffee.

"Do you got any sugar?" he asked. I did, and traded a little sugar
for a little of his powdered milk, a wary exchange by two men who
measured their remaining supplies in grams. I hadn't had milk powder in my coffee in ages, and the smell threw me back in a reverie to a
time ten years before when I had traveled over China by train. There
are no dairy products in the Chinese larder, and after a couple of
months of doing without I bought three packets of Nestlé powdered
milk in a tourist store and began mixing cups in any samovar I could
find. Late in the trip I'd spent a night high on the Tibetan plateau
with a clan of horse nomads on a pilgrimage. They served me yak
butter tea and I made them powdered cow milk. They shared many
of the physical features and even habits of dress and hairstyles with
the Peruvian Indian, who was a first cousin. They too lived in a world
whose cosmos spun overhead as it always had.

The same three women I'd fed with rice last night appeared
again and squatted down on the opposite bank of the stream, which
was very narrow here. It was light now. They talked among themselves, pointing shyly at the various devices: there were no words in
Quechua for powdered milk, for butane/propane fuel canisters, or
for gorp, which Franz issued in a precious dribble from a plastic bag

that he did not want me to get my hands on. While we stirred and sipped the women watched intently.

After my own dose of caffeine it was time to be ambassadorial, and I stirred up a fresh serving in the red plastic cup. I reached halfway across the stream and gestured toward the women. The boldest reached tenderly across to meet me, took the cup, emptied the coffee onto the ground, and put the cup in her pocket.

After some gentle prying I was able to get the cup back and, using sign language, explain that I meant for her to have the coffee in the cup, not the cup itself. Not only was she distraught at losing the cup—everyone had seen it, I had handed it right to her!—but she was also terrified of coffee, and reeled back when I approached with a second cup. Eventually I persuaded one of the other women to try it; she took a sip and spit it out on the ground with disgust.

I turned down their offer to buy my camp stove, which convinced them only that I was a tough negotiator. They came back twice in the next half hour with higher and higher offers, eventually totaling three dollars. I resisted.

All this time the women had spoken only Quechua, and in their attempts to buy my cookstove they had taught me the word for *pot* (*manco*). At the end, when I was packing up to leave, the youngest woman suddenly spoke in halting Spanish, with an accent so thick she sounded Russian.

"There are . . . beautiful things . . . in your country," she said.

I wished Franz luck, smashed through the ford, and drove up to the washout. It was much bigger than I had expected, some three hundred feet across. The last mile of road ascending to the cut was lined with the same colorful trucks and buses that had nearly killed me over the last two days. The passengers waited by the vehicles, but the drivers had all gone up to see the action.

The road passed across a cliff face here, or at least it had. When the rains came a huge chunk of road had slid down into the river. It was a spectacular spot, the drama spiced by the rusted hulk of a bus resting on the valley floor below. It was an old wreck; you take what consolation you can. I pulled right to the head of the queue, dismounted, and noticed the little goat path across the gap that Franz and his partner had transited while carrying their bicycles. The slope was made entirely of round, loose rocks, angling down at about forty degrees. They were brave men.

There was a mass outbreak of stupidity under way. Immediately on my arrival all the truck drivers began whooping and shouting for me to ride straight across the gap. They had seen too many episodes of *Knight Rider* and were gravely disappointed that the supergringo would not leap with snarling engine through the air. The repair crew also consisted of morons. Their method for fixing a washed-out road was simple and totally ineffective. First, they got three Caterpillar D-9 bulldozers, then parked two of them on the road and had the drivers fall asleep in their seats, mouths open to the heavens. The third Cat then began shoveling rocks and dirt into the gap, where they promptly slid down a thousand feet and made a nice addition to the pile already at the bottom.

They had tried this all day yesterday and advanced about ten feet. They went at it for a few more hours while I took a nap and then adjusted my monoshock under the tutelage of every truck driver in the camp, none of whom had ever seen an adjustable shock absorber before. The more everyone prattled—How fast? That's not fast! Put the wrench on the other way!—the angrier I got, and the angrier I got the more they seemed to close in around me, until I literally did not have enough room to work. I threw a fit, which convinced them all that I was crazy and increased the respect in their voices.

To keep them away I climbed up on a boulder with Ernesto's diary and began reading. I had only intended to escape the drivers, but after a moment I found a passage on this section of Guevara's itinerary. As he and Granado hitched up this road they too found it blocked:

> *. . . we were told there was a landslide up ahead and we would*
> *have to spend the night in a village called Anco . . . we reached*
> *the landslide and had to spend the day there, famished yet curi-*
> *ous, watching the workmen dynamite the huge boulders which*
> *had fallen across the road. For every laborer there were at least*
> *five officious foremen, shouting their mouths off and hindering*
> *the others, who were not exactly a hive of industry either.*

According to the sergeant's neat map, Anco was the very next village up the road. My head reeled for a moment with a bad case of timeslip, the grinding of the Caterpillar merging into the dynamiting that Ernesto described. Yet the coincidence that both of us would be stopped forty-four years apart on the same spot by the same problem was really no coincidence. The road was *always* falling apart here, right in the same narrow valley where the road could do nothing but clamber up the mountain faces. Anco had hosted this scene then, now, and every year in between. For travelers as for guerrillas, topography was destiny.

Around ten o'clock the machine operator finally changed his tactic and, instead of trying to fill a bottomless pit with rocks, began carving a new road out of the rock face above the cut. This was dangerous work, since debris tended to tumble down onto the tractor, but it was effective in the soft rock, and after half an hour he had almost finished the repair. The waiting drivers now reached pre-orgasmic heights of excitement. The whole time, as the Cat tottered on the precipice, flung itself back and forth, and churned up great billows of white powder, its every movement was shadowed by a cloud of thirty men who walked behind and alongside the thrashing, spinning treads of the machine. Every few seconds these men were on the point of being run over; they yelped and ran back, or dove to the side, or staggered about choking on dust. Yet each time they would close in again like a batch of buzzing insects. I sat there praying that the Cat would finally flatten one of them, leaving a pulpy smear as a lesson to the rest, or that the entire road would give way, sending the whole flock of bastards spinning down into the gorge, but that wouldn't be fair to the Cat driver and it didn't happen.

With each shove the Cat scraped its way toward the far side of the gap, and at a few minutes before 11:00 A.M. a path the width of a motorcycle was open. There was still a Caterpillar tractor grinding back and forth in front of it, but every truck driver in the valley began shouting with a kind of fever. They wanted me to floor it up the slope, swerve around the tractor, dodge its consuming blade, and fly over the narrow, loose track. I declined to slake their boredom this way, raising a kind of murderous resentment in their eyes. All the gringos on TV drove the way a Peruvian wanted to; I had to be some sort of coward to not fly across on my immense motorcycle. They shook their heads in disgust.

Finally, at precisely 11:01, the Cat backed up, the driver turned and waved at me, and I was given the dubious honor of proofing the repair. A chorus of truck horns erupted behind me. The road was only sixty seconds old, but as far as the drivers were concerned that was fifty-nine seconds too many.

"Vaya, gringo!" several voices yelled, and I went over.

CHAPTER TEN

HOLY WEEK

Ayacucho sat in a bowl surrounded by round hills, at the epicenter of the Peruvian tragedy. It was a startlingly beautiful city filled with stone churches from the earliest days of the Conquest, a syncretic gem that married high Catholicity with the final vibrant traces of Andean greatness. In the 1980s it was a charnel house, repeatedly seized and sacked by the Shining Path and the Peruvian army in exchanges of dynamite and lead. Ayacucho was where the Shining Path had come closest to achieving the dream of cell block B-4. Although there were remote villages that had been under Shining Path control for long blocks of time, Ayacucho was the heart of their rebellion for the simple reason that their leader, President Gonzalo, got his start here.

His real name was Abimael Guzmán, and he had come to Ayacucho in 1962 to teach Kantian philosophy at a new university set up to train rural people. The defining moment in his life was a long study trip to China in the 1960s while Chairman Mao's Cultural Revolution was in full swing. He was enraptured by this chaotic "revolution within the revolution" and returned to Peru in slow percolation. After years of preparation, his war began in 1980, on election day, here in Ayacucho Department. A group of peasant cadres descended on a rural town called Chuschi, burned the ballot box, gave an incomprehensible speech, and went away. The attack was noted in passing in Lima newspapers as another strange occurrence in the distant mountains. The next day they attacked in the city of Ayacucho itself; a month after that they launched four simultaneous attacks in the city.

Drawing on a mix of Marxist university students and desperate, disoriented peasants, Guzmán built a secretive guerrilla movement that spread with each year of the 1980s. Ayacucho Department as a whole was the Shining Path's main base, while the city itself was under only tenuous military control well into the 1990s. Twice the guerrillas had seized the town square and hoisted their red flag before being pried out again by the army's superior firepower. There was no clear way to deduce where the loyalty of the Ayacuchans really lay. Almost the entire population of Ayacucho had once turned out for the funeral of a top guerrilla, and many young Ayacucho men enlisted in the guerrilla ranks. Yet the guerrillas often forced such gestures of loyalty by assassinating their opponents and blowing up the houses or stores of businessmen who resisted. As usual, the ordinary people were forced by both sides to choose sides, and were thus both complicit and innocent by the mutually exclusive definitions of the guerrillas and the military. The only certainty was that the country bled and Ayacucho was its open wound. At night the guerrillas would light bonfires on the hills above the city, the flames tracing the shape of the hammer and sickle for all to see.

I took a cheap room in the late afternoon and parked the motorbike in the lobby where other guests could stare at it to their hearts' content. A shower, barely warmed by an electric coil wired to the spigot, awoke me to civilization just as it began to grow dark outside. Wandering into the central plaza, I sat among hordes of food vendors operating tiny gas burners and dishing peppery stews. I drank the Ayacucho special, a cup of milky coffee laced with Peruvian brandy, and bought the local paper. I opened it to find a large picture of Che Guevara laughing. The headline shocked me: Benigno had become a worm.

"Benigno" was the code name of Daniel Alarcón, one of Che's best soldiers. He'd fought in the Cuban revolution, then followed Che on a failed military mission to Africa, and in 1966 he'd been a crucial participant in the Bolivian guerrilla war. Che and most of his men had died fighting there, but Benigno and just two others had survived, fighting their way through the mountains of Bolivia, escaping repeated encirclements, and finally walking across the Andes into Chile. As the only survivors of the doomed expedition, the men were welcomed in Havana as heroes, and all three survivors were promoted to positions of high visibility in the revolution. Benigno had taken over the running of the school for international guerrillas that Che himself had founded. Later he headed Fidel Castro's personal security team. He was a colonel in the Cuban army.

Or had been. Thirty years after following Che to Bolivia, Benigno, comrade in arms to the patron saint of the revolution, had finally had enough. He now broke with the Cuban regime in the most public and embarrassing way: "Today," he announced at a press conference in Paris, "I have taken the decision of exile to make patently clear my position as a political refugee." He lashed out at the Cuban regime and said that if Che were still alive "he would be indignant to see how Fidel Castro has converted his image into a flag to make the people work more every day to change nothing." He added for good measure that Che "would never have accepted or allowed a dictatorship like that under which the people now live."

This symbol of what Cubans called "the heroic years" was now a traitor to the revolution—a *gusano,* or worm, as Castro called those who defected. The list of worms was long: most of the original leadership of the revolution had either gone into exile or served long prison terms within Cuba. The revolution has steadily eaten its children; Benigno was only the latest, and the Cuban government paid no attention to the defection. Right next to the article on Benigno was another article that reprinted some Cuban declarations on "reordering" the economy, "intensifying the struggle," and defending socialism "tooth and nail" under the leadership of the man they just called Fidel.

Ayacucho had its own life to worry about, and Cuban politics seemed far away. It was Holy Week, the highlight of the year in a city of churches and religious pilgrims. The vendors had ringed the plaza with their little tables, and pilgrims from all over Peru and as far as Brazil and Ecuador were gathering in, eating and laughing, expectant. They were waiting for the highlight of the week, a traditional event called the rug parade. The rugs—*alfombras*—were not woven but poured, their colors and patterns trickled directly onto the pavement of the plaza and the nearer side streets. The artisans were mostly young men, but each *alfombra* was sponsored by some piece of the civic spectrum—a youth club drew a Peruvian banner with red and white sawdust, filigreed with a white dove holding green laurel branches. Businesses sponsored the *alfombras* in front of their doors; the middle-class families in the houses closest to the plaza produced traditional family designs. As darkness settled in the creators were hustling back and forth, swapping colors with their neighbors, putting finishing touches on the elaborate drawings before the parade started. Now the entire old stone plaza was redrawn in vivid colors and texture, like an old woman with a careful makeup job. A few thousand people milled about, a delegation of priests and officials waited at the cathedral, and a group of soldiers in oversized hats tuned their brass instruments. The paraders would carry an image of Jesus up through the city, circle the plaza, and then receive a blessing by the church. The vendors were giggling at how much business they were doing; the pilgrims laughed with joy at their own luck in being present for one of the most famous religious processions in the Americas; the boys of the town darted around their artworks, proud perfectionists.

There was a sudden, crisp tearing sound in the air—an explosion—and everyone in the plaza ducked. Their response was instinctive, instant, and experienced. One moment they were standing about flirting, or trickling sawdust, or pondering the menus of the little food carts planted around the rim of things. An unendurably long millisecond later they were hunched, feet flat on the ground, ready to break for cover.

The long slow clap of thunder rolled down from the mountain, and everywhere people broke into relieved sighs. It was not a bomb, just the mountain gods who had always rattled Ayacucho. In a breath, the city discarded the fear. I had been too ignorant to duck and cover, which promoted me to the ranks of the courageous; I saw a band of teenage boys mercilessly teasing one of their number who had dropped his bag of sawdust out of fright.

We were so busy pretending that nothing had happened that for a moment all forgot that something had happened. The first raindrops fell after two minutes. This was a mountain storm, pouring over the nearest peak with undiminished force and thoughtless ease. In seconds, the rain became a downpour accompanied by the rattle of thunder bombs and the flash of lighting fire. Fat, heavy rain plummeted down on the city. In two more minutes the plaza was empty of people, who rushed to the colonnaded cover of the surrounding promenade. Thousands packed into the too-small galleries, where they jostled and squirmed backward, trying to escape the flagrant swirls of wind and rain.

In another two minutes—just at the point that people had gotten over the excitement of the storm—the *alfombras* began to wash away. First the water in the gutters turned green and red. Rivulets cut their way through the designs. Gradually the sawdust began to float away, so that each rug was bleached of its colors, then was cut through with cracks, then lost its edges. The crowd was quiet, watching this. The rain did not stop, nor lighten. After half an hour the rugs were in ruins. After an hour there was no trace of them.

Following the example of wet skeptics everywhere, I took shelter in the cathedral. I listened to the mass, hoping to glean some meaning in the clear words, but eventually my attention wandered to the physical structure of the church, upward to the realm of arches and flying buttresses. The cathedral was grand without being great, a modest size but filled with ornate filigree. The nave was almost doused in gold, and more gold gleamed from high points on the supporting pillars, the ceiling, and the crypts lining each side of the chamber. The church literally glowed with candlelit gold, and the parishioners sat with expressions of calm relief. At least there was one place in the wilderness that not only promised the richness of eternal life but actually showed it. There was a gap here I could not close. I had not found religion, and little suspected that it was about to find me. I rose and went back to the door to look outward.

The rain bucketed down, inevitable and careless in its power to ruin. The sawdust drawings were long gone, the parade canceled, the pilgrims depressed. Twenty or so Peruvians and a few foreigners in brightly colored synthetic clothing milled beneath the arch, letting the faint spray blow over them. The rain pulled this disparate tribe into an amiable, multilingual mob, and when a little voice penetrated our circle everyone turned at once.

A little blond girl, no more than five, stood crying. She had emerged from behind the first pillars of the church and stared about wildly, tears streaming down her face. Two fat Peruvian women descended on her with devotion in their eyes, but they could not speak to the girl. Clearly she was a foreigner, but where were her parents? Each of us was examined with searching looks. After only a moment the entire group realized this child was lost.

But the Peruvians all remained preternaturally calm as the child wailed away. They told me not to worry. Even here—perhaps especially here—they believed in each other. They were certain the little girl's parents would show up. Everyone took turns comforting her, and indeed she eventually calmed down. It rained and rained.

Who would hurt a child?

Resistance and survival had made Ayacucho strong, and when the rescheduled march began the next night, Thursday, the town re-emerged to display a vivid indifference to natural and man-made oppressions. The reassembled crowd packed into the side streets along the route of the bier; every single sawdust rug had been laid down in the same place again. In a world of uncertainty the rug parade was certain. It had always been done, and always would be. Pressed against the wall of an alley outside the plaza by a crush of hundreds of people, I asked a teenager how long the parade had been held.

"It's so old," he said, "our parents did it."

The procession itself proved underwhelming. A towering white bier came slowly up the street, carried on the shoulders of a dozen blue-sweatered boys in front and back, followed by the Second Infantry Division brass band. The float was covered with several hundred white candles and dressed with white bunting and white corn cobs, white birds, white pineapples, and white leaves all made of candle wax. The fruits and vegetables symbolized plentiful harvests, and the birds were doves of peace. The only thing I didn't recognize were the decorative leaves amid all the finery, and I asked the man next to me what kind of leaves they were. "Leaves of wax," he replied.

Jesus was on top of this wedding cake looking very unhappy. Aside from the very real possibility that the entire float would burst into flame and melt onto the sidewalk, murdering the blue-sweatered youth of Ayacucho, He was suffering as usual from a series of spectacular and bloody wounds, and had His eyes cast up to heaven. Ernesto had observed a similar procession in another town in the Peruvian Andes not far from here:

> *Towering above the groups of small Indians gathered to see the procession pass by, you can occasionally glimpse the blond head of a North American, who with his camera and sports shirt seems like (and in fact is) an emissary from another world in this lost corner of the Inca Empire.*

The crowd was fantastically dense and mostly female. Many of the women were crying, others tossed fistfuls of yellow petals into the street (Ernesto described red flowers), and at least two took advantage of the fact that Jesus wasn't looking to check my pockets for a little contribution.

The second time, I caught the woman. I simply reached behind me and grabbed her fingers as they probed futilely at my buttoned back pocket. I turned slowly; we locked eyes. She looked like a pious Indian grandmother dressed in a black shawl over cheap, dirty clothes that smelled of poverty. There were whole conversations in the second we measured each other, or at least I imagined so. She was not ashamed, and in the tightly packed crowd it was not entirely impossible to believe that her hand had been accidentally forced into my pocket, which is what I chose to pretend. I broke off the glance, secured my back pocket, and turned back to watch the float and the huffing, puffing faces of the Second Division band as they marched up the alley and turned left into the plaza, their feet completely obliterating the sand and sawdust pictures of what was supposed to be.

The longest day started badly with a burst of predawn rain. I waited for a hint of the sun and finally left Ayacucho at 8:30 A.M. heading southeast, toward Cuzco. The roads were thick with mud, and the day dragged on as I climbed steadily for four hours. The world seemed empty, whole valleys unpeopled and the curves in the road marked with crosses and shrines for those who died in transit. I rode up steep switchbacks and down again, along valley floors and then up again, always up, and in one place it rained and in the next it was hot and sunny, and the crosses on the curves passed in a kind of metric rhythm, ticking off the kilometers and lives in one gesture. At one point I entered a tiny town and stopped at the police garrison. Twenty-five young soldiers poured out of the building and stood around the bike. I asked them if the town had a pharmacy. Pharmacies were the surest barometer of guerrilla activity, because before launching any big attacks the Shining Path would build up a stock of bandages and medicines through robbery. This forgettable town didn't even have a medical outpost to rob, it turned out. The soldiers seemed calm but slightly amazed by my arrival ("How did you get here?" one asked me, unwilling to believe the obvious answer).

The air was so clear at this altitude that coming over the next pass I saw a village on the far side of the valley and guessed that it was perhaps five miles away. It turned out to be more than thirty miles. I went down and down, turning through thirty-three switchbacks, and then over the valley floor, and then up the next mountain flank. A dog would come rushing out of each hut and pursue me, yapping and snarling ineffectively at my heels on the pegs. By the time I wore that dog out his barking would have alerted the dog in the next hut, who would come rushing out and repeat the procedure. In truth I had decided by now that there was really only one dog in all of South America, a filthy, long-furred, half-starving mutt who could change color and travel between villages at the speed of light. This dog had been after me since that first day on the pampas. I escaped him yet again, and upon finally reaching the town I ate lunch in a fly-infested cantina as children watched.

The checkpoint that finally stopped me was in the flatland across the next ridge. I saw it from half a mile away, which was more or less the point. The soldiers could also see me from half a mile away. There was none of the mountain chill here. The valley was hot and dusty, and the road carried me with geometric precision through potato fields toward a hamlet of a few thatched shacks. A single wood pole was draped across the road.

A corporal and several curious infantrymen came out of the largest hut, which appeared to be made of twigs. Lying off in the potato plants, well camouflaged in battle dress, were two more soldiers with automatic rifles that could sweep both sides of any vehicle that pulled into the checkpoint. They squinted down the barrels at me as if President Gonzalo himself had ridden out of the hills at the head of a huge Shining Path column.

Their corporal led me into a twig lean-to standing precariously close to the road. He sat down at a tiny school desk graced with a manual typewriter. Wind and dust blew in through the open wall. The lean-to had the proportions of an outhouse with the door thrown open.

"Papeles," he said. I handed him the usual raft of documents— the registration, entry and exit permits, the *permiso de circulación*, the expired insurance certificate, whatever was floating around in the

tank bag. He took the *permiso* in both hands like he was gripping a steering wheel. He was holding it upside down.

I caught myself. I had been about to reach across the little desk and right the document in his hands, or perhaps I had been about to say something or even laugh. I'd only ever *read* about illiterate Third World flunkies holding documents upside down. Now that it was happening, it seemed like a joke on me, as if this rickety shack and the short soldiers with their huge rifles were all just a stage set for a parody. But I caught myself.

Nothing happened for a while, and I nervously explained in Spanish that I was en route to Cuzco. "Cuthco?" he said, pronouncing it properly. Then he added a comment I couldn't understand. Yes, I said hopefully, that's right. I was a foreign journalist visiting Peru to write about . . . tourism, actually. This was no moment to discourse on the relevance of Che Guevara to Latin American history. In truth, I could have said whatever I wanted. Not only was the young corporate illiterate, but he also could not speak Spanish. After realizing this I stood dumbly for a few minutes, disarmed of my one defense. I tried repeatedly to explain who I was; he and the privates stared at me blankly and talked among themselves in Quechua. They asked me questions in their language and tried a few words in Spanish, but very few. Our conversation consisted almost entirely of the word "Cuzco" passed back and forth as both question and answer. I tried to pronounce the word with the proper accent, and this seemed to relieve the corporal of some of his worries. He eventually righted my paperwork of his own accord and sat for some more minutes fiddling with the ledger book on the desk. Tension ebbed and flowed in the lean-to. When the privates stood over him, he was embarrassed. When they went away, he relaxed. A great deal of nothing happened.

I finally noticed his shoulder patch: the First Division. They were a notorious bunch of killers who had terrorized the highlands for years. The Shining Path guerrillas were even worse, of course, but all too often the First Division had been attacking civilians in remote villages, not hunting guerrillas. Allegations of torture, murder, and "disappearances" had followed the First Division for years.

"Primera División es número uno," I said. The tops! His eyes lit up. I'd hit the right button at last.

"Primera División es número uno," he repeated, and we exchanged thumbs-up. He did speak some Spanish after all.

He took the accounting ledger and, using a pencil and a laborious, crude hand, wrote "CUZCO" in the first column. He stared at the various papers for a while, and at last I took the passport and, as if it were a small matter of our mutual curiosity, opened to my photo and pointed out the serial number. This he copied into the ledger over the course of ninety seconds. When he was done I gently turned the ledger to me and filled in the rest of the entries—name, vehicle type, date, and so forth. I wrote slowly, so as not to offend him. He was watching from the corner of his eye to see if his privates could see us. They couldn't, mostly because they were busy staring at Kooky. He stood up, all five feet of him, and shook my hand. A private sat down on one end of the pole barrier, causing it to swing up and clear my way. The flankers were still out there, ready.

I rolled beneath the pole and down miles of dusty road, downhill, at a steady, flat angle. After an hour I came to the bottom, a clear blue river spanned by an ugly new steel bridge. A group of soldiers in T-shirts came out, inspected my papers, and stared at the bike. One private brought me a bottle of Inca Cola, the yellow bubble-gum soda that I'd drunk with David Medianero ages ago in Lima. They spoke Spanish, and told me that two Italians had passed by recently on motorbikes. I looked forward to meeting these fellows until the soldiers explained that by "recently" they meant last year. They could think of no more questions to ask me—not even how fast it went—so I went on.

It was a journey through solid light. Even the rain was luminescent at this altitude, and on the higher peaks I would simply climb up inside a cloud that glowed with the sun's radiation, every misty raindrop a tiny moon catching and reflecting the light that pounded through the thin atmosphere. When it stopped raining there were rainbows, one after another, sometimes double and once a triple, its three sections separated by vertical columns of colored light that flew up into the ether with rigid perfection. There would often be three kinds of light at once: a harsh, burning sunlight striking one part of a valley; a vague, soft, glowing light that came through mist and fog pouring over a peak; and then a warm yellow light that seemed to come from the moist ground itself. The clouds were divided into similar camps, with low fogs dribbling over ridges, above them a thick belt of rain clouds, and then—visible through small breaks or across the vast clear valleys and beyond some peak—a blue sky dotted with the fantastic nubs and grasping arms of cumuli.

Climbing out of a little village called Chincheros—hitching their way along this route, Ernesto and Alberto had spent an unremarkable night there—I stopped to take a few photographs. A cluster of shy children hid behind some trees, convinced I could not see them. A thick fog was beginning to pour over the top of the road, and I was hurriedly snapping pictures in the last rich golden light of sunset when I heard a faint jingling behind me. I turned. Upon the mountain a band of pilgrims was marching.

The minute they saw me, the entire procession changed course and began to close in. I idly snapped a picture before realizing that they weren't headed in my general direction but, in fact, were aiming right at me. There were more than forty of them, highland peasants dressed in their best clothes, a mixture of traditional petticoats and sweaters on the women and sober jackets on the men. Some wore felt fedoras, and a few sported red sashes. They were led by a girl carrying a banner of the Virgin Mary on a short pole topped with a cross and a couple of small bells whose jingling had alerted me to their arrival.

Before I could say or think anything they were on me. I panicked and tried to backpedal, but it did no good. The young lady and the first man in line took positions on each side of me. They shook my hand, loudly proclaiming "Good evening." In a confused rush, the other marchers grabbed my hand and repeated the phrase. All of them, one after another, down the entire line. An old woman got down on her knees, kissed my hand, placed it against her forehead, and began to pray. I was frozen in a strange mixture of fear, incomprehension, laughter, and guilt: suddenly I realized they were saying not "Good evening" but "Good evening, *Father*."

Before I could fully comprehend what this meant, the leader spoke. "Well, Father, thank you for coming to meet us."

I mumbled noncommittally, still trying to shake the praying woman off my hand. "Actually," I said, my mouth going dry, "I'm not the father."

"You are his assistant?" the man asked.

And here I sinned. These poor pilgrims had probably marched for hours over twelve-thousand-foot mountains to reach Chincheros. Some of them were barefoot. It was Good Friday, one of the most important days in their religious calendar. They had sacrificed much to get there. Of course they expected a welcome from the priest. Of course they weren't surprised that the priest was a tall white foreigner (they usually were) circulating through the parish on a motorcycle (they usually did).

I now realized that I was wearing black trousers and a black leather jacket zipped tight to the neck. From a distance I could be mistaken easily for a priest. It all made sense to them. They wanted their pilgrimage to be noted, to be important enough that a priest rode out of town to guide them in. They wanted me to be that priest.

"Yes," I responded.

As quickly as possible, I extracted myself, explaining that I had to go on to the next town, Andahuaylas. The lie was transparent, ridiculous, and offensive, but I had blurted it out in the confusion of the moment, unwilling to disappoint them. They, in turn, seemed content to hear that I was the priest's assistant.

"Where is the father?" the old woman who had been praying on my hand now asked. She was smiling.

"Uhm," I said, sure I was about to be exposed, "he's . . . he's waiting for you. Down there. In the . . . church." They promptly marched off to town, happy that their journey was over. But mine was not. I realized at once that I had to get out of the province. They could probably shoot you for masquerading as a priest.

It was almost dark now, and the road led up into that cruel bank of fog. I turned the key and stared at the emerald diode on the dash. I didn't know whether to laugh or be ashamed of myself. "Well, Kooky," I said to nobody, "we've been promoted."

I slunk over the mountains, driving into the night and a dense fog that wet me to my bones. The road was awful. Just after midnight—sixteen hours, but only a hundred and sixty miles after leaving Ayacucho—I dropped down a last set of switchbacks into Andahuaylas, chased the final two miles by a pack of furious dogs. There was a checkpoint on the edge of town. Roused by the barking, a sergeant came out and looked at my papers. He only asked me one question.

"Are you a priest?"

I denied everything.

Ernesto had been suffering an unusually bitter attack of asthma. His normal cure—shots of adrenaline alternated with heavy doses of black tobacco—could not contain the problem this time, and when their truck arrived in Andahuaylas the two G's headed straight for the little town's only hospital, where they received the usual rough lodging and hospitality from their medical colleagues.

I had to rely on the town's hotel, of which there were two. The better of these did not have whores streaming in and out of the front door, and cost eight soles a night. The bed was good and the manager—an adorable nine-year-old boy—let me ride Kooky up the front steps and into the lobby. During the days he sat by the front door watching Mexican soap operas, and at night he slept on the floor behind the desk. Sometimes he was eating a bowl of rice, but I never saw an adult in the place in four days. He stared at the motorbike sometimes, but looked away if I caught him doing so as though he were afraid of me.

I waited for the rain to stop falling, just as Ernesto and Alberto had waited days here for a truck that would carry them. In the meantime I toured the hospital and tried to uncover any records of asthma patients from 1952. The doctors looked at me with a vague discomfort when I explained that Che Guevara had once been a guest in their wards, and they said there were no old records. They preferred to talk about the lack of funding from Lima that kept medicines in short supply. It was a small, dirty hospital but they were not ignorant or backward in their skills. The entire staff was consumed at one point by a two-day seminar on neurological repair led by a physician from Miami. They had little interest in the past.

The Argentines had visited a leper colony—long since closed—in the nearby hills. Ernesto wrote with great feeling about the suffering of those locked inside, with no reprieve from the mosquitoes and the psychological isolation. They made the trip there on horses which Ernesto praised and Alberto criticized.

Once, leaving the front gate of the hospital to walk through the muddy streets toward the hotel, I heard drumming. I followed the beat past the farmer's market, stacked with oranges and potatoes, and came to a back street where a crowd of fifty had gathered. A terrified beauty queen sat in the bed of a pickup truck while various men leered at her, but most in the audience were watching a set of six male dancers reenact the conquest from the point of view of the losers. The dancers wore "helmets" of wool that mimicked those of the conquistadors, and donned papier-mâché masks painted with the unfamiliar physiognomy of those who had come to enslave them—pink skin, blue eyes, and yellow beards. Their costumes were decorated with gold braid, beads, pom-poms, and bright sashes, and they carried whips and cardboard swords. The overall effect was Gilbert and Sullivan meets the Holocaust.

In the first dance a small girl in a ruffled pink-and-white gown stepped through a slow minuet with the devil (his tunic identified him as EL DIABLO). Then the dancers pounded each other's legs with whips, and finally two men squared off, one posing as the bull, symbol of the Spaniard, the other as a condor, symbol of the Inca. In the dance, unlike in real life, their encounter was peaceful.

The audience, like the dancers, was drunk. Slowly, people in the crowd noticed me at the rear, and more and more red eyes turned to watch me. Bottles passed freely from hand to hand while a drummer pounded a relentless marching rhythm and the dancers swirled to the skirl of a fiddle and a *quena*, or pan pipe. The whips cracked the air, and the devil consorted with the crowd, trying to claim young ladies. A nauseating sense of time slippage invaded me, a kind of friction between the past and the present. My own blue eyes and eight-day beard mocked the papier-mâché villains at the center of the circle. The costumes were both ancient and modern—relics of a dance born five hundred years ago in a bitter conflict but updated with nylon fabrics and Adidas sneakers. There was no purity or simplicity in the way a historical memory was handed down by a people in dance and music. This was not, in fact, a ritual or even a tradition, which implied some kind of codified meaning, but a living dance, as much a document of the present as of the past. Some in the audience wore blue jeans; others homespun; a few town boys laughed at the ignorant mountain girl who had come for market day and stood at the edge of things, terrified by all the sights of the city. I had never seen them or Andahuaylas before; it was virtually certain that they had all seen New York City on the television many times.

The friction of time was also a friction of mutual expectations. Foreigners sought out the "pure" and "unspoiled" indigenous culture of the Andes but found the reality of modern intermingling even here. There was an ancient dance at the center of the crowd, and a boy in a Metallica T-shirt watched raptly. Just as subatomic particles were altered by the act of observing them, our own presence was a corruption of the thing we came so far to see. Maybe Douglas Tompkins was right: perhaps it was better to have no audience at all, to let a vacuum of silence fall over the last examples of a disappearing culture. If these dancers were going to be museum pieces, then at least lock the door to the museum and let them play in peace.

But that was impossible, of course. There was no escaping this friction, no closing off the complexities of a society interrupted and rerouted. The conquest had dropped like a rock into the pond of history, the waves still rippling out and bouncing back, doubling up or canceling one another in infinite combinations of past and present, nylon and wool, languages brushing past one another, the blue eyes of the observer locked, across the crowd, with the devil's own blue-eyed gaze in return.

The dancers were proud of their craft, and afterward posed for my pictures. They asked me to bring a video camera and put them on television, but night was falling, the crowd was increasingly drunk and the devil danced toward me, menacing me with a pair of shears and his dead gaze, so I moved on.

Early the next morning I said good-bye to the mute nine-year-old and stopped at a barbershop offering a haircut called "the John Travolta." I didn't need a cut but I did need to quiz the local drivers, who lounged about the place inspecting themselves in mirrors. I had a conversation there that stands in my mind for all the ridiculous conversations of this type that I had, day after day, on the entire trip. My goal was simply to learn how long it would take to reach Cuzco, but it was impossible to get a straight answer from these vain, loathsome men. Where I wanted information they offered boasts: Cuzco was not in any fixed place, apparently, but moved closer or farther away depending on the mood of the respondent, his estimate of my driving skills, a visual inspection of the motorcycle, and other incalculable factors such as how many other drivers were listening. No professional driver could stand to admit how long it actually took to reach Cuzco; his fellow drivers would mock him if he spoke the truth, so all engaged in a round of fictional calculations. The answers rained down on me: Cuzco was six hours, or four hours, or only two hours away. They informed me that I could "fly" there on such a big motorcycle. I persisted, asking for hard kilometer figures rather than wishful thinking, but the dozen men who drove from there to Cuzco regularly could simply not agree. The best I could learn was that a bus took about twelve hours to make the trip; still, they insisted that I could do it in as little as six or even four, or maybe in just two hours on "that thing." I left town no better informed than before the discussion.

A couple of hours after I left, climbing up a high rampart of mountains, it began to rain. I spent the day bouncing over a moonscape of valleys and ridges, the road pockmarked with holes and lined with wallows of mud so deep that I often had to ride on the shoulder—which was sometimes an area just six inches across with a steep drop on the other side. The world was deserted, except for the hourly trucks slamming in the opposite direction or, once, an astonished teenage herder standing with his llamas in the middle of the road. He called out to me in shocked Quechua and then laughed and jumped up and down, as though he had never seen a gringo on a motorcycle before.

In a dark downpour late that day, at roughly twelve thousand feet, the smell of something burning roused me from my trance, and I stopped the bike and discovered that the luggage rack had snapped, allowing the saddlebags to fall inward. The friction of the wheel had then burned a large hole in the fiberglass of the left case. After five minutes of staring at this insoluble problem I heard an engine in the distance, and eventually a red pickup truck approached. The driver was a fortyish fellow with curly hair. He discussed my options with me and agreed I had none. I could not move with the saddlebags where they were; the bags could not fit anywhere else on the bike; nor was it possible to repair the break without welding. The driver commiserated briefly and then offered the only solution that seemed possible: he would carry all the luggage to Cuzco in the crowded bed of his truck, and I could ride on by myself and collect the gear in a couple of days.

A couple of days? "You won't make it tonight, believe me," he said. I put everything into the bed of his truck. He handed me a slip of paper with an address on it and got behind the wheel. We shook hands through the window, and he drove up a set of switchbacks into the freezing rain, the little red truck disappearing into the bottom of a cloud.

I was left alone, with only my wallet and a map. My boots had soaked through and the rain drummed on my helmet. The clouds swirled around me and I stood there trying not to feel anything. *This is fine. This will be fine.*

Incapable of anything else, I merely kept breathing. Each breath was the cleanest I had ever tasted. After a while the relentless coming and going of mountain air did its work. An ember of defiance caught slowly and glowed faintly. Take whatever you want, world. Take it all. I don't care.

This moment of life, alone at dusk in the rain at twelve thousand feet with nothing, is still enough. A slow dread spread through my bones, warming me, as I realized that I would go on regardless. I could live through the rain and the darkness and the bad roads and everything I owned disappearing into the bottom of a cloud. But I could not live without the trip, without some movement. In a life of restless longing, the only hope lies somewhere ahead.

Key on and look for the green light. Kickstand up, clutch in, left foot on the peg. Throttle in, clutch out, and then pull away. I climbed up into the bottom of the cloud and rode a long time in those mountains, and then spent the night on the floor of an abandoned gas station. I went on after that, and saw many more things, and eventually I crawled into Cuzco twelve days after leaving the coast.

CHAPTER ELEVEN

THE NAVEL OF THE WORLD

"AT LAST: CUZCO!" Ernesto crowed with capitalized pleasure upon reaching this clean, cool city at 11,500 feet. His diary described three separate places, all layered on top of one another. The foundation stones were the massive blocks laid by the Incas; the conquistadors were next, raising cathedrals on the ruins they had created; finally there was mestizo Cuzco, the origin point of half-breed South America.

The city had changed, but only to become even more what it had been. The acceleration of the modern world was everywhere: Boeings roared into the valley from Lima and, balanced on their wing tips, turned inside the mountain range and dropped onto the runway like bricks to disgorge tourists in bright coats with water filters and phrase books and bits of paper leaking from their pockets like straw stuffing from a scarecrow. There were pubs full of drunken Englishmen, and restaurants with the menu in Hebrew, and many, many young people arguing about who got a better exchange rate in Bolivia or where the drugs were best in Ecuador. I found a small hostel that I remembered from years before, the kind perennially filled with languid young women from northern Europe, ice climbers shouting in various languages, and guitar-strumming troubadours. Over it all hung a sign: PLEASE TO BE QUIET, THE TOURIST IS SLIPING. The staff seemed terrified of us.

A *kibutznik* who missed his motorcycle offered to buy Kooky on the spot but settled for a free ride around the plaza. He went around and around, crying out *"Thank you!"* each time he passed, while I sat on a bench and had a ten-year-old bootblack clean my footwear. He carried a little wooden box filled with polish and rags, and scrubbed ferociously. I asked him who Che Guevara was. "Who?" he replied. I ate pizza in a five-hundred-year-old temple and later that night drank beer in an African disco thrumming on top of some old Incan building. There were beautiful women everywhere; I fell for a Dane, and then three different Quebecois girls in a row. At 4 A.M., entirely beyond myself, I scrambled up a hill and then down an obscure cobblestone alley and then stood there in the dark, running my fingers around the edges of the twelve-angle stone, a huge and precisely fitted masterpiece of Incan engineering that was replicated on the label of Cusqueño beer.

Very late the next morning I calmed down and went looking for 1952. My first stop was a battered doorway in a collapsing Spanish home on Márquez Street, which led to the studios of Martín Chambí, the photographer laureate of Peru. Chambí had patrolled the mountains, villages, and society weddings of the province with an enormous bellows camera and a box full of glass plate negatives. He died in 1973, but his elderly daughter, Julia—dressed in a checked wool skirt and jacket, wizened and tottering but still vain enough to dye her hair brown and conceal her age from me—answered the door. She was glad for a visitor, and led me through a series of wooden portals to a small dim room in the back lined with filing cabinets. These were the archives, tens of thousands of images. Most of his pictures were either landscapes printed as postcards (his early series on Machu Picchu helped popularize the ruins; it took him a month each way on foot to reach the site) or formal portraits for the wealthy. Yet his silvery, composed images transcended their antique appearance and local content to offer a genuine vision of the human condition. ("It is dangerous to dwell too long on the documentary value of his photographs," Vargas Llosa warned.) Chambí's portraits of the Cuzco demimonde alternated between sympathy and malice, while his eye for emotion—in a mistreated street urchin, a group of arrogant cavalrymen, or a coca-chewing peasant working a foot plow—was universal.

I told Julia Chambí that I wanted to see the Cuzco of 1952. "Oh," she said, slightly disappointed. Her father's best works were from the '20s and '30s; he seemed to lose his bearings right around the time Ernesto and Alberto passed through town. She began rifling through the cabinets, squinting and plucking at the brown Agfa envelopes, each containing a single five-by-seven-inch glass negative. She held one of the negatives up toward the window. "Ah, here it is," she said, and passed it to me. It was called "After the Cuzco Earthquake," and it showed a front loader clearing a street of rubble while men in shapeless felt hats watched.

The earthquake struck two years before Ernesto and Alberto arrived, but they saw its legacy everywhere: their diaries noted the broken frames of paintings, the doors hanging crooked on their hinges, and particularly the toppled bell towers of the Chapel of Belén. Ernesto wrote that the chapel "lay like a dismembered animal on the hillside."

I asked Julia if she remembered the quake. "Of course," she said. "I was sitting down to lunch with my father in the old house. I'd won a tennis tournament that morning, and he was so proud. I'd just taken a sip of beer from the trophy cup when it happened. It was two-fifteen in the afternoon." The house shook. Buildings around town collapsed. The church spires plunged to the ground. The streetcar tracks—and here she plucked another negative from the stack, showing exactly this scene—bent in crazed wiggles through the plaza. The photos were filled with barefoot, filthy children, and incompletely whitewashed homes, and pompous magistrates in ribbons and cornaded hats, and everywhere peasants in beautiful homespun clothes. Perhaps it was the effect of the black-and-white images, but it seemed a world of simple gestures and closed façades. Even an earthquake did not penetrate the exterior of these stoic mountain people, although their grim, unsmiling expressions betrayed a subtle amazement at the world.

After an hour of holding negatives up to the window and flipping through boxes of loose prints, I rose to leave. "Wait outside for me a moment, please," she said, and I stepped into the anteroom. She didn't close the door behind me, and I could see her fussing with something in one of the cabinets. She emerged with an old negative envelope, which she handed to me as she pushed me out the front door.

I turned uphill one block, made a right, and collided with a man coming around a corner. He was chewing coca. His clothes were entirely homespun, from the top of his pointy wool cap down to his knees, where his crumbling pants ended. A moment ago I had been looking at this same avenue in a glass negative; like some reverse development, my mind overlaid a black-and-white image on the colored world in front of me. Here, where the traffic divider now sat, there was once a row of dirt with trees. There, on the far hillside now settled with one-story homes, there should have been an empty slope.

Standing on the corner, I opened the envelope Julia Chambí had put in my hands. The picture slid out, a simple contact print of a five-by-seven-inch negative exposed at sunset one cold afternoon. It was a picture of a man in a white lab coat astride a beautiful V-twin Indian motorcycle, one of the legendary and extinct American brands. The rider had a jaunty smile on his face and a pair of goggles over his checked wool cap. A Peruvian flag on the handlebars snapped in the breeze, and his feet were on the pegs as though he were riding past the cobblestones and whitewashed buildings, past the barefoot boys who stared at the Indian with the expression I had seen a hundred times. When I looked closer I saw that the kickstand was down; he was posing for the photographer.

I turned the print over. On the back, she had written, "First Motorcycle in Cuzco, Marco Pérez Yañez, 1930."

In exchange for all my worldly possessions I had been given a small slip of paper with an address, and I rode Kooky down the gentle slope of the city, past the old Temple of the Sun, its walls now the base of the Santo Domingo Church, until I reached the cheap districts. There were neither foreigners here nor things they wanted to see, just ordinary, modern, struggling Peruvians.

The address led me to a garden- and home-supply store filled with bags of cement and faucets, everything coated with the gentle dust of commerce. Tito, my curly-haired savior, was behind the counter. He led me upstairs to his apartment and prepared a pot of tea. He turned out to be a former journalist; his wife owned the garden business. He handed over the two black cases and the backpack that normally rode strapped across the back seat, tied to each saddlebag. Everything was as I had last seen it, down to the enormous hole burned in the back of one case by the rubbing of the tire, and the mud that had entered inside, coating my clothes.

Tito listened to the story of my trip and sat back in his chair. He adopted my cause as his own. There were people I would have to see, he said. He would arrange everything. Also, since my saddlebag needed fixing, he would take care of that. He had a friend who had a friend who did these things. Probably I also needed a better hotel— he knew several. Also, if I needed any garden or home supplies, I could get me a discount. There were women, too, who—

I had to flee the place before he handed over the keys to the pickup or tried to marry me to one of his cousins. I spent the afternoon in a garage he recommended on Manco Capac Avenue, surrounded by preening truck drivers who wanted to trade their transcontinental rigs for mine. They bought me the worst lunch I have ever succeeded in eating, but it was a beautiful, warm afternoon, and we stood around in the sun, a bunch of lonely men talking about tools. The sparks from the welding of the luggage rack zinged into the mud with a satisfying sizzle.

It took a couple of days, but eventually Tito arranged for me to meet with Dr. Yuri Valer, an old survivor straight from the pages of *The*

Secret Life of Alejandro Mayta. Valer was a handsome, chubby lawyer and the top bureaucrat of the Cuzco city government. He wore a sweater vest and square glasses as he received me in his tilted, creaky office in an old wood building. Mounds of papers tied in crazed bundles covered his desk and were stacked on chairs, side tables, filing cabinets, and anywhere else flat, and there were five boxes that said IN but only one that said OUT.

"Peru used to be famous for Machu Picchu," he said as we shook hands. "Now it's famous for guerrillas."

You had to offer people a way out of their past, in case it was a bad one. I began by asking Valer if he knew about the early years of the sixties, when the area around Cuzco had been crawling with various vanguard leaders in search of a movement to lead. Among them were Javier Heraud, a prize-wining poet from the upper class; the son of a prosperous land owner named de la Puente; and Hugo Blanco, the son of a lawyer. Blanco was the most credible of these would-be revolutionaries, since he was an agronomist who lived among the peasants and spoke Quechua. Sometimes they called him the Che of Peru, but his Trotskyist guerrilla cell had failed and Blanco went first to jail and then into exile.

"Of course," Valer said, shifting in his seat a bit, "I know something about it." Picking his words carefully, he said that he was "part of the movement" but never a guerrilla. He was *almost* a guerrilla, he said. Back in 1959 he went out for drinks with a friend who had just returned from Cuba. At first his friend was full of cryptic statements ("The era of words is over, the era of deeds has begun!"), but after a few more beers he coughed up the plan. Despite the fact they were Peruvians, he and some others were going to Argentina to launch a guerrilla revolution, just like Castro and Che had done in the Sierra Maestra, the mountains of eastern Cuba.

"He kept insisting, 'We're going, we're going,' but I didn't join him. I told him, 'I'm not joining you, but not because I'm afraid.' A month or two later"—and, *crack,* Valer slapped a palm on a bundle of papers—"the group appeared."

A few months later, *crack*, they were all dead. That was the history of the Uturuncos, those first guerrillas to rise in Argentina. "We were just drinking," Valer mused quietly.

He could not remain sad at the recollection, though, because it had been such a remarkable time. From 1962 to 1964 he had been a top officer of the peasants' union in the Cuzco area. He wasn't a peasant, but on the other hand he'd done his law school thesis on peasant organizations. The big issue at that time—as at most times in Latin America—was land distribution. Some of the *haciendas*, or farms, had existed in an almost unchanged condition since their founding by the conquistadors four centuries before. The peasants were nothing more than serfs; rich families owned thirty-five thousand acres at a clip. Cuzco Province was a hothouse of land invasions, evictions, seizures, and violent demonstrations. The union, a nexus of peasants and intellectuals, became the recruiting center for Hugo Blanco's budding war. I asked Valer what motivated Blanco to turn to the guerrilla path.

"It's evident Ernesto Guevara had a tremendous influence on him," he said. "The influence of the Cuban revolution was tremendous at that time. There were three leaders—Fidel Castro, Ernesto Guevara, and that other one who died in a plane crash. The greatest influence, more than Fidel, was Guevara." Valer talked on for a while about the man he first called "Ernesto Guevara," then after a few minutes "Che Guevara," and then "Che," and finally "El Che." His enthusiasm for the old days crested as Valer stood behind his desk, wagging his finger in the air while reenacting Guevara's 1961 speech in Uruguay, a blistering assault on John Kennedy's new Alliance for Progress aid program. Just months after the failed Bay of Pigs invasion, with the hemisphere rapidly polarizing, Kennedy had proposed a $100 billion development program (about five times the size of the Marshall Plan for Europe) designed to counteract the growing influence of the Cuban revolution across Latin America. In reply, Che stood up—all the other delegates spoke while seated—and delivered one of his most famous orations:

> *We cannot stop exporting our example, as the United States*
> *wants, because an example is something spiritual that pierces*
> *all borders. What we do guarantee is not to export revolution,*
> *we guarantee that not one rifle will leave Cuba, that not one*
> *weapon will go to another country. What we cannot ensure*
> *is that the idea of Cuba will not take root in some other . . .*
> *country, and we can assure this conference that unless urgent*
> *social measures are taken . . . the Andes mountains will*
> *become the Sierra Maestra of [Latin] America.*

Valer's dramatic reenactment of the scene was interrupted by a young aide with a paper that needed signing, and the bureaucrat plopped back into his chair with a thud, struggling to regain the breath he had lost over thirty-five years. When he turned back to me, his line of thought had become more personal.

"We had a kind of fever," he said wistfully. "A guerrilla fever. Groups sprang up in all parts of Latin America, and here in Peru. The theory behind most of them—no, all of them—was Che's."

He rattled off the names of Guevara's books—*Guerrilla Warfare, Man and Socialism in Cuba,* and *Episodes of the Revolutionary War.* I let the list hang there for a moment, and then asked if it was really the theories—doctrines about mountain *focos* and the stages of socialism—that had created that fever. "No," Valer said. "It was El Che. He was a symbol. A symbol of a new type of leader, of a new era. He wasn't a bureaucrat or a union leader or a politician but a romantic type. He crossed from country to country, traveling by foot or horse or motorcycle like you, getting to know all of Latin America."

It was dark outside now, and Valer made it visibly clear that the assigned time for our interview was up. I rose reluctantly and we swapped business cards. I was about to leave when Valer spoke. "He was here, you know. In Abancay." I told Valer that Guevara had been all over Peru, and showed him *Notas de Viaje,* with its pages and pages on Cuzco.

"I've never heard of all this," he said, flipping through the book. "I'm startled this hasn't been seen or discussed here in Peru. Startled." He asked to borrow the diary and told me he would return it soon with something else that I should have. I asked what it was. "I'll give you the names of some people you should talk to," he said. "People who know more about this than I do."

Foreigners were required to travel to Machu Picchu on a special tourist train that rode out each morning and came back the same evening. With a few days to kill while awaiting my next interviews, however, I decided to attempt the same, slower itinerary that Guevara had followed. At dawn the next day I laid siege to the jovial station master, burying him in flattery and waving around a set of expired Peruvian press credentials while claiming to be someone important. In a few minutes I was ensconced with about a hundred Indians in a carriage of the inexpensive, slow, and crowded local train. We seesawed up a set of switchbacks above Cuzco and then began rumbling slowly down the Urubamba River Valley. Over three hours the valley grew steeper and narrower until the railroad had to cling to a reinforced shelf along the side of a cliff, with the brown water tumbling beneath my window. We stopped for a while so that the crew could clear a small slide of black earth from the track, and the Indians used the interruption to buy boiled corn on the cob and roasted guinea pig on a stick. Ernesto's scatological eye could not help noticing that the petticoats of the Indian women were "veritable warehouses of excrement."

I debarked at Aguas Calientes, the town nearest the site, and at 7:30 the next morning caught the workers' bus up to the mountaintop. We debarked at a hotel built discreetly into the hillside. When they arrived here in the parking lot, Ernesto and Alberto joined a pickup soccer game with some of the hotel players. The manager was so impressed ("I admitted in all humility to having played first division football in Buenos Aires," Ernesto wrote) that he offered these eminent Argentines free room and board while the hotel was empty.

Like Ernesto, I played goalkeeper, but it was too early to find a match on some narrow ancient terrace. The busboys and porters went to change into their uniforms, and I set off on foot to see the ruins. When I topped the last rise between the hotel and the site I stopped. Ten thousand people had lived here, and despite the orderly walls and careful terraces, it was still the setting that overawed me. High on a saddle between peaks, the empty city sat awash in a sea of summits and wrapped in a roaring river so deep below that its foaming rapids sounded like a distant breeze.

At Machu Picchu, Ernesto confidently dove into the archaeological debate over the nature of the lost city, pointing out that the lack of defenses facing Cuzco showed that the city was built during a time of confident expansion, not as a refuge from the Spaniards. For a better view of the layout he ascended the small peak called Hauyna Picchu that towers over Machu Picchu. It seemed inescapable that I would have to climb up, and when I saw the two-car tourist train screech into Aguas Calientes far down the valley, I started up a steep path of tiny steps, wheezing for oxygen the whole way. After an hour, muddied by crawling through a small tunnel near the peak, I emerged some six hundred feet above Machu Picchu. There was a small clearing surrounded by trees, and a Peruvian woman was busy hacking her name in one trunk with a pen knife. I found the highest point, a granite promontory that had been carved into a throne, and sat down to read for a while.

The Irish-Argentine aristocrat was now suffering from recurring bouts of Pan-American solidarity. On his birthday—he turned twenty-four during the trip—he got drunk on clear *pisco* brandy with some Peruvians and launched into a rambling toast insisting that "the division of [Latin] America into unstable and illusory nations is a complete fiction. We are one single mestizo race. . . ." He now called the ruins "a pure expression of the most powerful indigenous race in the Americas," which "practical" North American tourists could not appreciate. He claimed that "only the semi-indigenous spirit of the South American can grasp" the significance of the place.

Mountaintops induce hallucinations in everyone, of course. The dream of reuniting the Spanish-speaking Americas into one single nation was as old as Simón Bolívar, and a perennial trope in Latin American politics born long before Guevara and still alive today. It was an emotional, utopian vision that he had in the Peruvian mountains, perhaps driven by the immense vista visible from this peak, and he would continue to speak of this Bolivarian dream as he moved to Cuba and then took to the world stage. The notion appealed to the worst myths of his twin ancestry—the Celtic affinity for lost causes and a Hispanic idealism realized only in full flight from reality. His best instincts contained evidence of the very flaw that would undo him: the realities of different political systems, races, and economies were "illusory," the rivalries and distinctions among nations a "complete fiction." He grasped for some connection to what he saw by lumping himself among the mestizos as a "semi-indigenous" South American. He was reaching for solidarity with others, but wishful thinking like this would soon kill him.

On top of Hauyna Picchu, the two semi-Argentines hid a bottle in the bushes with their signatures tucked inside. They meant to come back and reclaim it someday. I dug around in the underbrush, but the peak was full of trash now, and the woman with the penknife soon came over to ask what I was looking for.

"A souvenir," I told her, and went down.

Back in Cuzco, I recovered Kooky from a garage and rode through the slippery, cobblestone plaza up to the same little hotel again. There were two notes waiting for me. Tito wrote to say the saddlebag was ready. The other was from Dr. Valer, who had made a call on my behalf, and I was instructed to be at a certain coffee shop at a certain time the next day. I was told only the name of the man I was to meet: Néstor Guevara.

Tito drove me across town the next morning in the red pickup; we went first to a workshop down an alley. Tito's friend's friend had molded black fiberglass over the hole in my saddlebag. I paid him twenty dollars and held the case in my lap as we drove to the coffee shop, opening and closing it with glee. I was starting to believe I might actually make it.

In the coffee shop, Tito pointed silently to a lanky man sitting alone at a linoleum table. Néstor Guevara—no relation to Che—was approaching retirement age, a weary man dressed in a faded gray sport coat. He wore thick glasses, and his hair fell black and flat across his head and down toward one ear. We sat down and introduced ourselves. I mentioned Valer's name, but Nestor looked vaguely displeased. "He was a Trotskyist, and still is," he muttered.

"I trained with Che," Néstor began, and then launched into his story. As he talked he turned over a sheet of paper—the syllabus of the economics course he now taught at a local college—and drew an outline of South America with a ballpoint pen. He sketched the rough borders of Peru and then drew a scraggly oval that represented Cuba.

"We believed that the Cuban revolution was the only way forward," Nestor explained, and drew an arrow arcing north toward the Caribbean. Néstor was a student in 1959 when Fidel Castro had driven into Havana. By 1960, Havana was filled with young men from all over the hemisphere, eager to drink at the revolutionary wellspring itself. Che, the regime's designated internationalist, assumed leadership of these like-minded recruits. The talk was of freedom and justice, and there was as yet little evidence of how things would go.

"We were young," Néstor said. "We believed in the mystical Cuban revolution, the mystical Che, the mystical Fidel Castro. We thought the experience could be repeated in other places. For me—pardon me, but for me, Che was a saint."

He spent six months training under Guevara in western Cuba, an activity he described as "hiking in the mountains." I asked him if this was really all they had been doing. Weren't they trained in arms? Guerrilla tactics? Ambush and recon? "A little," he said dismissively, "but it was more a romantic thing," mostly physical conditioning and endless discussions about socialism.

This idyll was interrupted by the Cuban missile crisis of October 1962 (*"CRISIS OCTUBRE,"* he now wrote). The foreigners were sent home. Néstor said this was done to protect them in case of a Yankee invasion, although it might also have been part of a larger retreat from the embarrassing international commitments that had brought on the crisis in the first place.

"The Guatemalans left for Guatemala," Néstor said, "the Ecuadoreans for Ecuador, the Peruvians for Peru." At each of these phrases, he drew an arrow out of Cuba to the appropriate destination on the page. The map was starting to fill up, but Nestor kept drawing, adding in the Argentines, Brazilians, Venezuelans, Dominicans, as they all flowed homeward with Che's doctrines in their pockets. There were some Colombians, for example, who had gone home to form a guerrilla group called ELN, which exists to this day. Their commander cultivates a thin Che beard and likes to pose for photographers in a beret with his eyes cast upward, a precise and deliberate reenactment of the most famous image of Che. The ELN mostly lives off ransom money from kidnappings now.

Once home in Peru, Néstor joined a new guerrilla force called the MIR. There were forty-one fighters, and the group was quickly wiped out. His best friend was killed, but Néstor escaped, hid in Bolivia, and then enlisted in a second group, also called the ELN, in Ayacucho. In 1965 he "fell in battle," he said. I looked up from my notes. The phrase meant the opposite in Spanish and English. To fall in battle in Spanish meant to fall prisoner. Disgrace was worse than death.

His huge, bony hands hovered over the paper throughout this account, filling in each detail. He wrote the Spanish initials of various groups over the body of Latin America—ELN, MIR, PCB, UMSM, MNR, COB, JPC, MTR, URJE—and then the places—Bolivia, Peru, Puerto Maldonado, Catavi, Nankawasi, Ayacucho, Concepción, Cuzco, "Battle of Puente Uceda"—and then the years—'56,

'59, '60, '61, '62, '64, '65, '68, '71, '72. There were notations on the losses in battle ("41 − 7 = 34" or "80 percent"). He wrote in "HB" and drew hash marks over Hugo Blanco's theaters of operation. From Colombia to Chile, from Lima to Rio, all of South America had come alive with dynamite and groups competing for some new combination of the words *national, army, liberation, united, revolution,* and *party*.

In early 1966 Néstor was released from prison and fled to Bolivia. Tens of thousands of tin miners were in revolutionary ferment in Bolivia, organizing strikes and forming militias and issuing demands. Nestor sought out the most militant miner groups and tried to help them organize. "The revolution was coming," Néstor said. "There was a lot of theory, but it was . . ." His thought trailed off.

Bolivia was never Che's preferred destination. He had left Havana in secret, still loyal to Castro but fed up with the unheroic life of meetings, speeches, and Soviet-style bureaucracy. He tried to prop up a guerrilla army in the Congo but found the Africans unwilling to fight and interested mostly in scholarships to Cuba. Castro put off questions about Che's whereabouts for almost a year ("You will find Major Guevara where he can be of service to the revolution," he said) but then suddenly broke his silence. In late 1965 Castro read to the nation a letter addressed to "Fidel" in which Che resigned his position of leadership in the party, his ministerial rank, and his army commission. He wrote that other nations called for his "modest efforts," and the letter ended with a maudlin promise: "If my final hour finds me under other skies, my last thought will be of this people and especially you."

In the Congo, Che flew into a rage when he learned that Castro had read the letter aloud. After announcing his own martyrdom—the letter was obviously intended to be read only upon his death—Che could hardly return to Havana alive and defeated in Africa. He was trapped: unlike his careful cover story on the motorcycle trip of heading "only" as far as Chile, he had left himself no wiggle room this time. After five months in Africa he returned to Cuba in secret.

Committed by his own hand to pursuing revolution elsewhere, to leaving rather than arriving, he now needed an elsewhere. Thus a fatal chain of events began to get under way.

The first step was to choose a battleground. Néstor recalled a glancing conversation in Cuba when Che asked him two questions, one about Hugo Blanco, the Peruvian guerrilla, and then this: "How does Bolivia seem to you?" Unlike so many who had told me about Che but never known him, Néstor's eyes did not glow with excitement as he recalled this moment. He did not leap from his seat or gesture wildly—in fact, other than inking his outline of guerrilla history, Néstor made no gestures at all. He didn't even look at me as we talked.

"Poverty," Néstor had answered. This was all that he had told Che. Even to a Peruvian the poverty of Bolivia was shocking. People lived in Stone Age conditions in many parts of the country, still enacting the ordered cycles of life, planting communally with foot plows just as they had done under the Incas half a millennium before.

Néstor did not then know how close he was to the course of history. He went back to Bolivia in 1967 to organize the tin miners—an arrow arced south again—and while there he began to hear rumors of a guerrilla cell operating in the south of the country. Eventually, there were reports—which Néstor believed—that the guerrillas were led by the famous internationalist Che Guevara.

"I told them, 'Che is here,' but he was received with—" Néstor searched for the words—"a bit of indifference. The peasants did not respond."

There was no coffee left in my cup. I stared at the grounds, uncomprehending. According to Che's own Marxist analysis, Bolivia was a tinderbox awaiting a spark. I asked Néstor how it was possible that the tin miners—a ripe socialist force, organized for action and fueled by the "objective conditions" of poverty—had been indifferent to the arrival of the world's most famous revolutionary.

He searched again, uncomfortable, for something to say. Finally, quietly, in tones of disgust, he said, "The miners had never heard of him." He repeated himself, slowly and precisely: "The miners had never heard of him."

Never heard of Che Guevara? By 1967 Che was in the crosshairs of history. He was condemned by *both* superpowers, labeled the man "most feared" in Washington, and denounced as an "infantile adventurer" by the Soviets. He was the founder and keynote speaker at the Tricontinental Congress, an attempt to unify all the revolutionary governments of Africa, Asia, and Latin America. He'd appeared on *Face the Nation* and conducted secret negotiations with John F. Kennedy. He was venerated in speeches that compared him to San Martín, the South American liberator; he was imitated and worshipped by young rebels the length of the Americas; he was even celebrated in a poem ("Thus, Guevara, strong-voiced gaucho, moved to assure/his guerrilla blood to Fidel") by Nicolás Guillén, the Cuban poet laureate.

But the Bolivian tin miners had still never heard of him. "Remember," Néstor explained, "this was an area where never had come a single publication, not one magazine or newspaper. Nothing. Che was known only by university types."

The page was now littered with half-forgotten acronyms and arcing lines of retreat, with dates and names and places that had dropped into the rearview mirror of life. The outline of South America was obscured by the crowded field of events; Peru itself had disappeared beneath repetitive circles of insurgency, zones of operations drawn and drawn again, dots of blue ink where graves now lay. History was merciless with the mistaken, cruelly indifferent to our illusions, more ruthless in its verdict than even the dialectical Marxists had assumed.

"Now all those heroes are being replaced," Néstor said, scanning the list of names on his clouded map. "Poverty continues in Peru. Misery still exists." He said nothing for a while, and I took his map, folded it in half, and pocketed it. He watched the paper disappear and still said nothing, but his hand was furiously rapping the ballpoint pen against the linoleum tabletop, a drumbeat of disillusion, death, and disaster.

"We failed," he said at last. *Rap rap rap.* "He sent us, and we failed." *Rap rap rap.*

"We were young," Néstor said.

Early in the morning the gravel road ran up the *altiplano* with the mountains pushing farther and farther away to east and west. Dust dropped through the airless void like powered lead. After a few hours I grew feverish and my hands trembled on the throttle. By noon I was vomiting in a cheap hotel in a town daubed with Shining Path graffiti. I spent the afternoon and evening imprisoned in my bed by a catastrophic fever. As I twisted with agony and soaked through my sheets, Peru's worst rock band rehearsed right outside the window, playing through a set list of classic rock at deafening volumes for five hours straight. The mattress became a puddle.

At one point two children broke into my bungalow through the bathroom window. When they came out of the bathroom and saw me lying in bed, so racked with muscle spasms that I could neither sit up nor speak but merely stared at them with wall-eyed fury, they turned and ran for it.

The morning after that the road rolled up the plain and topped, at a gentle rise, 14,176 feet. Herds of llamas broke and ran at the sound of my engine. The air was too clear at this altitude. You could see Lake Titicaca in the distance, blue and cold down at 12,000 feet. Beyond that were all the great towering peaks of Bolivia, some of them 20,000 feet tall. The light bent with the curve of the atmosphere, and you could see all the way to where the world fell away from itself.

CHAPTER TWELVE

THE WIT AND WISDOM
OF CHE GUEVARA

The plateau shattered and died at last. After crossing the border at a wretched little post, I floated across the narrowest part of Lake Titicaca on the last barge of the day. The ferryman asked me if it was true there was salt in the ocean, and why.

Driving across the last miles of the *altiplano*, I bought gas that an attendant swore was 71 octane—lower than anything I'd ever heard of. Then the earth died and fell off the map. There was nothing much to warn you, just a scattering of brown adobe houses and some stores like in any little village, and then the road became a divided highway and abruptly fell over the edge.

La Paz was at the bottom. The city was built into the side of a crater, shielded from the cold wind of the *altiplano* a thousand feet above. It looked like a child's invention, tiny and fragile. I took a big highway down, an elevator-drop ride that made my ears pop and delivered me into the heart of the city at an inadvisable speed, and quickly I found an enterprising hotel full of Israelis that allowed me to ride La Cucaracha up the front steps and into the lobby.

I set off for a walk down the steep streets, past the hanging carcasses of the butcher shops and the old women in bowler hats everywhere, and soon I came down onto the flat floor of the city. The main avenue changed names every dozen blocks or so, but was mostly called the Prado. It ran like a vein down the central arm of the city, slowly dropping as the city moved away from the *altiplano* and becoming more and more modern with younger buildings. I began at the top of the avenue, near the Basilica of San Francisco, a lovely old stone church and monastery dating from 1549, just a few years into the conquest. The façade of the church was a brilliant mestizo pastiche in which the usual baroque vines of European styling were adorned with the Andean touches of carved fruits, plants, birds, and little animals. The plaza was full of interesting faces, but I moved on because there was shopping to do.

La Paz is a city of vendors, and walking steadily downhill I began with a set of batteries at one stand and a newspaper a block later. Down a few more blocks I found a blue stall selling flag pins, and I was reaching for Bolivia's little red, yellow, and green tricolor when my hand passed over him. There he was: tiny, pressed into tin, the same iconic face as always. The pin was well made for something small, capturing all the necessary elements: his eyes burning up into the distance, his hair in disheveled rebellion, the little star clearly visible on the beret. The background was red enamel, of course. It was a reduction of an impression of a memory of a photograph, not the image of the young Ernesto but that of a fiery Cuban major on the cusp of middle age, a legend in his own time. I bought two pins. A block later I found a stall selling a crummier version, where his face was slightly melted and the star had been blunted into a dot. But it was still him, no matter how badly they pressed it.

Another block and his face was peering from book and magazine covers. Two competing vendors took up the challenge of selling me their Che books, but there were more than I cared to read. There was a special on *My Son El Che*, written by his retroactively adoring father. I picked up a copy of *My Friend Che*, an exaggerated account by Ricardo Rojo, an Argentine who spent some months traveling with Che in 1954 and had never stopped talking about it. Still, I couldn't resist seeing what Rojo had to say and began haggling with the two men, each more determined than the next to sell me a copy. Finally I struck a complex but inexpensive deal: the Rojo book and a copy of *Che's Letters of Farewell* from the uphill stall, and from the downhill one a cheap paperback called *The Diary of Che in Bolivia*. This was Che's battle diary from the 1967 campaign.

Che had not made it to La Paz on his 1952 trip. He'd kept his promise to return home and finish his medical degree, but in 1954 he was on the road again, searching. Rojo met him in the confines of La Paz and Che warned him that traveling companions had to bear the total absence of money, walk everywhere, and have no concern for clean clothes.

In a restaurant, I ate potato soup and read. The newspaper was silent about Vallegrande, Che's resting place, but I saw there had been a ten-day strike at Chuquicamata, back in Chile. From there I turned to the Rojo book. Like Alberto Granado, Rojo had to be taken with a grain of salt, but he knew Che when Che wasn't cool. When they first met, Che described what had happened to him while traveling South America before. Che referred to the 1952 journey as a "serious trip," as opposed to previous skylarking adventures, and Rojo believed it was rugged travel that made the man:

> *Before he had read any theoretical writings, his own observation and analysis gave him a new perspective: he saw at first-hand the importance of economic events in the history of nations and individuals. His travels through Latin America showed him the social panorama created by economic events. If I had to describe Guevara as he was then, I'd say he was only yet feeling his way toward what he wanted to do with his life; but he was absolutely sure of what he did not want it to be.*

There it was: that lost moment when he knew what he was against but not what he should be for.

Che's eventual answer was sitting only a few inches away: *The Diary of Che in Bolivia* was *documental*, the cover helpfully declared. Back home I had two copies on better paper, a Cuban version called *The Bolivian Diaries of Che Guevara* and an American version called *The Complete Bolivian Diaries of Che Guevara*, which included the passages Castro had edited out. All of them told, in one way or another, edited or not, cleaned up for posterity or elaborated with photographs and supporting documents, the sad story of Che's final days, written in his own hand. From his first diary I had now progressed to his last.

This was a Che who knew what he was for. The pulper began with a balanced introduction by the editors ("For millions of young people, Guevara is a romantic revolutionary, a martyr in the struggle against oppression. But older people believe he symbolized anarchy . . ."), passed through the windy and unnecessary "Necessary Introduction by First Minister Fidel Castro," and then began on November 7, 1966, with Che's first entry: "A new stage begins today."

In fact, the "new stage" had begun almost a year before. The man who once swore in public that "not one rifle" would leave Cuba now directed an enormous, cross-continental logistical effort to export a revolution to Bolivia. The operation had been under way since January 1966, when Castro had met with communist leaders from South America to discuss the establishment of a guerrilla base in South America. In February, Cuban agents in Bolivia began constructing a support network; in March several Bolivians began training at a guerrilla camp in Cuba; in June the Cuban advance team purchased a farm in southern Bolivia, close to Argentina, and began stockpiling arms and food; in July the Bolivian Communist Party leader, Mario Monje, agreed to supply twenty local fighters, and the Cubans made an overture to one leader of Bolivia's militant miners. There were endless disputes over where to locate the *foco,* or "focus" of guerrilla action. In his books, Che had outlined a theory of guerrilla warfare in which a small vanguard element could pin down large numbers of conventional troops; by gradually dragging out the war, hitting the enemy wherever he was weakest, the guerrillas would force the government to use repressive measures. This deepening of the contradictions would, in turn, increase popular support for the guerrillas, and eventually the rotten regime would collapse. He hoped to draw the United States into open combat in South America, creating a new Vietnam war. But Bolivia was merely a pawn in this international struggle; Che the Argentine dreamt of using Bolivia as a platform to reach his homeland. The Peruvian recruits wanted to fight in Peru; the Bolivians were willing to sacrifice their lives and country in this cause but were internally divided between the Maoists, who supported Che's strategy of fighting in some remote place, and the Muscovites, who had ties to the miners and wanted to be close to the urban support networks. The farm in southern Bolivia was originally supposed to be a rear-area camp for training and resupply, but Che issued contradictory orders about locating a new base, and in the end no other camp was set up. A kind of deadly inertia began to take over the mission. Che let the real-estate market partly determine one of his most important decisions.

Finally, on November 3, Ernesto Guevera de la Serna landed at the airport above La Paz, exhausted by an aerial odyssey from Havana to Prague to São Paulo to here, a journey designed to conceal his tracks. The plan worked, and the arrival of what my new pulper referred to as "the world's No. 1 guerrilla" went unnoticed, thanks to a brilliant disguise: Che was now bald. He shaved not only his famous beard for the trip, but the center of his head, too. Cuban disguise experts then highlighted his remaining hair with silver. In a black suit and tie he was the perfect image of "Adolfo Mena," the bald, bespectacled, middle-aged Uruguayan businessman his fake passport claimed to present. He strolled through customs, an invader in wingtips.

Disoriented by jet fatigue and the thin air, Che took long walks around the city, visiting tourist sites and playing with his camera. He snapped photos of himself in a hotel mirror and had himself snapped buying a newspaper in front of the train station. This was an early indication of the fatal flaw that would undermine and eventually destroy his mission and the men and women in it: Che was now obsessed with his own place in history. He had himself photographed in La Paz and then in the field. He urged others to document the campaign on film and in diaries. The guerrillas even posed for a group shot in the jungle, arrayed like a class photo. Che took many of the photographs himself, but this was not simply the innocent shut-

terbug of 1952 clicking away. Back then Che had taken all the pictures, which were therefore mostly of Alberto Granado or those they
met on their route. Now, as his snap of a hotel mirror showed, Che
had to be the *subject* of the pictures.

The photos were, inevitably, captured. Bolivian and CIA intelligence officers used them to confirm Che's presence, identify his fellow guerrillas, and draw vital conclusions about the strength, location,
membership, and disposition of the enemy. There were other, almost
childlike incidents of egotism. A local supporter named Whiskers was
assigned to drive Che from La Paz to the farm in the south, and the
two men rolled off in a white jeep for the two-day trip. Whiskers had
no idea who his bald, silver-haired passenger was, and this apparently
annoyed Guevara; near the end of the trip Che blurted out his real
identity just to see what reaction he would get. Whiskers was so
shocked that he literally drove over a cliff. Although this must have
been quite satisfying to Guevara, the jeep was stranded on the
precipice and the two men had to walk the last twenty kilometers to
their base. In only the first days of his new venture, Che was endan-
gering himself and those around him in order to document, polish,
and plumb his own myth.

Everything had changed between Cuzco and La Paz, between
Guevara's first trip and his last, between the Ernesto of 1952 and the
Che of 1966. In the intervening years the world had exploded with
frustrated social movements as diverse as Asian liberation wars
and the sexual revolution, African decolonization and rock and
roll. Armed with globe-wrecking weapons, the superpowers—a new
term—engaged in a dangerous game of brinkmanship over Cuba.
The Bay of Pigs invasion in 1961 and the Cuban Missile Crisis in
1962 had put the island at the center of a maelstrom. Guevara had
changed with his times. Fighting in the Sierra Maestra mountains,
he had become hardened to the uses of power. When the rebels
caught their very first traitor—a guerrilla who had informed on

them—Castro ordered his execution, but none of the Cubans would step forward to carry it out. Only Che volunteered, blowing the man's brains out with a .32-caliber pistol during a thunderstorm. When he later led his own column of troops, those who were guilty of disloyalty or cowardice—in Che's own judgment—were killed. In wartime such summary judgments can be justified, but between his dauntless attacks in battle and his harsh "revolutionary justice" behind the lines, Che left a trail of dead men wherever he passed, and he earned a reputation for cold-bloodedness. The doctor had learned to take lives as well as save them.

Administering victory proved even more difficult than promoting struggle. At the instant of triumph, Guevara was appointed commander of the La Cabaña fortress in Havana. Under the title of Supreme Prosecutor, he oversaw a bloody purge of Cuba's regular army and police. About fifty men were shot on Che's personal orders at La Cabaña after trials that lasted only a few hours. In the following years, Che served variously as the head of the National Bank and as Minister of Industry, but his real role was as the revolution's roving ambassador, always traveling, the Trotsky to Castro's Stalin. He signed the new national currency with a jaunty "Che" but insisted that Cubans, who called even Castro by his first name, had to address him always as Comandante Guevara. His personality was seen as arrogant, distant, and typically Argentine. (Cuban joke: "How does an Argentine commit suicide?" "By jumping off his ego.")

Guevara moderated such resentment with his personal rectitude. He lived abstemiously, volunteered for hard manual labor, and gave inspiring speeches about what he called the "New Man," his vision of a citizen motivated not by lust for money, goods, or comfort but by love of justice, sharing, and struggle. Despite the hijacking of the phrase by Castro—in practice the New Man turned out to be a secret policeman—the *idea* of the New Man remains Guevara's one lasting philosophical legacy.

One of the New Man's most salient characteristics, Guevara warned, had to be hardness. An abstract love of humanity left little room for love of actual human beings. His speeches were filled with images of violence, death, and hatred. His belief in worldwide revolution was embodied in a famous statement: "How bright and wonderful the history of the peoples would be if two, three, many Vietnams appeared on the face of the earth." But rarely did anyone cite the rest of the quote: ". . . with their daily quota of death, tragedy and heroism."

"We mustn't be afraid of violence," he said then. And: "Hatred is an element of struggle; relentless hatred of the enemy that impels us over and beyond the natural limitations of man and transforms us into effective, violent, selective, and cold killing machines."

The speaker was obviously not the same man as the anti-authoritarian smart-ass of 1952, yet the first trace of what Vargas Llosa would call Che's "precursory character" was found right in the final pages of the road diary. After returning home from the motorcycle trip in late 1952, the man who now insisted on being called Che sat down to study for his medical exams and to rewrite his road journals into *Notas de Viaje*. The now-twenty-four-year-old Guevara began by drawing a clear line between the man who had left on the trip and the man who returned from it. "The person who wrote these notes," he stated in only the second paragraph of his literary effort, "died the day he stepped back on Argentine soil. The person who is reorganizing and polishing them, me, is not the me I was. Wandering around our Americas has changed me more than I thought."

The most curious entry in this manufactured diary was also the very last. After recounting the adventures of the trip in chronological order and setting down his lusts, hungers, illnesses, doubts, and dreams, Guevara closed the book with a final chapter only two pages in length. Titled "As an Afterthought," the entry described a conversation around a campfire in "that little mountain town." Granado was not mentioned; only a mysterious man who had "fled the knife of dogmatism in a European country" and now offered Guevara a "revelation."

The revelation was revolution. The man at the campfire explained that a just society could only come about through violence, and that those who could not adapt to a new world—innocent or not—would perish. "Revolution is impersonal," the mystery man warned, "so it will take their lives and even use their memory as an example or as an instrument to control the young people coming after them." The man then predicted that Guevara would die with his fist clenched, "the perfect manifestation of hatred and struggle."

The final paragraph of the diaries acknowledged that the European exile had "foretold history," and writing in 1953, fifteen years before it would happen, Guevara predicted his own death clearly:

> *I know that when the great guiding spirit cleaves humanity into two antagonistic halves, I will be with the people. And I know it because I see it imprinted on the night that I, the eclectic dissector of doctrines and psychoanalyst of dogmas, howling like a man possessed, will assail the barricades and trenches, will stain my weapon with blood, and consumed with rage, will slaughter any enemy I lay hands on. . . . I feel my nostrils dilate, savoring the acrid smell of gunpowder and blood, of the enemy's death; I brace my body, ready for combat, and prepare myself to be a sacred precinct within which the bestial howl of the victorious proletariat can resound with new vigor and new hope.*

Barricades and trenches. Rage and slaughter. A knife stained with blood and nostrils dilating at the smell of gunpowder. The "Afterthought" explained nothing but contained everything. He had foreseen what he would become. With its unrevealed prophet, the absence of any time or place, and a tone completely different from the rest of the diary, I could conclude only one thing: the conversation had never occurred. It was not a documentation of what had been but a declaration of what would be. Just as he had insisted on his new name, the revelation was his own willful creation, a literary transformation as much as a real one.

In 1953, home safe in Buenos Aires and reflecting on the trip, Ernesto had sat down and written a character called Che into existence. Now, as 1966 tailed into 1967, all that remained was to collect his band of soldiers and put the prophecy of his own "Afterthought" to a final test. It was time to head south.

Somewhere short of Mataral, Bolivia, a thick hoarfrost had settled over the land during the night, hiding everything within a crystal cloak. When I woke up in a ditch at dawn the ground around me was white; the hillsides were white; the fields were white; my sleeping bag was white. The motorcycle, dismembered and balanced on its center stand, had lost its usual blue, orange, and black tones and turned a perfect white as well.

I reached a hand out of the bag, swiped away an armful of what resembled snow, and sat up. The sun was just beginning to break the horizon at 7 A.M., and in only a few minutes the first horizontal rays injected color back into the world. The quinoa on the lower slopes was first, emerging in separate patches of red, yellow, and purple, and then the potato leaves on the upper slopes began to appear as lines of dull green tracing the contours of the hills. The frost on the flat tire next to me was among the last to clear.

I boiled a cup of water for instant coffee and stared at the tire. It had blown explosively just as I crossed a pass into this valley at the last moment of daylight. One minute I was riding by a village wedding procession, the next I was wobbling all over the road, headed for the verge of a steep ravine. I skidded to a stop and shivered with an adrenal rush that told me I was still alive.

In the last moments of dusk I had pushed Kooky off the road and dug out my tool kit. I then put the bike on its center stand and removed the rear wheel. In darkness, I had popped the worn tire off the rim, pulled out the punctured inner tube, and put in the one spare tube that I had been carrying for months. Night interrupted the work, and I lay down in a ditch and listened to the distant music of the wedding party high up the valley. Sometimes a girl would come walking down the road, followed by a mooning young man flirting with her in Aymara. They couldn't see me in the ditch, and I drifted off when the party ended around midnight.

By the time my morning caffeine had kicked in the frost had sublimated into the sun's rays. I applied a pair of shims to the wheel. The black rubber slipped over the rim reluctantly and popped into place. I removed the seat from the bike and reached under the gas tank. The pump rested inside a metal tube welded to the frame of the bike, and I drew it out, applied the hose to the tire, and pumped. Nothing happened.

I tried again, with the same result. The nozzle on the pump and the nipple on the tire were not the same size. I'd come almost four months without a flat tire. I'd considered myself extraordinarily lucky so far, but all my good luck had brought me was a long way with the wrong pump. After half an hour of fierce effort I managed to force a little air in, but when I put the wheel back on it was a pitiful sight—the weight of the bike left it completely flat. There was no way it would support me, let alone the saddlebags and backpack.

I hid all the luggage in the bushes and talked to a gigantic peasant who was sorting potatoes in front of the nearest shack. He barely spoke Spanish, and his cheek bulged with a thick wad of coca leaves, his version of morning coffee. He pointed to a cloud down at the far end of the valley, where the sun had first risen to smite me. He said there was a gas station beneath that cloud. How far? "Six or seven kilometers," he said.

The bike started on the first try. I had been dropping all day yesterday and was somewhere around eight thousand feet now. I would have to switch back to the low-altitude carburetor jets soon, but for now the bike purred like a well-fed cat. Leaving all the bags behind, I set off for the gas station, which in these parts always did tire repairs. For six or seven kilometers there was no sign of a town, let alone a fuel depot. Every now and again there was a single shack visible above the road, and once a two-room house with a pickup truck. The owner came out and told me he had no gasoline, no air pump, and no patch kit. I wobbled on. After six or seven miles the tire went flat again.

I got out the patch kit, unhitched the wheel, dismounted the tire, pulled out the tube, and glued on a patch. It was possible to force a little air into the tire by placing the pump at a certain angle, almost removing the little key inside the nipple, and putting a pebble inside the pump nozzle. I heaved like a madman for half an hour and the tire was inflated, just barely. I felt smug at the way I could solve my own problems, even here. Then the patch popped right off and the tube sighed and collapsed. I started over. The sun was up high now, and I stripped off my shirt and used the second half of the tube of glue to put on a second patch. I remounted the tire on the wheel, reinstalled the pebble in the snout of the pump, and then heaved madly for another half hour until the tire was partly inflated. This time the patch held. The tire was still soft, but better than before, and it seemed possible to drive. I remounted the wheel onto the drive-shaft, donned my shirt and helmet, and then drove back up the valley, plucked my bags out of the bushes, and set off again toward Vallegrande.

After ten more miles I found a man with a pump who filled the tire up to regulation. After another ten I found a *gomería*, a roadside shop where they patched inner tubes. The trucker in line ahead of me was getting his sixteenth patch. I had both tubes neatly vulcanized, put some extra air in the wheel, and rolled on.

After another ten miles the tire blew again, and the bike wobbled all over the gravel and slid to a stop at the very edge of a ravine overlooking a beautiful valley. The mountain dropped a thousand feet down from the front tire, and my eyes had never felt sharper. I could pick out the round, smooth pebbles bouncing down to the next switchback. I was becoming habituated to adrenaline now; a kind of searing afterburn crawled through my skin.

I took off the wheel, popped the tire, extracted the tube, put in the recently patched one, remounted the tire, and pumped furiously for half an hour. The result was pathetic. I got a hundred yards before it went flat again. Now I was out of glue, patches, palms, and patience. I hid Kooky down a dry arroyo scrubbed to its red rock bottom by rain, then pulled off the wheel. I uprooted several bushes, camouflaged everything, and began walking. After an hour, mostly walking downhill with the wheel on my back but sometimes rolling it and chasing after it, I got to the first town. There was no *gomería*. An old man told me I could find one in the next town. When I asked how I could get to the next town, he pointed back up the mountainside I had just come down. "Take that bus," he said, and I could just see, a thousand feet above us, a bus passing the spot where the motorbike was hidden. In twenty-five minutes the bus arrived and I caught a lift to the next town, sitting amid peasants for an hour and letting the wheel rest, I later discovered, in vomit.

I got off at the town and pushed my flat wheel toward the *gomería*. This is when I discovered the vomit. The mechanic let me wash my hands in his toolshed. He got to work and within seconds had destroyed my inner tube. He hadn't noticed that the air valve was held on by a nut, and when he went to pull out the tube he yanked so hard that he ripped the tube right out, but not the valve, which stayed attached to the metal wheel.

I blew up. I threw one of those gringo fits that I despised in others, sputtering away in my best Spanish about what a complete and utter ass he was. I explained, in carefully enunciated tones, that in my country we were very careful with tires, and didn't pull stupid stunts like ripping the valves out. I was still shouting at him about how he'd just ruined my only spare tube when he reached inside the now-empty tire, poked around with his fingers, and extracted a thin, rusted nail.

The nail that had given me four flats in twenty-four hours. The nail I had never thought to check for. He patched the hole in the old tube perfectly, reinstalled it in the tire, and then inflated it to load-bearing hardness. Since I couldn't bring myself to apologize, I vowed to keep my mouth shut.

Long after nightfall I caught a ride on a truck filled with potatoes and peasants chewing coca. The truck loitered in the first village, and I rode on with two Bolivian policemen in an open jeep who were heading off to investigate a rumored bus crash. They dropped me high on the mountain again, and I rolled the now-firm wheel down the arroyo.

Kooky was unmolested beneath the camouflage of bushes. I slept on the stones of the wash, next to the bike. Off through the dark air you could see a few lights of the first town and then, way beyond that, at the far end of the valley, a single light marking the second.

In the morning there was no frost, only a few loose feathers leaking from the rotted sleeping bag. I made a cup of instant coffee and put the wheel back on and then drove down into the valley and through the first town and into the second. The same mechanic I had yelled at was sitting outside his shop.

He asked me what country I was from. "Canada," I said.

CHAPTER THIRTEEN

TEN THOUSAND REVOLUTIONS

The road alternated between dirt and gravel as it ran south. As the altitude dropped the llamas gave way to cows and the headgear of peasants in the distance switched from the pointy wool caps of the Andes to the straw cowboy hats of the *vaqueros*. It took two more days, but eventually a long valley yielded to a minor set of ridge lines, and I went up and down and in the early afternoon came around a bend and there was a gas station and the beginnings of a town of red roofs and white walls. This was Vallegrande.

It was a matter of habit now to pull into any and every gas station, regardless of how much was in my tank, and I did. The attendant came out, wiping his hands with a rag. *"Qué tal, Che?"* "How's it going, Che?"

I asked him why he called me that. He looked surprised: "You are from Argentina, right?" Like Ernesto, I'd been exposed as an outsider the instant I arrived. After topping up, I reached for the key and my hand passed over the odometer. After a look in my notebook I did some quick math. The result was hard to believe: I'd ridden more than 9,900 miles since departing Buenos Aires four months ago. I rode up the last hill and into Vallegrande. A couple of men sitting in the plaza watched while a pair of black dogs chased me around and around. I found the hotel that all the journalists had stayed in when they were watching the excavations. It cost four dollars a night, was clean, and had hot water and a view of the valley. I lay down on the bed and thought about staying here for the rest of my life.

I was almost the only foreigner in town—there was one resident Peace Corps volunteer—and the news of my arrival rippled through the streets. Even before I had time to wipe the dust off, the president of the local civic council came around to ask me why I was there. When I told him, he said, "Of course. El Che. We assumed that was the case."

We took a walk. His name was Calixto, but everyone in the street called him "Professor" because he had once been a teacher. Calixto took me to his municipal office, which turned out to be a tiny school desk in the back of the general store he now ran. The room was stacked high with eggs, noodles, candy, and toilet paper. The desk was covered by a foot-high pile of papers that Calixto pushed toward me. There were newspaper clippings from as far back as 1967, files on the recent search for Che's bones, and a few books, including *My Son El Che* by Ernesto Guevara Sr. Flipping through the stack, I came across a worn little booklet that resembled one of the ration books that Cubans carry. Inside was a neat photograph of a young man—Calixto himself—in uniform. It was his military service *libreta,* dated 1967. He'd been a private in the army at the time of Che's campaign, but, he hastily added, he'd been stationed right here in Vallegrande, where he spent the months of the insurgency pushing paper on a desk and standing guard duty in the middle of the night. Calixto took the little booklet and gazed at the picture of himself as he had been. The paper was wrinkled and worn soft. So were his hands as they held it. A tiny transistor radio played in the background.

"The people are still living the psychosis of those times," he said, popping open a liter of lemon soda from the store's cooler. "They won't talk. Somebody comes forward with a story once in a while: 'I saw three people buried over there. It was El Che.' But there's nothing there, or it turns out to be somebody else. We found four like that."

The search had been quite an affair, the biggest thing to hit Valle-grande since 1967, the last time somebody was looking for Che here. When the retired military officers came to lead the search for the body there had been forty or fifty journalists with them, and the Cuban ambassador had shown up with two coal-black bodyguards whom Calixto called, with a kind of hushed awe, *"los Burundi."* A news crew from Globo, the Brazilian television conglomerate, had arrived in their own airplane, making an even greater impression. Most of the journalists left after a week or so, but a hard core of fif-teen or twenty had stayed for two months while the Argentine foren-sic experts dug and dug. Calixto showed me some pictures of a party the journalists threw on January 26, a month into the search and while I was deep in Patagonia. The guest of honor was Loyola Guz-mán, a Bolivian woman who had briefly joined Che's guerrillas and survived to an old age of dancing salsa with foreign correspondents. Calixto remembered it as a fun time. "Look," he said, pointing at the photo, "that's the man from radio in La Paz."

Everyone used Che for something. The journalists wanted head-lines or, in my case, a mirror. The Cubans and Argentines wanted the body. In Vallegrande, the civil council had hoped, briefly and naively, that the remains would stay right in town and attract tourists like some Lourdes of the left. There was already a smattering of Che tourism. For years young people—mostly Latin Americans but also some European socialists—had been coming to town on pilgrimages, usually for the official anniversary of Che's death, October 8.

"The young people that come here," Calixto said, "talk about taking up arms, going into the hills. I hope it's only talk. But there is great misery, it's true." He said the province was slowly stagnating. They were in the sixth year of a drought and there were no more har-vests. People were fleeing for the big cities: the school system had declined from two thousand to one thousand students. I asked him what the young people should do if they wanted to Be Like Che and put an end to injustice. "Learn," he replied. "Study. Help someone. But to go into the hills with a rifle doesn't serve anything. What good is a rifle when the government has so many more?"

We were still flipping through the papers, and I came to a photograph, the famous shot of Che lying dead in a laundry shed behind the local hospital. The Bolivian military had put his body on display to prove to the world that the famous invader was really dead. The photograph showed Che, shirtless and disheveled, stretched out on a cement table used for scrubbing blood out of surgical gowns. His arms were thrown out to the sides, and his lifeless eyes seemed to stare at the camera. There were small cuts in his torso where the bullets had gone in. It was an obviously Christ-like image (in fact, Dr. Valer, back in Cuzco, had referred to it as " the image of Christ").

"I was there, you know," Calixto said, taking the photo from my fingers. Calixto had joined a line of two hundred people waiting to see the body that day. Some of the women ahead of him clipped small bits of Che's hair. I asked if the mourning and memorializing showed that the people in the area had genuinely supported Che.

Calixto shook his head. "No," he said. "They didn't know who El Che was." Many local families had actually informed on the guerrillas. It was only curiosity that brought them to see the body, he explained. Like the tin miners, they'd never known or loved their would-be savior until he was dead.

Che proved more influential in his afterlife. "The people up in La Higuera, when they have an illness now, they light a candle to El Che and say it cures them, like a miracle. Students here in Vallegrande do it when they have an exam." We walked down the hill to the airfield. We passed a small parking lot, and on the gate was a faded red graffito: VIVO COMO NO TE QUERÍAN GUEVARA. I couldn't understand the phrase and asked Calixto what it meant. "I don't know," he replied, stumped. The wording was ungrammatical in Spanish, and meant, loosely, "Guevara, you are more alive now than ever." Calixto said it must have been painted by a foreigner.

He was a brooding man, and as we passed beyond the last buildings and saw first the windsock and then the grass landing strip his mood grew even heavier. It was a huge field, far larger than I had ever understood from reading the news reports. There was a hangar built like a Quonset hut, and inside it was a small plane owned by a family of American Pentecostal missionaries. They didn't live here, but occasionally flew in to witness for Christ. On the far side of the field was a high wall containing the town cemetery, but in most directions the field simply ran under a split rail fence and kept going, out into the valley floor. They always said that Che had been buried "under the airfield" at Vallegrande, but that meant nothing. The airfield was just a swath of valley floor. He could be anywhere.

"Where in all this are you going to find El Che?" Calixto asked.

In the morning I went to see the Che museum. Calixto took me to the plaza, where we marched up the front steps of the municipal building, climbed up the second floor, and went into the main room that overlooked the plaza. There was a desk, and Calixto opened it and took out a Plexiglas case about the size of a typewriter. Inside it was a pair of old leather sandals.

That was the Che museum. "We are hoping to get some more things to add to this, but right now this is all we have," he said. These were the sandals worn into the grave by one of the four guerrillas whose bodies had been recovered so far. It was the footwear of someone who served under Che. A piece of the true cross.

Out on the steps of the municipal building a Bolivian man in a blazer and jeans did a double take as he passed me, and Calixto stopped and introduced us. He was the town's radio reporter, responsible for broadcasting a daily show on the provincial station. The station was headquartered just across the plaza, and he dashed off and minutes later returned with a microphone and a cassette deck. He put on a pair of headphones and stuck the microphone in my face.

"Who are you and what is the purpose of your trip?" he asked once the tape was rolling. I rambled on for a while about how I was heading up to La Higuera tomorrow to see the place where Che Guevara died, how I was studying the life of the young Ernesto Guevara and what people thought of Che now. Since the radio host didn't stop me, I kept talking. I had been spending a lot of time alone and apparently needed to get a few things out. In the end I talked continuously for half an hour about where I'd been, what people had told me about Che, how I thought he had started out great but gone wrong, terribly wrong, and how everything was lousy in Cuba and, in the end, violence got you nowhere. The revolution always ate its children, and so on. I explained that the *foco* guerrilla strategy was a dim-witted notion, a foolish attempt to refight the battles of the Cuban war in a radically different political context. At the end I said that it was understandable that people admired Che because nobody else seemed to give a damn about the poor. At last he snapped off the tape recorder.

An hour and a half later, I sat down to lunch in the town's only restaurant. There was an article in an old newspaper about the Zapatista guerrillas in Mexico. They'd held a meeting with the French author Régis Debray, one of Che's old advisers. Debray had once written books about the inevitable triumph of Marxist guerrillas around the world; now he advised the Mexicans that their strategy of propaganda stunts and Internet dispatches was "more realistic" than Che's plan of recruiting a guerrilla army from Bolivian peasants.

All this time, as I read, the radio in the restaurant was on. I was into my soup when I head a familiar voice: "... *investigación del joven Ernesto Guevara, antes de que el fue conocido como 'Che' ... que opinión tiene la gente ... empezó bien pero al final ... opresión en Cuba ... cada revolución come sus hijos ... un plan idiótica.*"

It was me and I sounded like a moron. My entire speech on the steps of the municipal building—visible out the door of the restaurant—was on the radio, run not in the edited snippets I had expected but stem to stern, thirty minutes long. I slowly spooned through my soup and then waited for my fried steak. You could hear only two things: me blabbing on the radio in ungrammatical Spanish and the forks and knives of a half dozen customers as they ate. They listened and watched me surreptitiously. It was the longest meal I have ever eaten.

I spent the afternoon looking for Che memorabilia, but there was none. No postcards, no T-shirts, no lapel pins, no books of any kind. I marched from one general store to the next, but the merchants all said that they had never seen such things and asked if it would be a good way to make money.

That night the village was stilled by a soccer game between Bolivia and Argentina. The Argentines were heavily favored, but when Bolivia scored early the streets of Vallegrande erupted. You could hear people screaming, car horns tooting, and teenagers running around the plaza whooping. In the end the Bolivians were crushed by their neighbors. They'd lost their empire to the Spanish, their coastline to Chile, and their soccer game to the *ches*. That's how it went in Bolivia. They were used to losing. In Latin America there are many things worse than defeat.

On the morning of the third day I drove south out of Vallegrande, through the dusty fields, heading for La Higuera to see the last of what Che had seen. It was a dry, clear morning. Calixto had drawn me a little map on a cocktail napkin. It showed two intermediate towns, and all I had to do was make a right, a left, and then another left.

The first right was ten miles down the road, and following the new track I climbed up and over a series of ridges, each higher than the next, until I had left the flatlands far behind. The ridges ran in long parallel lines, as though Pachamama, the Earth Mother, had dragged the tines of her golden rake across the face of the world. There was not a house or a line of smoke as far as the eye could see, just dark green and brown hills rippling off toward the curve of the earth.

There was supposed to be a town along here somewhere, and when I came to a house I asked the sole resident—a shirtless teenage boy—where El Cruce was. He looked about him. "This is it," he said. The road branched right and became even thinner. Snarling up and down the hills for another half hour, I came up a particularly steep set of switchbacks and entered Pucara, a village made entirely of stone. I circled once around the cobblestone plaza, counterclockwise, looking for the exit, but by the time I had come back around to my entrance point a lean young man in blue jeans was standing in the road, arms folded, blocking my path. I stopped.

"First of all," he said, handing me an envelope, "take this letter up to La Higuera. Second of all, I heard what you said on the radio yesterday, and you are wrong." He turned out to be the local schoolteacher, which also made him the postmaster and village administrator. He invited me inside and produced a mason jar full of moonshine that we passed back and forth across a desk while debating socialism, the New Man, and the Bolivian political scene in 1966.

After half an hour I left drunk. I flailed at the kick starter for a while before realizing that I had forgotten to turn the key on, and no sooner had I veered out of the plaza and bumped a few hundred yards down the road than an old man in a straw hat came running out of a shack, flapping his arms with excitement.

"You must be the gringo on the radio!" he shouted toothlessly. "I talked to Che Guevara right on this spot thirty years ago!" I sat astride the bike, chatting with him. He recalled—suspiciously well—how he and some other peasants were rounded up by the guerrillas and Che gave a talk about the coming revolution. The man claimed that he had given food to the guerrillas, but as I departed after ten minutes, leaving the thrilled fellow in the middle of the road, I recalled that Che had complained bitterly in his diary about how the peasants were overcharging him for supplies.

Relations between the guerrillas and the peasants they had come to liberate were terrible. The expected support "does not exist," Che confided in his notes. "Not one person has joined up with us." There were all too many reasons for the failure that was now enclosing him. Unlike in Cuba, many peasants in Bolivia had plenty of land and identified with the country's president, a brown-skinned military strongman who spoke Quechua. Although Che had been careful to "Bolivianize" the struggle by recruiting a slim majority of Bolivian guerrillas before starting his operations, casualties and desertions quickly whittled his force down to a hard core dominated by Cuban combat veterans. Instead of swimming through the peasant sea, these guerrillas flopped about like fish out of water. None of them could speak the local dialects, and some of the Cubans were black, a skin color most Bolivian peasants had never seen before. Perhaps even more important, the guerrillas were led by a white man, and an Argentine to boot—exactly the kind of person who had been exploiting brown-skinned peasants in this region for centuries. Che's skin marked him in a way no ideology could: he was what rural Bolivians call *la rosca*, a bitter term for a white outsider with power and wealth. With typical realism, the peasants often fled whenever this motley band of foreigners and sun-burned city boys appeared. Morale in the guerrilla column plunged. Once, they seized the town of Alto Seco, just up the road from here, and Che gave a propaganda lecture on Yankee imperialism and Marxist liberation, and then asked for volunteers. Only one local man stepped forward, but he was told quietly by one of the guerrillas, "Don't be silly; we're done for."

In his diary, Che wrote coldly and with little sympathy for his men, but the facts were clear even to him. The Bolivian volunteers were deserting. One guerrilla drowned while crossing a river. The rear guard got lost, wandered through the hills for weeks, and was then wiped out in an army ambush. By July, Che was down to twenty-two fighters, "three of whom are disabled, including myself." In August their base camp was uncovered, cutting them off from supplies, including the last doses of precious asthma medicine ("A black day," he wrote). They were surviving on rotten anteater carcasses and horse meat—eating Rocinante, rather than riding her. Two diary entries for August use the word *desperate* in their opening sentences—August was "without doubt the worst month we have had so far in this war." But then September proved even worse. The situation on the ground was "a big mess," Che conceded to himself.

The insurgents wandered aimlessly through this barren landscape, often lost, usually thirsty, sometimes starving. Che's tactics were curiously passive: instead of attacking vital infrastructure, like the oil fields in nearby Camiri, he staged small ambushes and then listened to the radio to see if the world had noticed. The high-water mark came when the guerrillas briefly seized a small town on the main highway through the region, sending the Bolivian government into a panic. In La Paz, they didn't know that Che had ordered the attack only because he hoped to steal some asthma medicine from the town pharmacy. His condition had become so severe by then that he could no longer walk; he was leading the revolution from a lame mule.

When he learned from the radio that a Budapest daily had criticized him for engaging in guerrilla warfare, Che's frustrations finally exploded. "How I would like to rise to power just to unmask cowards and lackeys of every sort," he wrote, "and squash their snouts in their own filth."

The New Man was running out of hope.

The road dropped for a while and then off to the right you could see the Río Grande, far down in the valley bottom. I had to refocus my eyes before I realized what I was looking over: there, a half mile down the hillside in the same vista, was a meadow filled with tall white and yellow crucifixes. They were death markers. This was where the final battle had taken place—the guerrillas trapped in a shallow ravine without cover as the army rained bullets on them from above. The crosses marked where Che's men had fallen. Che knew that the only way out of an ambush is to attack, not retreat, and he tried to push his few remaining soldiers up the hill to a position with better cover. But the time of theoretical tactics was over. Che had been hit once already in the leg, and was wounded again when the rifle was literally shot out of his hands, burying splinters in his arm. A loyal guerrilla named Simón Cuba tried to lead his commander to safety, but the army troops charged down the hill. Wounded, disarmed, and defeated, the "world's No. 1 guerrilla" was captured. In the confusion, three guerrillas crawled through the underbrush and escaped, led by Benigno, the same man who had recently defected from Cuba and denounced Castro for abusing Che's image.

It was a sad spot, and I fled it, but I had bounced no more than a hundred yards down the road when I came over a small hill and there he was, Che himself, alive and well and a little shorter than I had imagined. Also his beard was red, but other than that it was definitely him. He was marching up the hill toward me, the jaunty beret cocked on his head, the little star clearly visible on his brow. I pulled to a halt, convinced that the moonshine was responsible for this vision, but the figure only grew more solid with each step. Che approached steadily, and as he came closer I noticed he was wearing a Che Guevara T-shirt. I sat on the motorcycle, frozen in fear.

"Hallow!" he said in an approximation of English, and then burst into tears and handed me fifty dollars. The fellow's real name was Jans van Zwam, and he was a Dutch tourist in his forties. He was just returning from a morning in La Higuera. He shoved the two twenties and a ten in U.S. currency at me and said, "Please, you will take for the doctor in the town," and then burst into tears again.

When all the crying was over I asked him what he was doing here. "For twenty years I dream of coming to Bolivia," he said. He had passed through four airports in two days, jumped into a taxi and come straight to La Higuera. Against his driver's advice—which Jans did not fathom, since he did not speak any Spanish—he dismissed the taxi. He had planned on catching a bus back to Vallegrande, but there were no buses or taxis on this road, so now he was walking.

He had about fifty kilometers to go. With the exception of Pucara, five kilometers up the road, there was no shelter along the route, nor any place to find food and water. I told him to flag down any trucks that passed, although there would almost certainly be none, and promised to pick him up on my return if he was still afoot.

He rolled up his sleeve and showed me his left biceps. There was a tattoo of Che on it. When he made a muscle Che's face bulged a bit and the eyes of the "world's No. 1 guerrilla" surveyed the future even more intensely than usual. I asked him how to get to La Higuera.

"You will see it easy," he said. I pulled away, and indeed, the route wasn't missable. Downhill a half mile the road forked. A tall pole stood at the divide with a crude hand-lettered sign attached.

CHE, it said; 10 KM.

Twenty-nine years too late, I followed a grassy path over the hills. Aside from a weekly truck no vehicles came this way. A tiny bridge of rotten logs spanned a dry creekbed, and then the road went up and over one last ridge line and there it was, down below me.

La Higuera was not a town or even a village, but just a hamlet, a cluster of brown, one-story buildings draggled along the sides of the only street. The settlement sat on the slopes of a vast, gentle valley, guarded on the left and at the far end by a steep, brush-covered ridge. Below it were sloping fields of tall, golden grass, some trees, and far, far below that the Rio Grande. I powered slowly up the main street, looking into the empty houses. A coupe of immense pigs slept against a wall beneath a slogan in red paint that said EL CHE VIVE.

The letter I had been handed in Pucara was addressed to the most substantial house in La Higuera. The building was made of cement and had a chain-link fence around it to keep out thieves. The schoolteacher lived inside. She was a rather elegant white woman with dark hair down to her waist, and she made me tea. She did not ask why I was there, since there was only one reason foreigners came to La Higuera. She talked for a while about life in the village, which had no electricity. There were only twenty-two families left now, she said, about half the number who lived here when El Che came. They mostly raised cattle and were slowly going broke. About half the people in the area had Chagas disease, the heart-eating condition spread by beetles. I left the letter with her and set off on foot to find the doctor Jans had mentioned.

His office was in a long, low hut at the top of the hamlet. This was the same building where Che had been murdered. In 1967 the army had carried its wounded captive to La Higuera and put him in the hut, which was then a schoolhouse. At one point several Bolivian soldiers took Che outside and posed for a picture with their trophy— he looks wildly disheveled, and his captors are leaning in toward him like guests squeezing into the frame at a party. A local woman was allowed to feed him some soup. He sat on the floor, his back to the wall, his wounds bleeding but not fatal.

Via radio, the soldiers received a coded order from headquarters in La Paz: "Fernando 700." Decoded, this meant "Kill Che Guevara." The Bolivian government did not want to risk a show trial full of posturing and speeches. The date was now October 9, 1967. A sergeant was given two cans of beer to fortify his courage and was then sent into the schoolhouse where Che was waiting. There are various accounts of what Guevara did or didn't say at the end. Supporters claimed that his final words were "Shoot, coward, for you kill a man!" Enemies said it was "I am worth more to you alive than dead." There were also claims that he denounced Castro, or refused to speak at all, or sent a farewell to his family, or cried out "Long live the revolution!"

It doesn't really matter what was said; the sergeant put an end to words by shooting nine bullets into Guevara.

Now there were a few children standing outside the door of the former schoolhouse, which had been fixed up and whitewashed. They were brown-skinned boys with ratty sweaters and shorts. They loitered, listening to the screams of agony coming from inside. The doctor had his hands in the mouth of an old peasant woman in a black-and-blue poncho. She sat in a chair, her head tilted back. The doctor was prying at her teeth with a set of sharpened pliers like those used to pull nails out of horse hooves. He gave a great heave, and a bloody tooth came sliding out while the old woman twitched in her chair and pleaded for mercy. *"Dios mío!"* she cried out in a muffled, wet voice. The doctor added the tooth to a collection of saliva-damp molars in his left hand. There were five of them glistening there in his palm. "Well," he said to the woman, after spotting me, "why don't we get the rest in a few days?"

The doctor was a barrel-chested, handsome young man, dark in skin, eyes, and hair. He rhapsodized about the man he called *"el Guerrillero heroico"* and said plainly that he was in this village, providing care to the poor, because he wanted to Be Like Che. His medical education and salary were both funded by the Cuban government. This, too, was a legacy of Che.

The walls in the little room were decorated with posters about polio and inoculations. There was a plaque above the spot where Che died with a bad poem about him, and below that a framed pop art collage that showed his face and a section of the Argentine flag.

I handed over the fifty dollars, making sure that the boys at the door heard me explain that the money was a gift from the Dutchman for the medical care of the villagers. The doctor held the bills in front of him and then smiled—and then laughed. I asked him what he was going to spend it on. "Medicine," he said at once. "Or supplies. We need bandages, and scalpels, and antibiotics. And needles. Also a battery for the radio." He showed me the radio. It was a ratty two-way model, the only connection between La Higuera and the outside world. Some German leftists were raising money to install a solar panel to power it, he said. The Cubans were even talking about paying to bring electricity to the village. He took me outside and showed me a red 125 cc dirt bike that he used to make his rounds. It was in terrible shape. He said he needed new tires—but that could wait, since the dry season was here. With the Dutchman's money he could stock up on some medicine. He would worry about tires later.

I gave him another twenty out of my own wallet. It was one of the last bills in there, but still, it is amazing how cheaply we can value our debts.

———

(he came to La Higuera twice. The first time had been three days before the end, not as a captive but as a fighter. His column was half the size of when he started, but the men were still on the offensive. Arriving after dawn, they found the hamlet eerily calm and the mayor missing. Despite these bad omens Guevara ordered the column to move forward. The advance guard walked up the main road toward Pucara while Guevara and the others waited in town.

"The army started shooting from that ridge line up there," the doctor said, pointing to the hill I had crossed to enter town. We were walking in the same direction that Che's men had been moving when the shooting broke out. The vanguard was decimated. Three of Che's most able men—"magnificent fighters," he wrote in his diary— were killed at once. Two others were wounded, and two Bolivian rebels took the opportunity to desert to the enemy. The survivors retreated into the center of town, to where we now stood.

The doctor made a left down a narrow lane, signaling for me to follow. The path headed downhill and was shaded by overhanging trees and shielded by stone walls on each side. "It took some time to get the mules organized but then they came down here," he said. "This was their route of escape."

The ridge line was almost out of rifle range from here. The guerrillas had slipped down the lane, using the walls for excellent cover. I squatted down behind one and cocked a finger at the army troops who had been on the ridge that day. You would need a telescopic sight to hit anything from here. Following the path, laying down a barrage of covering fire from behind its walls, the survivors slowly worked their way out of the village, down the hill, into a ravine, and then eventually disappeared with the arrival of darkness. They hid in the valley below the town for three days, almost dying of thirst. A new unit of Bolivian army rangers was deployed in the area. There were two hundred of them, freshly trained by American Green Berets. They had intelligence information gathered by the CIA, including Che's photos of himself in disguise. Listening to his radio while hidden in the underbrush, Guevara heard a broadcast about the deployment of "hundreds" of troops to encircle him. "The news seems to be a diversionary tactic," he wrote on October 7.

It was the last line in his last diary.

The good doctor took my picture while I stood next to the statue of El Che in the town plaza. La Higuera was too small to actually have a plaza, but that is what residents called the traffic circle in their one and only dirt street. There were a few trees inside the circle, and inside them a bust of Che on a white pedestal. It was the worst representation of him I had seen yet. Only the obvious adornments—the trademark beret with star and the word *Che* in red across the pedestal—made it clear who it was. In the photo my boots are streaked with oil, my jeans ripped from the crash in Chile, and my head sunburned by four months of travel. I look like I'm posing with Omar Sharif on the set of 1969's *Che*. In that Warner Brothers production, Sharif played Guevara, of course; Jack Palance was Fidel Castro.

There had been a different and better likeness of Che in this exact spot, but one night in 1990 a jeep full of Bolivian soldiers pulled into town. They threw a lasso over the head of El Che, tied it to the back of the jeep, and then drove out of town as the bust bounced behind them like a tin can at a wedding. The replacement had been made by some art students of dubious talent. Neither the art students nor the soldiers were from around here. Nor were the young leftists who mourned here in La Higuera each October 8, just managing to miss the right date the way they just missed everything else about Che.

Which is as close as I could come to explaining the miserable mood that had settled on me with my arrival in La Higuera. We didn't belong here. Not the soldiers nor the art students. Not Jans, the Che tourist, not Che himself. We were all meddlers, outsiders who thought we knew better. Except for the doctor with his palms full of bloody teeth, we—Argentines, Bolivians, rightists, leftists, CIA agents, Cuban diplomats, journalists, pilgrims, and tourists—were all here as soldiers in some cause, imposing our wills on a group of people who needed rain and batteries, not a place in history.

It was mid-afternoon now, and conscious of how swiftly darkness would cover the country, I thanked the doctor and began a very long journey home. I rode slowly down through the houses, past the EL CHE VIVE scrawl and the pigs lying contentedly in the sun, and then went over the ridge. A few miles on the other side of Pucara I came around a corner and saw Jans striding purposefully along. When he heard the sound of my motor coming he turned and waved his arms over his head as though I might somehow miss him. I pulled over, lowered the rear foot pegs, and Jans climbed aboard. He put a stiff hand on my shoulder and sat bolt upright during the trip.

Because of the road we drove no more than fifteen miles an hour, and this made it possible to talk. I kept the visor of my helmet open to hear him better. Like all Che fans, Jans had a parable about the man, and he first apologized for his bad English and then launched into it. "I didn't have no education," he said. "At fourteen I am going to work. After much time I pick up a book. It is about Che Guevara. I see he is a doctor, from good family. He have everything, he could be a good life, but he give it up to fight for the poor. So I think he is a good fellow, and I read another book." End of parable.

Jans knew everything about Che. As we rode along he mentioned Che's birthdate, what he'd done in the Cuban war, his missions to Africa and Bolivia, what he'd said at the Tricontinental Congress, whom he'd written his farewell letters to, on and on. Back in Holland, Jans was a minor politician—a vice-mayor of a community of seventeen thousand people—and said he was known as the "Che mayor" because of his fascination with Guevara. He made me pull over long enough to show me some articles he kept in his jacket. They were from a Dutch paper and I couldn't read them, but they showed Jans wearing a beret and a Che pin on his lapel as he stood in front of a Che poster in his home. According to Jans the first article said that Che Guevara was "the one who set Jans van Zwam right." I recognized the Dutch word *pelgrimage* in the text of the second piece. When we started again I asked Jans if he had read about Guevara's 1952 motorcycle trip.

"*Ja,*" he said. "This is the trip when he begin to wake up. He start to think about how people is living."

We didn't talk much after that. We just rolled slowly over the ridges, one after another, and consumed the views. Somewhere that afternoon, while my eyes were busy, I passed through the ten thousandth mile since leaving Buenos Aires.

We flew up the valley floor and into Vallegrande, a long rooster tail of dust chasing our arrival. I slammed on the brakes seconds after we hit pavement at the outskirts. Jans tumbled forward onto my back. "It's the hospital," I said.

"Which hospital?" he asked.

"The one where they put his body."

We left the bike at the curb and wandered up some stairs. It was just a small clinic, really, called Nuestro Señor de Malta, with the price of services listed on the front door. Guevara's inert body had been lashed to the skid of a small helicopter and flown down from La Higuera to be put on display here. BOLIVIA CONFIRMS GUEVARA'S DEATH, read the lead headline in *The New York Times* the next day; BODY DISPLAYED. After the journalists were gone, a pair of wax death masks were cast, and then Che's hands were sawed off so that his fingerprints could be verified later against Argentine records. Sometime before dawn on the eleventh he was stuffed into a grave dug at random near the airstrip.

The laundry shed was now surrounded by weeds and trash. It was open on one side, with a cement table in the middle that held a pair of shallow sinks with fine ridges laid into the sloped bottom. It had drains and a single dead spigot. There were rings of candle wax around the edges, and the blue plaster walls were covered with messages. The majority were in Spanish, but there were a few in Por-

tuguese and others in German and French. Some people just left
their names on the wall ("Charito 19/1/92"), but most of the space
was taken up with very personal messages, letters to Che himself,
often cast in the intimate *"tú"* tense rather than the respectful
"Usted."

"Che: you are a star guiding us," one said. *"El Che Vive,"* read
another; and "Che Is Present"; and up high that old suspect, "Be
Like Che." I stopped counting after a hundred. The messages went
up to the rafters and even covered the support column dividing the
open side of the shed. Up top it said:

> AT THE FEET OF
>
> OUR DEAD
>
> A FLOWER IS
>
> WHAT GROWS
>
> OUR HAND
>
> PICKS IT
>
> OUR RIFLE
>
> PROTECTS IT
>
> CHE LIVES

And lower down:

> For the liberty of all
> the Latin American people
> El Che lives
> and the struggle continues.
> The commander of the Americas
> has not died
> until the final victory.

That last line—*"hasta la victoria siempre"*—was Che's own signature exit line, a dramatic way of sending his comrades off with
confidence that, ultimately, victory was theirs. There would be a final

triumph, a happy conclusion to their journeys. It made the revolution seem less like a remote possibility and more like a real condition that would come to exist—soon. If you said that the final victory would come, then it would. Then we would all live in a peaceful world populated by New Men and New Women.

Behind this illusion there might need to be a little squashing of cowards and lackeys—as there was in Cuba—but there was literally no room on the walls of the laundry shed for details. It was a place of slogans, of aspirations, and of hopes, not of asterisks. Nobody came here twice.

Jans unsheathed an enormous Bowie knife and began carving something on the wall in Dutch. He scraped at the plaster for quite a while, patiently digging each letter into the surface with the tip of the blade. White dust trickled onto his boots while he worked. When he was done, I asked him what the phrase meant.

"You are my light," he said.

The last mile, something like the 10,013th in a series of them, began at the hospital shed and ran through the cobblestone streets of Vallegrande and then came down the hill, returning to dirt as it passed the entrance to the airfield and around back, ending only when it had to at a barbed-wire fence. I stopped Kooky cold by putting my thumb on the kill switch. Jans was on the back, and we sat there staring over the field while the engine dinged and pinged. The sun had gone down some time ago. Now the sky was dark blue.

Jans dismounted first, and we went through the barbed wire and across the grassy expanse, both of us stumbling a bit in the dusk. The holes were where the excavators had left them when the search had been interrupted two months before. The retired army officers had pointed, the Argentine forensic experts had dug, and the journalists had watched, but day after day the digging had produced nothing. They expanded the search; the Cubans sent help; old peasants were interviewed; and then a ground-imaging radar was pushed over the field like a lawn mower, plumbing the clay soil for traces of history. Eventually teams of soldiers joined the dig, and finally a bulldozer turned up long tracts of the soil, peeling it back like the lid on a can of sardines that somehow proves empty. Most of the journalists left after a few weeks. The computer printer for the radar unit broke, making it impossible to interpret the results. The Argentines left, promising to come back when they had more money, which they eventually did.

But for now, beneath the planets and stars of the blue night, the only signs of this excruciatingly slow exhumation were the coffin holes. There were just over a hundred of them in the field. Many had filled with rainwater. Already one child had fallen in, and the villagers were demanding that the government refill the holes before someone got seriously injured.

Jans stood around, peering into some of the holes and taking pictures. After a while he burst into tears again. I sat down, thoroughly uncompassed by this moment of arrival. It was hard to look at the holes and not feel cheated, somehow. I had to accept that the farther I traveled to see him, the less close I got. He was here, certainly, cornered one last time but still holding out a bit longer, as uncompromising as ever. It felt like a fine resting place, and I wished they would just leave him here, but they wouldn't. They had long ago absconded with his life; now they would take his death, too.

Before coming here, Che had explained his actions—his various wars, departures, and sacrifices—to his children in a careful letter of farewell. He wrote to his three sons and daughter that the revolution was more important than any individual, that service to the cause stood above any one life. "Each one of us, alone," he told them, "is worth nothing." Now, sitting in the falling darkness amid the holes that had swallowed all the ideals, all the blood, and all the bodies, this seemed to me exactly backwards. Each one of us, imperfect and little and terribly alone, is worth everything. People are ends, not means.

Like La Higuera with its doctor, however, Vallegrande did get one inadvertent benefit from Che's efforts. Because of Che—because Che came here, and then the army came after him, and then the tourists like Jans also after him, and now me, too, after him or whatever was left of him—the government had been shamed into installing electricity in the town. Now up on the hillside, as the black night settled on us, Vallegrande glowed white with streetlamps. The town seemed to bask in this privilege amid so much darkness.

FINAL VICTORY

We rolled east from Havana after breakfast, missed the exit, and spent the morning wandering back and forth, asking directions, chatting with bicyclists and horsemen and police officers and patiently waiting would-be bus passengers. Eventually we got the rental car pointed in the right direction and sat back for the ride to Che's funeral.

They had found him, or at least some of him. A year after I passed through Vallegrande the Argentine-Cuban forensic team had returned to the grassy airstrip with new funding. They'd dug and dug some more, and eventually, in June 1997, they had found enough bones to fill a small coffin. The arms lacked hands; these, then, were the bones of Ernesto Guevara de la Serna, known at various points in his life as Little Ernesto, the Shaved Head, the Sniper, the Pig, Big Che, Mongo, Fernando, Fernández, Adolfo Mena, El Puro, and El Che. It wasn't the whole Guevara, only an elusive portion, but it was enough to construct a symbolic extravaganza. The remains of six other guerrillas who fell in the battle at La Higuera were also, at least theoretically, identified.

Che had been bundled off to Cuba just in time for the thirtieth anniversary of his death, in October 1997. The remains of the seven were put on display inside the José Martí Monument at the heart of the vast Plaza de la Revolución in Havana. They put a flag identifying the nationality of each guerrilla on the appropriate box. Che was draped in the red, white, and blue flag of Cuba. He might have renounced his Cuban citizenship and died an internationalist Argentine fighting in Bolivia, but he was going to be buried a Cuban.

Thousands of people were in line to see the remains when I walked toward the plaza at night in the company of a *Newsweek* reporter and a bottle of rum. Havana is a dark city; we held hushed conversations at intersections with invisible men who did not identify themselves. The uniformed police deferred to these civilians, who extracted a pull from the bottle and let us pass their outposts in the night.

The line stretched from beyond the edge of visibility, up a long avenue, over a bridge, alongside the plaza, and then curled around the vast parking lot that was the heart of official Cuba. The line passed beneath the electric gaze of a six-story neon Che blazing from a blank wall. The same little groups of mysterious civilians stood around, supervising everything via radio. We approached, seeking permission to poke and prod the public for comment. By the light of Che I could see that these men with their cloaked authority wore tiny lapel pins reading BRIGADA ESPECIAL. The special brigades are the enforcers of the revolution, the plainclothes police who specialize in pounding Cuba's square pegs into round holes. They scolded us for drinking rum while observing the "act of homage."

The line of mourners continued around the plaza, moving at a quick march and never stalling for even a moment. After passing beneath the illuminated Che it snaked right and ascended a gentle, lengthy staircase into the base of the monument itself, a tasteless stupa erected by the Soviets. The uniform line that entered in a compact, speedy thread emerged from the other side as a disordered throng. Little clumps of families and dots of solitary people wandered out of the viewing chamber, moving at different speeds in various directions, as though lost. In death, Che converted the Cuban masses back into individuals.

I thought about joining the hour-long line and marching up the stairs and into the monument to see the box holding his bones, but I didn't. It was all too much. Loudspeakers overhead blared with

Socialist-Realist music that seemed, at a distance, indistinguishable from the liturgical tones of a Holy Mass. The disembodied voice of Fidel Castro echoed from the heavens, reading Che's farewell letter to the Cuban people in an endless loop interrupted only by Che songs ("Hasta Siempre") and Che poems ("Thus, Guevara, strong-voiced gaucho . . ."). Forty-four years ago, a young Ernesto had scribbled a final warning in his notebook that revolution is impersonal, that it consumes the innocent and guilty together, and then manipulates the memory of the dead as an instrument of control.

The Cubans in the queue did seem deeply moved. A lean black man told me that Che was "one of the men of the twentieth century, of the twenty-first century." He pointed to his twelve-year-old son. As the boy skipped about, the father said, "He was born to come here." A woman with her two daughters said, firmly and steadily, "This is not just an act of homage to Che but an expression of solidarity with the revolution by the entire nation as the eyes of the world are upon us," and went on in that vein for another two minutes.

But away from the plaza, my Cuban friends only groaned when I described the crowds at the event as "spontaneous." I knew two brothers who lived in the old Chinatown, and they had been skewered neatly on the horns of a Cuban dilemma. Their problem was simply that they had two funerals to attend, that of Che here in Havana and that of a grandmother who had just died in Cienfuegos. The brothers were smart young men, products of the revolution, educated and hardworking and dedicated to Cuba, if not necessarily to those who ran the island. At their job sites, the brothers explained, those who "volunteered" to go to the plaza to see Che received a checkmark in their files. Those who didn't, didn't, and the consequences were clear, if unspoken. Cuban communism is a system for micromanaging every aspect of life, and failure to earn enough of these checkmarks indicates a "poor attitude" toward the revolution in a society where your attitude affects what you eat, where you live, and how much gasoline and education and pay you receive. Caught between family and state, they had divided the consequences. One brother had dutifully gone to see Che—and he showed me his pay slip with a notation of his attendance. The other brother had gone to Cienfuegos.

Unlike in the rest of Latin America, where Che was a symbolic outsider, in Cuba he was the Establishment, stripped of his rebellious appeal by the coercive government demand underpinning his post-mortem existence. Toddlers literally napped under his gaze in day-care centers. Children promised en masse to "Be Like Che." There were portraits of him in every school, and the officially sanctioned lessons of his life were taught on every blackboard. Anything he had done or touched was sacrosanct. He'd once spent four hours operating a cigar-boxing machine; the machine was now retired, decorated with placards, and painted silver because Che had used it. All Che's books were available in Cuban bookstores, and there were always new books about him—Granado's diaries, memoirs by others who knew him or claimed to, plus profiles of Che the guerrilla fighter, Che the economist, Che the journalist, Che the doctor, Che the Argentine, Che the photographer, and Che the traveler.

Che was everywhere, not just as political propaganda but as profitable consumer good: there were Che posters and lapel pins, Che refrigerator magnets, Che T-shirts, Che cigarette lighters and Che nail clippers, Che postcards and Che photo albums. The Swiss watch company Swatch put out a Che Swatch bearing his photo and the slogan "Revolución!" The Cuban government bought the entire production run and begun flogging the watches at José Martí International Airport, outside Havana, for fifty dollars apiece.

I called Alberto Díaz Gutiérrez, the photographer known as Korda, who'd snapped that most-famous picture of Che one overcast day in March 1960. He demanded money for an interview but gave a short rant free of charge about all the royalties he was owed. He offered to sell me a signed original of the shot—cropped or uncropped, it was my choice—for three hundred dollars, but I already knew that you could knock the price in half if you went to his house with a bottle of rum and convinced him you were a friend of the revolution.

On October 9, 1997—thirty years to the day after Che died in La Higuera—the Cuban daily newspaper *Granma* ran the headline CUBA WILL NOT ENCOURAGE TOURISM WITH THE FIGURE OF CHE and quoted vice-minister of tourism Eduardo de la Vega as he assured the nation, "We don't believe the figure of Che should be commercialized." I bought a pair of Che maracas and tapped out my rhythmic applause for the vice-minister.

Having thus praised Alberto Granado, I went to bury him. The *Newsweek* guy and I hired an old Cadillac and rumbled through the pitch-dark city and then into the suburbs on the broad Quinta Avenida. Granado had sent me a couple of letters explaining that he couldn't talk with me because he'd sold his life story to an Italian movie company. His address was on the envelopes, though, and we found the street in a neighborhood of luxurious American-style homes from the 1940s. Granado's turned out to be one of the largest. The house was unlit, but in Havana that meant nothing, and I banged on the front door and waited and banged again. After a while a child answered, we were let inside, and there was a lot more waiting and then discussions and movement upstairs. Some relatives were in the backyard watching a pyramid of wood burn down to the proper con- dition for an Argentine barbecue. It takes a lot of meat to make one of those *asados;* the official ration in Cuba is the equivalent of two ham- burger patties a month.

Alberto Granado received us upstairs, on the balcony. He wore a green shirt and shorts, was almost bald, and had a small mustache. We sat on lawn furniture and I presented the bottle of Havana Club that had gotten us into trouble at the plaza. His wife went in search of glasses; she didn't talk during the interview but stayed within reach of the bottle, which we all began to consume neat. I was so stunned to finally meet Granado that I did not know where to begin, but he did, and he started into his story with easy familiarity.

"The journey was my idea," he began. The purpose was "to

know the world, but first Latin America. We read books about Chile and Peru, but we needed to see it to really know it." The phrasing sounded familiar and indeed was almost word for word what he had written in the introduction to his diary. Granado made a lot of appearances now and gave scripted remarks about his friendship with Che to international groups. He'd been in Venezuela addressing unionists, and went to Temuco in Chile to speak at a university. He was allowed a passport, one of many benefits of being an official Friend of Che. I'd seen a photo of him in a Spanish newspaper recently, part of an article about tourism to Cuba. The caption said, "Alberto Granado, an old friend of Che, tests the golf links at Varadero."

We started with Patagonia, listing towns we'd both visited decades apart, and then progressed to Chile. "Temuco has changed tremendously," Granado said. I suggested that they had had a lot of fun in Chile. "Che was very attractive," he said, nodding. "He was always interested in women, but he was also interested in reading, in travel, in thinking. We didn't have so much time for girls." He agreed that the name "Che" had stuck to Ernesto for the first time in southern Chile, although: "We Argentines are known as Ches in all Latin America, Chile, Peru, Venezuela, wherever." The conversation went easily for a while, as long as we stuck to geography and our mutual motorcycle memories. But there was one odd detail that had been bothering me for a long time. It was so obscure that I was almost reluctant to mention it, but I told Granado that there was a curious discrepancy between the two diaries, a small matter about th—

"Who rescued the kitten?" Granado said. He didn't need reminding. "It was him who rescued the kitten from a little roof. He attributed it to me and I to him." When I wondered aloud how this could happen, he gave only a vague answer—"It was an endearment we shared"—and took a pull of rum. *Newsweek* and the wife were sitting quietly, sipping at the sweet, fiery liquor. I drank the last of my glass and poured refills for everyone. Even in the dark the rum was golden. I asked him about the final chapter in Che's diary, the strange declaration of martyrdom around a campfire. "I can't locate where it was," he answered. Still thinking literally rather than literarily, he insisted that it must have been a real episode, or at least "a synthesis of many people we knew."

I'd drunk enough to loosen my Spanish, and I deployed a thesis that the motorcycle journey of 1952 had awoken Che to the world and led inevitably to his subsequent travels, when Che had set off again to Bolivia and Guatemala, studying revolutionary movements and finally having his fateful encounter with Fidel Castro. One trip begat the next; one journey led to another. He was a traveler to the end.

"This is a well-developed thesis," Granado replied. "The first voyage was to ask questions. The second was to find answers. I think travel sensitized him to injustice, to the lack of respect for the humanity of Indians, to the poverty. These were the roots of all his Marxist theories."

I asked if he, Granado, wasn't something of an influence through his early Marxist beliefs. He scratched his head, sipped, and said, "Not a great influence, but yes." The main difference between himself and Guevara was one of temperament. "There are two types of people. One thinks he can change the world in small steps. Then there are those who think they can change it in one grand action."

The bottle was mostly gone now. We'd been talking slowly in the hot night, gradually getting drunk. Granado had a lot of wrinkles, and because he was sitting in a collapsing lawn chair his round head barely came up over the table. I poured another round. *Newsweek* spoke up now, asking about contemporary Cuba.

"We're passing through hard times," Granado answered. "We lost ninety percent of our markets, but the Cuban community has dignity. Fidel knows the people. Many people think Fidel is a grand pastor with a big flock, but the reverse is true. The people lead Fidel. Before, we had one school of medicine and zero centers of medical investigation. Now, thirty-six years later, we have eighteen schools of medicine, fifty thousand doctors, and twenty-five centers of medical research. We don't offer a Buick. We offer schools, medicine, employment, and work." He went on for a while about how Cuba had "practically no" political prisoners and only a few *delincuentes* were sent to jail for causing trouble. Peru and Argentina were both in much worse shape than Cuba. The last time he was in Argentina he'd been shocked—shocked—to find people selling things in the street.

I asked him about Stalin. "We must put it in historical context," he said, and then did so, talking about World War II and the necessity of defeating the Nazis. Stalin's only error "was that people had no part in power. That doesn't happen in Cuba. Here, the people have the last word, not Fidel."

At the end, when the bottle was nearly empty and we were rising to leave, he signed my copy of his diary, the same one that had come originally from Havana to New York, then passed over the Andes and traveled ten thousand miles, only to return in the end to the hand that had written it. "For Patricio," he now scribbled across the title page, "dignified emulator of my voyage with El Che. Affectionately, Alberto Granado."

On the way out he told me that his son and Che's son had talked for a while about teaming up on a pair of motorcycles to retrace the journey but that nothing had ever come of the idea.

Che's final road trip began at dawn the next day. I staggered down to the waterfront with a splitting headache. I'd been partying in a bar full of whores and Germans until 3 A.M. The city was filled with European and Canadian men who didn't even know about the funeral. They bought Che T-shirts and listened to trios sing "Guantanamera" and then went off to private houses to screw the girls for twenty dollars. They slept through the mornings and then started over again.

Che's bones were going to parade out of the city in a motorcade, passing along the length of the Malecón seawall and then heading for Santa Clara, to the east. At 7 A.M. the tropical sun was already too harsh for my eyes, but a serpentine crowd had assembled along the length of the waterfront and was keeping to a respectful murmur. There were probably ten thousand people waiting, craning their necks for any sign of the cortege. Children climbed onto the pedestals of street lamps, and some fathers held toddlers on their shoulders. A middle-aged *mulata* named Ana Portela asked me where I was from, and I told her. "Anyone who invaded this country," she promptly volunteered, "would find blood and sweat and rubble left in Cuba, but not one Cuban." She was with an older friend, also an Afro-Cuban. I asked this woman what she thought of Che, but she answered another question. "I am eighty-five years old," she said, "and here we are all equal. There is no racism or discrimination here. We are united."

At last the little column of vehicles approached, passing first under the shadow of Meyer Lansky's Riviera Hotel, then by the Nacional, where Capone stayed. The crowd stood straight and silent as a few motorcycle cops passed, and then came seven military jeeps pulling seven glass-topped caissons bearing seven wood boxes under seven flags. When the procession was gone the Cubans disbanded to their schools and places of work.

The seven jeeps were headed for Santa Clara, the scene of Che's great victory over that armored troop train carrying more than four hundred government reinforcements. That was in late December 1958. After Santa Clara surrendered to Che, the dictator Batista fled the country within days. While Castro loitered in the east, Che formed a convoy of commandeered vehicles and rolled up the highway with his guerrillas toward Havana, greeted by cheering throngs along the route. In those days history was flowing in the opposite direction.

After breakfast and aspirin, we hired a white Subaru with the smallest tires I had ever seen and fled the city. It took an hour of wandering to find the country's major highway, which turned out to be behind a tree, totally unmarked. We headed east and then south, and came by mid-afternoon to the Bay of Pigs. Our rooms were in a bungalow built on the spot where the Cuban exiles had come ashore in 1961, hoping to overthrow Castro. We went across the street to the small museum where detritus from the battle was on display. We signed in and put "USA" in the nationality column of the guest book, which generated a satisfying jolt in the eyes of the elderly attendants. The exhibits were filled with hectoring denunciations of the invasion, the exiles, and United States imperialism. After an hour in this hothouse climate of martyrs and villains, I needed a drink. *Newsweek* and I went back to the hotel and sat down in the bar. We ordered piña coladas, and I tried to pay with Cuban pesos, but the bartender waved them away. "Dollars only," he said.

There was a documentary about Che on television. "All Che," *Newsweek* said, "all the time."

Santa Clara was where my own journey had begun. Just like six years before, you could still see the bullet holes from Che's shootout on the façade of the Santa Clara Libre hotel. We drove in past the plaza, past the benches where the *gusano* with his home-brewed beer had expressed the conviction, "If he were still alive, none of this would be happening."

Now that statement was literally true. The funeral was already under way, and the side streets near the plaza were packed with pedestrians walking out toward the new mausoleum. I wove the Subaru gently through the bodies, tooting the horn like imperialism personified. On the radio we could hear the speeches beginning, and just around the time I found a parking space Fidel Castro came on. I could hear his voice on the car radio; looking down the hill, I could see a crowd of perhaps fifty thousand people and on the far side a tiny green figure addressing us from the podium. The mausoleum dominated everything. It was capped with a twenty-two-foot-tall bronze statue of Che striding forward, rifle in hand. The statue rested on a high stone pedestal that was hollow. At the end of the ceremony they were going to stick him inside it.

We pushed through the crowd, but with the event already under way it was impossible to get near the front. Policemen manned fences that cut us off from the press gallery. The sound system was breaking down, and Castro's voice boomed in a kind of unintelligible abstraction. In the car, I had heard his every word; in person, I couldn't understand anything he was saying. It didn't matter; when I read it in the paper I saw that he had declared that Marxism was advancing across the globe and that Che and the other six guerrillas in the funeral were "a reinforcement brigade" come home to bolster the revolution.

I began to panic. I had come all this way to watch Che buried, but I couldn't see or hear anything but a crowd of tens of thousands of sweaty regime loyalists. We slogged around the outside of the event looking for the press center, hoping for access to the bandstand, but had to settle for a spot behind the event and to one side, along a fence. The mood was tense, and even though I don't smoke, I wanted a smoke. There was an old man with a cigar box standing mutely to one side, and I bought two cigars that he had rolled himself for twenty-five cents. I hadn't yet struck a match when two New Men approached. They wasted nothing but a sour look on a foreigner, but the old man was treated to a cruel harangue about denigrating the occasion with buying and selling. I could see how thin the old man was, how hungry, but the revolution was an absolute. Even a twenty-five-cent flaw had to be squashed.

The words *imperialism* and *immortal* floated over us from time to time, and eventually Castro stopped talking and some cannons rattled off a salute. I saw a group of soldiers march past, turn sharply, and disappear over the little rise that separated us from the reviewing stand. More groups marched by; different types of soldiers, a phalanx of policemen in blue, more green, and finally a group of model workers who wore their own clothes and could not march in step, although they tried. Over they went, doing their best to keep together as they passed the rise and went down the other side, dropping into invisibility.

Slowly, the field emptied out. The crowd became thin, and then there were just isolated clusters of people, and after an hour all that was left was a muddy expanse of trampled grass. At long last we were all done. El Che stood alone against the tropical sky.